# Teaching History

## Developing as a Reflective Secondary Teacher

***Reflective Teaching and Learning: A guide to professional issues for beginning secondary teachers***

Edited by Sue Dymoke and Jennifer Harrison

Reflective practice is at the heart of effective teaching. This core text is an introduction for beginning secondary teachers on developing the art of critical reflective teaching throughout their professional work. Designed as a flexible resource, the book combines theoretical background with practical reflective activities.

***Developing as a Reflective Secondary Teacher Series***

These subject-specific core texts are for beginning secondary teachers following PGCE, GTP or undergraduate routes into teaching. Each book provides a comprehensive guide to beginning subject teachers, offering practical guidance to support students through their training and beyond. Most importantly, the books are designed to help students develop a more reflective and critical approach to their own practice. Key features of the series are:

- observed lessons, providing both worked examples of good practice and commentaries by the teachers themselves and other observers
- an introduction to national subject frameworks including a critical examination of the role and status of each subject
- support for beginning teachers on all aspects of subject teaching, including planning, assessment, classroom management, differentiation and teaching strategies
- a trainee-focused approach to critical and analytical reflection on practice
- a research-based section demonstrating M-level work
- a comprehensive companion website linking all subjects, featuring video clips of sample lessons, a range of support material and weblinks.

*Teaching Mathematics*
Paul Chambers

*Teaching History*
Ian Phillips

Forthcoming:
*Teaching Science*
Tony Liversidge, Matt Cochrane, Bernie Kerfoot and Judith Thomas

*Teaching ICT*
Carl Simmons and Claire Hawkins

*Teaching English*
Alyson Midgley, Peter Woolnough, Lynne Warham and Phil Rigby

# Teaching History

## Developing as a Reflective Secondary Teacher

Ian Phillips

Los Angeles | London | New Delhi
Singapore | Washington DC

First published 2008
Reprinted 2012



SAGE Publications Ltd
1 Oliver's Yard
55 City Road
London EC1Y 1SP

SAGE Publications Inc.
2455 Teller Road
Thousand Oaks, California 91320

SAGE Publications India Pvt Ltd
B 1/I 1 Mohan Cooperative Industrial Area
Mathura Road
New Delhi 110 044

SAGE Publications Asia-Pacific Pte Ltd
3 Church Street
#10-04 Samsung Hub
Singapore 049483

**Library of Congress Control Number: 2008922314**

**British Library Cataloguing in Publication data**

A catalogue record for this book is available from the British Library

ISBN 978-1-4129-4790-9
ISBN 978-1-4129-4791-6 (pbk)

Typeset by C&M Digitals (P) Ltd, Chennai, India
Printed in Great Britain by the MPG Books Group
Printed on paper from sustainable resources

# CONTENTS

# LIST OF FIGURES

# LIST OF TABLES

# ACKNOWLEDGEMENTS

I would like to begin by thanking the Faculty of Education at Edge Hill University for allowing me a period of sabbatical leave to complete this book. In particular I would like to acknowledge the help and encouragement of Dr Graham Rogers who has proved to be a particularly astute colleague over many years, whose considered advice is always invaluable. His ideas about teaching and learning history in higher education have helped to shape my ideas about working with Postgraduate Certificate of Education (PGCE) trainees.

Tony Crowley and Cynthia Miles, my colleagues on the History team have been valued friends and workmates. Phil Rigby and Francis Farrell as successive Heads of Humanities have also provided a great deal of support and encouragement.

I am also grateful to Lesley Ann McDermott, Head of History at St Patrick's Comprehensive Thornaby and Jason Brierly, Head of History at St George's Church of England Business and Enterprise College, Blackpool for their contributions to the ideas on thinking skills.

Particular thanks are due to Peter Duffy, Assistant Principal at North Liverpool Academy and his willing and unselfconscious students. Without his assistance and their co-operation the filmed lesson sequences would not have been possible. The North Liverpool Academy students proved to be the real professionals being filmed at the end of the school year on one of the wettest July Mondays.

Finally I would like to thank the History PGCE trainees, past and present from Edge Hill University who have invariably proved to be enthusiastic new history teachers and colleagues. However particular thanks are due to the classes of 2005–06 and 2006–07 who became willing collaborators and contributors to this venture.

I also hope that the completed volume will go some way to convincing my three sons that writing at home does involve hard work and long hours but little pecuniary advantage – which they still find hard to understand.

# HOW TO USE THIS BOOK

As you start your training to become a teacher, you will be faced with a bewildering array of information and requests for your personal details. A lot of the information will come from your training provider, and will give details about the course that you are starting. Your personal details will be required in order to compile a curriculum vitae (CV) that can be sent out to your placement schools; they will also be needed so that you can receive clearance to work with children from the Criminal Records Bureau (CRB). Very early on, you will learn that your success on the training course depends on your ability to demonstrate competence in the Professional Standards for Qualified Teacher Status (QTS) that are laid down by the Training and Development Agency for Schools (TDA).

This book is designed to help you to make a success of your training course. It shows you how to plan lessons, how to make good use of resources and how to assess pupils' progress effectively. But its main aim is to help you learn how to improve your classroom performance. In order to improve, you need to have skills of analysis and self-evaluation, and you need to know what you are trying to achieve and why. You also need examples of how experienced teachers deliver successful lessons, and how even the best teachers continually strive to become even better.

The book has a practical focus. It will help you to feel more comfortable about what is expected from you on teaching practice, through demonstrating good practice in history teaching, but also through putting that good practice into a whole-school and a national context. You will, for example, find suggestions about how history lessons can contribute to whole-school initiatives such as developing pupils' thinking skills.

A key feature of this book is the accompanying website (www.sagepub.co.uk/secondary). The icon shown in the margin will appear throughout the text where additional material is available. The website contains simple links to all of the websites featured in the various chapters, together with additional links to sites that provide useful support for your history teaching. The book makes extensive references to three history lessons. On the website you will find documents that give you a breakdown of the teaching and learning sequences for each lesson. Commentary in the text will refer to an incident or detail by the time; for example, you might be asked to view a teaching sequence which runs from 4 mins 30 secs to 7 mins 15 secs. The filmed lessons demonstrate key aspects of planning, teaching and student learning but the commentary will also draw your attention to particular aspects of a teacher–student dialogue or perhaps to a series of resources which are being used in a lesson. The video clips are in Windows media video file format (.wmv), and give the best quality visuals if viewed with Windows Media Player. (Players that support this file type are Windows Media Player 7 Windows Media Player for Windows XP, Windows Media Player 9 Series, Windows Media Player 10 and Windows Media Player 11.)

Although the focus throughout is on improving your professional skills, there is no attempt to provide a 'tick list' of how to achieve each of the individual Professional Standards for QTS. I believe that a more holistic approach is more suitable for this sort of publication. The book addresses professional attributes, professional knowledge and understanding, and professional skills in a more holistic way than the way they are presented in the Standards. You will, however, find frequent reference to the Standards, and it is hoped that through using the book reflectively, you will acquire the general skills required to gather and present your evidence against each of the Standards statements. A rough guide to where the book addresses individual Standards is given in the following chart.

**Table H.1** Professional Standards for Qualified Teacher Status

**Professional attributes.** Those recommended for the award of QTS should:

| | Standard | Opportunities to learn more |
|---|---|---|
| Relationships with children and young people | | |
| Q1 | Have high expectations of children and young people including a commitment to ensuring that they can achieve their full educational potential and to establishing fair, respectful, trusting, supportive and constructive relationships with them | Chapter 1, 'You and your subject: a personal perspective'<br>Chapter 2, 'You and your curriculum: a public perspective' |
| Q2 | Demonstrate the positive values, attitudes and behaviour they expect from children and young people | Chapter 1, 'You and your subject: a personal perspective'<br>Chapter 2, 'You and your curriculum: a public perspective' |
| Frameworks | | |
| Q3a | Be aware of the professional duties of teachers and the statutory framework within which they work | Chapter 1, 'You and your subject: a personal perspective'<br>Chapter 2, 'You and your curriculum: a public perspective' |
| Q3b | Be aware of the policies and practices of the workplace and share in collective responsibility for their implementation | Chapter 1, 'You and your subject: a personal perspective'<br>Chapter 2, 'You and your curriculum: a public perspective' |
| Communicating and working with others | | |
| Q4 | Communicate effectively with children, young people, colleagues, parents and carers | |

| | | |
|---|---|---|
| Q5 | Recognize and respect the contribution that colleagues, parents and carers can make to the development and well-being of children and young people and to raising their levels of attainment | |
| Q6 | Have a commitment to collaboration and co-operative working | Chapter 1, 'You and your subject: a personal perspective'<br>Chapter 2, 'You and your curriculum: a public perspective' |
| Personal professional development | | |
| Q7a | Reflect on and improve their practice, and take responsibility for identifying and meeting their developing professional needs | The idea of reflecting on practice is a theme that runs throughout the text |
| Q7b | Identify priorities for their early professional development in the context of induction | |
| Q8 | Have a creative and constructively critical approach towards innovation, being prepared to adapt their practice where benefits and improvements are identified | The idea of reflecting on practice is a theme that runs throughout the text. However Chapter 5, 'Managing teaching and learning' has a specific focus on innovative approaches |
| Q9 | Act upon advice and feedback and be open to coaching and mentoring | Chapter 11, 'Where do you go now?' |
| **Professional knowledge and understanding**. Those recommended for the award of QTS should: | | |
| Teaching and learning | | |
| Q10 | Have a knowledge and understanding of a range of teaching, learning and behaviour management strategies and know how to use and adapt them, including how to personalize learning and provide opportunities for all learners to achieve their potential | Chapter 3, 'Planning to teach and learn'<br>Chapter 4, 'The elements of teaching and learning history'<br>Chapter 5, 'Managing teaching and learning'<br>Chapter 6, 'Assessing for learning history' |
| Assessment and monitoring | | |
| Q11 | Know the assessment requirements and arrangements for the subjects/curriculum areas in the age ranges they are trained to teach, including those relating to public examinations and qualifications | Chapter 6, 'Assessing for learning history'<br>Chapter 7, 'Teaching across the ages: GCSE and A level' |
| Q12 | Know a range of approaches to assessment, including the importance of formative assessment | Chapter 6, 'Assessing for learning history' |

*(Continued)*

*(Continued)*

| | | |
|---|---|---|
| Q13 | Know how to use local and national statistical information to evaluate the effectiveness of their teaching, to monitor the progress of those they teach and to raise levels of attainment | Chapter 6, 'Assessing for learning history'<br>Chapter 7, 'Teaching across the ages: GCSE and A level'<br>Chapter 8, 'Inclusive history teaching' |
| Subjects and curriculum | | |
| Q14 | Have a secure knowledge and understanding of their subjects/curriculum areas and related pedagogy to enable them to teach effectively across the age and ability range for which they are trained | Chapter 1, 'You and your subject: a personal perspective'<br>Chapter 2, 'You and your curriculum: a public perspective'<br>Chapter 3, 'Planning to teach and learn' |
| Q15 | Know and understand the relevant statutory and non-statutory curricula, frameworks, including those provided through the National Strategies, for their subjects/curriculum areas, and other relevant initiatives applicable to the age and ability range for which they are trained | Chapter 4, 'The elements of teaching and learning history'<br>Chapter 5, 'Managing teaching and learning' |
| Literacy, numeracy and ICT | | |
| Q16 | Have passed the professional skills tests in numeracy, literacy and information and communication technology (ICT) | |
| Q17 | Know how to use skills in literacy, numeracy and ICT to support their teaching and wider professional activities | Chapter 4, 'The elements of teaching and learning history'<br>Chapter 5, 'Managing teaching and learning'<br>Chapter 8, 'Inclusive history teaching'<br>Chapter 9, 'Information technologies and history teaching' |
| Achievement and diversity | | |
| Q18 | Understand how children and young people develop and that the progress and well-being of learners are affected by a range of developmental, social, religious, ethnic, cultural and linguistic influences | Chapter 4, 'The elements of teaching and learning history'<br>Chapter 5, 'Managing teaching and learning'<br>Chapter 8, 'Inclusive history teaching' |
| Q19 | Know how to make effective personalized provision for those they teach, including those for whom English is an additional language or who have special educational needs or disabilities, and how to take practical account of diversity and promote equality and inclusion in their teaching | Chapter 8, 'Inclusive history teaching' |

| | | |
|---|---|---|
| Q20 | Know and understand the roles of colleagues with specific responsibilities, including those with responsibility for learners with special educational needs and disabilities and other individual learning needs | Chapter 8, 'Inclusive history teaching' |
| Health and well-being | | |
| Q21a | Be aware of current legal requirements, national policies and guidance on the safeguarding and promotion of the well-being of children and young people | |
| Q21b | Know how to identify and support children and young people whose progress, development or well-being is affected by changes or difficulties in their personal circumstances, and when to refer them to colleagues for specialist support | |
| **Professional skills**. Those recommended for the award of QTS should: | | |
| Planning | | |
| Q22 | Plan for progression across the age and ability range for which they are trained, designing effective learning sequences within lessons and across series of lessons and demonstrating secure subject/curriculum knowledge | Chapter 5, 'Managing teaching and learning'<br>Chapter 6, 'Assessing for learning history'<br>Chapter 7, 'Teaching across the ages: GCSE and A level' |
| Q23 | Design opportunities for learners to develop their literacy, numeracy and ICT skills | Chapter 4, 'The elements of teaching and learning history'<br>Chapter 9, 'Information technologies and history teaching' |
| Q24 | Plan homework or other out-of-class work to sustain learners' progress and to extend and consolidate their learning | Chapter 6, 'Assessing for learning history' |
| Teaching | | |
| Teach lessons and sequences of lessons across the age and ability range for which they are trained in which they: | | |
| Q25a | use a range of teaching strategies and resources, including e-learning, taking practical account of diversity and promoting equality and inclusion; | Chapter 3, 'Planning to teach and learn'<br>Chapter 4, 'The elements of teaching and learning history'<br>Chapter 5, 'Managing teaching and learning' |

*(Continued)*

*(Continued)*

| | | |
|---|---|---|
| Q25b | build on prior knowledge, develop concepts and processes, enable learners to apply new knowledge, understanding and skills and meet learning objectives; | Chapter 3, 'Planning to teach and learn'<br>Chapter 4, 'The elements of teaching and learning history'<br>Chapter 7, 'Teaching across the ages: GCSE and A level' |
| Q25c | adapt their language to suit the learners they teach, introducing new ideas and concepts clearly, and using explanations, questions, discussions and plenaries effectively; | Chapter 3, 'Planning to teach and learn'<br>Chapter 4, 'The elements of teaching and learning history'<br>Chapter 5, 'Managing teaching and learning'<br>Chapter 6, 'Assessing for learning history'<br>Chapter 7, 'Teaching across the ages: GCSE and A level'<br>Chapter 8, 'Inclusive history teaching' |
| Q25d | manage the learning of individuals, groups and whole classes, modifying their teaching to suit the stage of the lesson | Chapter 3, 'Planning to teach and learn'<br>Chapter 4, 'The elements of teaching and learning history' |
| Assessing, monitoring and giving feedback | | |
| Q26a | Make effective use of a range of assessment, monitoring and recording strategies | Chapter 6, 'Assessing for learning history' |
| Q26b | Assess the learning needs of those they teach in order to set challenging learning objectives | Chapter 6, 'Assessing for learning history'<br>Chapter 8, 'Inclusive history teaching' |
| Q27 | Provide timely, accurate and constructive feedback on learners' attainment, progress and areas for development | Chapter 6, 'Assessing for learning history'<br>Chapter 8, 'Inclusive history teaching' |
| Q28 | Support and guide learners to reflect on their learning, identify the progress they have made and identify their emerging learning needs | Chapter 5, 'Managing teaching and learning' |
| Reviewing teaching and learning | | |
| Q29 | Evaluate the impact of their teaching on the progress of all learners, and modify their planning and classroom practice where necessary | Chapter 5, 'Managing teaching and learning'<br>Chapter 6, 'Assessing for learning history' |
| Learning environment | | |
| Q30 | Establish a purposeful and safe learning environment conducive to learning and identify opportunities for learners to learn in out-of-school contexts | Chapter 5, 'Managing teaching and learning'<br>Chapter 6, 'Assessing for learning history' |

| | | |
|---|---|---|
| Q31 | Establish a clear framework for classroom discipline to manage learners' behaviour constructively and promote their self-control and independence | |
| Team-working and collaboration | | |
| Q32 | Work as a team member and identify opportunities for working with colleagues, sharing the development of effective practice with them | Chapter 1, 'You and your subject: a personal perspective'<br>Chapter 2, 'You and your curriculum: a public perspective' |
| Q33 | Ensure that colleagues working with them are appropriately involved in supporting learning and understand the roles they are expected to fulfil | Chapter 1, 'You and your subject: a personal perspective'<br>Chapter 2, 'You and your curriculum: a public perspective' |

As the title of the series suggests, this book aims to help you to develop into a reflective practitioner. Each chapter contains several points for reflection. These encourage you to break off from your reading and consider the issue being discussed. Sometimes you are asked to compare the information in the text with your own experience; sometimes you are asked to complete a small task. It is hoped that you will not be in a hurry to read through the whole book; take your time, reflect on the issues presented and, if possible, discuss the issues with other trainees.

The main focus of the book is on practical advice, but there is another area of your course where I hope that you will find the book useful. If you are undertaking an award-bearing course (for example, leading to a PGCE or a degree with QTS), then you will have to do some assignments.

# 1 YOU AND YOUR SUBJECT: A PERSONAL PERSPECTIVE

This chapter considers the following issues:

- history as an academic discipline and a school subject
- developing a critical and reflective approach to your understanding of history
- the professional identity of a history teacher
- subject knowledge: doing history or learning history
- the components of subject knowledge
- understanding professional craft knowledge.

## A SUBJECT CALLED HISTORY: DEFINING A ROLE IN THE NEW CURRICULUM

During the course of writing this text, changing ideas about the nature and purpose of the school curriculum have had an impact on the emphasis and direction of some of the chapters. So much so that this opening discussion is the last part of the book to be completed: an introductory epilogue perhaps? Every aspect of the school curriculum is 'up for review' and history teachers face the prospect of beginning to introduce a new Key Stage 3 National Curriculum, coping with a reformed GCSE regime and a new A Level structure at the same time. History teachers therefore have tended naturally to focus on these curriculum changes at the level of the history department: how will the reforms affect the history we have to teach? There is, as ever, a bigger picture which has the potential to influence the nature and the role of history in the wider curriculum. An apocryphal account of Captain Cook's first encounter with the coastal population of what is now New South Wales recalls that the aborigines living by the sea ignored HMS *Endeavour*. The ship was so large that it was beyond anything they had ever seen and was beyond comprehension.

They therefore turned their backs on the large ship and continued with their lives. It was only when the crew embarked on smaller rowing boats that they could see something that was within the realms of their cultural experience and possibly recognize a threat. This may, or may not be an appropriate analogy but perhaps history teacher's traditional commitment to the integrity of the subject, as well as trying to cope with the new reforms, has failed to recognize, yet again, more new threats; but as always there are also new opportunities. The PowerPoint of Mick Waters's Curriculum Review at the end of 2006 would, on the face of it, appear to threaten, or at least marginalize, history as these extracts appear to suggest:

- 'Let us finish with the traditional school curriculum in which subjects are served up as ends in themselves.'
- 'Resist institutional and organizational habits.'
- 'Support schools and settings in building their curriculum.'
- 'A shared emphasis on "doing better"; raising standards in literacy, numeracy and ICT as well as citizenship, health, enterprise, creativity and internationalism.'

Mick Waters then as some latter-day Danton condemning the subject-centred *ancien régime* and its defenders as myopic and conservative, not fit to serve the needs of a new dynamic nation in a new exciting century. As historians we know how to respond in a typically ironic and cynical manner. We can recognize the new curriculum, forged in the white heat of the new technological revolution, which might more resemble a clapped out microwave or a VHS video recorder but let us not be too hasty to rush to judgement. There are real opportunities and it is time to recognize them and make the most of them. Let us resort to some neat rhetorical trickery and see what else Mr Waters has to offer:

- 'Let us dig deeper and use subjects as the vast and inspiring resources they are for serving the educational goals we value. (Geographical Association)'
- 'Rethink subjects from concern about subject content to concern about the nature and impact of subjects.'
- 'Address difficult issues (that) affect the person(al) and (the) social.'
- 'Do not shrink from controversy, deal with emotions and relationships.'
- 'Help young people face fears.'
- 'See things from different view points.'
- 'Focus on the effectiveness of learning.'

Of course we could be cynical and claim that we have heard all this before but this response, in the end might be fatal and we could never know until it was too late. As history teachers we need to recognize that we perform a number of different tasks and take on a number of different responsibilities and just perhaps this new vision for the curriculum gives us an opportunity to define our role on our terms. A hedgehog-like response is no real defence, particularly when you are on the six-lane superhighway of the new curriculum. Does this prove that you can be ironic and enthusiastic at the same time?

Citizenship appears to be written into the new curriculum like never before, Mick Waters's presentation has two Curriculum Outcomes which appear to be citizenship-led: civic participation and responsible citizens. Lord Adonis, in response to requests for history to stay in the curriculum to the age of 16 muttered something about history being delivered through the citizenship curriculum. This prompted a comment to the effect of: 'great, the best taught subject in the curriculum is given up to be delivered by the worst taught subject in the curriculum'. This is one area where the new direction for the curriculum offers opportunities for history teachers and history departments but not, perhaps in the way that Lord Adonis might think.

History and citizenship as discrete curriculum subjects have always enjoyed an ambiguous relationship. In the early years of citizenship it was viewed by some as a means of salvation. There was a hazy assumption that much of the curriculum could be delivered through history. Political literacy would be covered by studying the Parliamentary Reform Acts, the Chartists and the suffragettes; while topics such as the slave trade and the Holocaust would obviously deliver the human rights 'bits'. Finally, modern-world GCSE could deliver international co-operation by studying the League of Nations and the United Nations. Citizenship is beginning to define itself as a subject in the school curriculum, but as Peter Brett readily admits: 'there are important lessons to be learned by citizenship educators from developments in History pedagogy' (2005: 16). This distinction is important, citizenship is not a defined academic discipline and as such it does not work within distinct conceptual and methodological frameworks. If you were to compare the citizenship and history key concepts and key processes you would see that the former might best be described as aspirational rather than embedded in the tradition of an academic discipline. This doesn't mean that *ancien régime* historians should feel superior to New World citizens. It demonstrates one of the key points in Waters's curriculum review: how the nature of history has an impact on the wider curriculum. The new curriculum is all about thinking differently and thinking creatively, perhaps responsible citizenship does not have to be shorthand for citizenship. What we need to define, and be clear about, is the way that history teaching itself contributes to 'responsible citizenship'. It might also be appropriate to consider how the clarity of purpose and direction embedded in the history key concepts and key skills can provide flesh and bones for the very amoebic concepts and skills slopping about on the pages of the citizenship curriculum. In other words if you are a beginning citizenship teacher is the academic rigour which underpins the study of history going to give your teaching more sense of direction? Chapters 2 and 3 explore the key concepts and key processes in further detail and explore ways in which these

can be used to provide a focus for students' learning. As you develop this understanding it would be worthwhile looking at the equivalent structures in the citizenship curriculum and trying to work out how you can turn liberal ideals into learning objectives. In a similar vein the focus in Chapters 4 and 5 on thinking and learning provide a more substantial diet for citizenship teachers who might want some practical advice about what constructing 'Critical thinking and enquiry tasks' might actually involve.

It is important that as your understanding of history teaching and the history curriculum develops you keep the larger curriculum model in mind. As a history teacher you have to accept that your 'day job' is more complex and involves more than simply teaching your subject. Even from the narrower standpoint of your subject you need to accept that teaching history is concerned with the transmission of cultural values and the curriculum has a socializing role. There will always be discussion and disagreement about the nature of the cultural values and the purposes of socialization but that is tied up in the notions of civic participation and responsible citizens.

## BECOMING A HISTORY TEACHER: DEVELOPING A PROFESSIONAL IDENTITY

Beginning a course in teacher education is a daunting prospect, from the start you are entering a new and a very different professional world. If you have come straight from university you probably spent the previous three years in the company of other history undergraduates in a history department which had a clear sense of its identity. You might still be at university, but an education department, school or faculty is quite distinct. If you are used to the world of work and have decided to become a history teacher after a few years, or many years of experience elsewhere, again the differences between one world of work and the professional world of the teacher are very different. Your group of fellow (beginning) history teachers will undoubtedly develop a sense of identity but for most of your PGCE year you will spend a significant amount of time in the company of other beginning teachers, or associate teachers, or interns, or trainees, as novices in history departments and schools. Your PGCE year is important for any number of mainly obvious reasons but one which is probably less obvious at the start of the course is the idea of developing a professional identity.

To develop your ideas about professional identity and to get you into 'reflective mode' it is worth starting with what you feel knowledgeable about in order to provide a practical framework or background for your critical reflection. It is more than likely that you understand how to take a critical, analytical and reflective approach to researching and writing a history dissertation. In the different world of education you will inevitably find yourself in an unfamiliar or challenging situation: having to justify the position of your subject in the school curriculum. Your first task as a beginning history teacher might be to develop a critical and reflective perspective on your subject, you need to be able to articulate clearly why you think history is important. This is not just an exercise; as a member of a university history department you were probably never challenged in this way; there was, after all, strength in numbers. In schools, history departments are small, history teachers are a minority – in some places an endangered minority. History is not like mathematics or English or science; pupils apparently need to study these subjects because they are self-evidently important. As a history teacher in a secondary school you have a different relationship to your subject and you will find that you have to justify the place of history in the curriculum. In the opening discussion which focused on the recent curriculum review the case was being developed for history being an integral part of the new school framework. At the same time a functionalist deputy head might look at Mick Waters's, PowerPoint and decide that if history is not mentioned it is not going to be there. After all the review allows schools to make their own local decisions. It is therefore even more important that you both understand the new curriculum framework and that you understand and can argue for the place of history in the curriculum. Just how do you make those arguments?

Can you use the arguments or the reasons which influenced your decision to study history at university? The chances are your reasons for taking a degree in history will be very different from the reasons put forward by a law graduate or an accountancy graduate. Presumably history interested you, although you did not necessarily see it as a vocational subject, an ideal preparation for a career – except perhaps as a history teacher. So why is history useful in the school curriculum? Practically you may feel that a study of history provides you with a series of reference points for understanding the present through the past. You might also believe that history serves a useful cultural purpose: a sense that history is part of a shared or commn heritage which helps to define or understand communities whether they be local, regional, national or international.

You might also like to consider what history you studied; how did you make your choices?

- Was it down to curiosity about the unknown or comfortable familiarity with a region or era?
- Were your choices dictated, to some extent, by available modules, or what your friends were opting for, or the reputation of a particular lecturer?
- You might like to consider why you avoided some areas of history, the unfamiliar: the black holes in your road map of the past?
- Were they areas which you felt were too difficult, less interesting, downright tedious or were they simply unavailable?

A line of argument appears to be developing which implies that there is an element of self-indulgence involved in studying history. You can, of course, argue successfully that history is a useful subject, that history graduates are actively recruited to any number of graduate professions; a history degree opens more doors than a narrower vocational degree which strangely might be seen as more useful. Reading history involves thinking in a defined way, it involves working with a range of sources, it encourages an attitude of mind and mental agility. In short historians might be considered as just too smart – or for 'smart' read 'cynical' or 'questioning' – perhaps we are dangerous as well.

### Points for reflection

Points for reflection

- As an undergraduate did you ever think about the point or purpose of a historical education?
- If you did think about the purposes of a historical education how relevant are your reasons now or does teaching history to young people below the age of 18 demand a different kind of rationale?
- Finally when a young person's historical education ends, whether at 14, 16 or beyond, what should that young person know, understand and be able to do as a consequence of their historical education?

## YOU AND YOUR SUBJECT: THE PERSONAL PERSPECTIVE

The focus for the rest of this chapter is you: you as a successful learner of history at university, you as an intending teacher of history. There is a good reason for this, you will understand when you begin to teach that one of the essential ways to move your students forward is to begin with what they know, or what they are familiar with; what is known as prior knowledge. You might think that your prior knowledge consists of the facts accumulated over the years of your historical education; more significantly the 'professional' knowledge which comprises the courses or modules you followed as an undergraduate. If you were asked to list what you had learnt at university you might well recite a list of topics. You would probably also be able to describe the more general skills which you feel a history degree helps you to develop: working with evidence, the ability to construct an argument, the ability to work as a member of a group, perhaps even some ICT skills. If we asked you to reflect on how you became a successful learner of history, that might be more difficult

- you just do history
- you eventually become good at doing history
- you know, instinctively, how to approach a historical problem
- how to work with evidence
- how to write a good 2.1 essay.

Becoming a good history teacher is far more than knowing the facts and then picking up a series of handy tips from already experienced teachers. You need to develop:

- an understanding of how your subject works
- an understanding of how children's perceptions of history are both a barrier and the key to developing historical understanding.

Developing these different areas of understanding is part of becoming a reflective teacher and it is why the initial focus of becoming a reflective teacher is on you. It is about helping you to think and to connect with your subject. This discussion is deliberate, it is working with your prior learning, trying to help you focus on the subject of history and learning history. If you are going to be a good reflective history teacher you need to develop an appreciation of how history works and how school history might 'work' differently. This involves developing a more self-conscious understanding of historical methods and procedures and inevitably imposes demands that you can articulate. You have already been introduced to the ideas of key concepts and key processes; even at the level of Key Stage 3 they demonstrate how history is a more systematic and organized form of inquiry. You need to develop a conscious awareness of what might best be described as your graduate view of history or your graduate construction of history.

Moving away from the focus on an end product, the dissertation or essay is about thinking in a more deliberate, or deliberative, way about the processes which led you to that end product; in short, to get you thinking about your own thinking. Inevitably the Greeks have a word for it and it is likely to be one which becomes familiar over the course of your teaching career: metacognition.

Thinking about your thinking as a beginning teacher of history is difficult, there are so many new experiences, initially it is difficult to make sense of what is happening in the classroom. You have few reference points; in a classroom, in a history lesson, so much is taking place. Until you become a more experienced observer and then practitioner your understanding has few contexts. Reflection on what you have observed or reflection on your teaching can be difficult. By starting with the familiar, and hopefully comfortable, world of history you can begin to develop an understanding of what reflection involves and how reflection can help you to become a more effective teacher.

Becoming a history teacher, then, is not about learning a script or picking up a series of handy tips and useful advice along the way, it should be about questioning and reflection. The end product of a teacher education course should be far more than an newly qualified teacher (NQT) who has passed the latest version of the qualified to teach Standards (QTS). A good teacher should be able to:

- reflect on their practice. This involves evaluating and thinking through lessons they have taught – it might be self-reflection, or it might be reflection prompted by a critical friend, a subject mentor or university tutor
- develop a critical perspective of their practice, to ask questions as part of their reflection which help them to explore why a particular element of a lesson did or did not work
- develop an analytical approach to all elements of their teaching, where critical reflection and critical thinking can help to inform their future teaching and their pupils' future learning.

Becoming a reflective teacher is difficult, but approaching your subject with an open mind is important. You are new to the world of history teaching but there is a great deal of work out there which can, and should, inform your practice. In some places critical reflection and critical thinking are also referred to as practical theorizing. They mean much the same: practical theorizing implies a practice which is actively informed both by external research evidence and the ability of teachers both to relate theory and practice but also to see how practice can exemplify theory.

This does have some bearing on you as a beginning teacher of history. In your school all pupils will be taking history in Key Stage 3 between the ages of 11+ and 14. Beyond Year 9, pupils might decide not to take history, which will depend very much on the status and reputation of your history department. Research by Haydn (2005) provides a useful perspective on pupils' views of the value and purpose of learning history:

'They teach us history because they think we MIGHT enjoy it.'
'To fill up space on our timetable.'
'I don't think we need it, yeah it's OK for telling stories but that is it. (I think they make us do it to bore us all).' (Haydn, 2005: 13)

These views are inevitably in sharp contrast to those you are likely to hold about the value and purpose of a historical education. Such views are an indication of the difficulty of the task facing you as a beginning history teacher. No matter how successful or dynamic the history department is, there will be fewer clients taking history at GCSE, and despite the intention to allow schools to design a more innovative curriculum, it is highly likely that some subjects will never be optional. Options are not optional as far as science, mathematics and English are concerned. Beyond GCSE, if your school is an 11–18 school, you will be able to teach an even smaller group of high-flyers and, who knows, you might then be responsible for inspiring some 18-year-olds to read history at university. Clearly your 'job' as a history teacher is not to provide cannon fodder for university history departments, it probably would not even figure as a footnote in your first job description. This is why it is so important to be able to articulate why pupils should study history in Key Stage 3, at GCSE and beyond.

The status of history as a curriculum subject and its role in society is paradoxical. History educators are continuously fighting a rearguard action to defend the status of history. With the exception of Albania (supposedly), the UK is the only European nation where it is possible for a young person's historical education to end at 14. You might think that no one would care too much about the history taught in schools. Inexplicably, history remains a very popular pastime. Just look through a week's television listings and work out the number of history programmes on air: even discounting two digital history channels, history might come fifth behind sport, soaps, reality TV and the news. Some programmes such as *Who Do You Think You Are?* and *Great Britons* have an impact beyond the airwaves and result in another horde of family historians descending on local record offices or fevered debate on Radio 4. Both the BBC and Channel 4 have dedicated history zones on their respective websites. The BBC history zone is so impressive that it ought to be a regular port of call for any aspiring history teacher (but no mathematics zone on the BBC website). Some of the most popular visitor attractions are museums and heritage sites – history, it seems is big business and has never been so popular. In autumn 2006 the National Trust launched a nationwide campaign 'History Matters: Pass it On'. While this had its focus on national heritage, it struck a chord with history teachers across the country, emphasizing again the very public nature of history.

This section has had a deliberate focus on some of the widest aspects of history. The matters discussed raise a number of issues which have a direct relevance to the role and status of history as a subject in the secondary school curriculum. It would be worthwhile thinking about some of the issues below. It may be that you have never considered these before but they are directly relevant to your role as a history teacher. Besides, as a beginning history teacher you need to have some passion for your subject and you should be able to articulate a clear philosophy for teaching history. For pupils and sceptical head teachers at interview you should to be able to put together a convincing and articulate response to the question 'Why teach history?' To be more convincing you might like to consider not 'Why history?' but 'What can history contribute to the new curriculum?'

## YOUR CHOSEN SUBJECT: 'THE DISCIPLINE OF HISTORY'

At the start of a PGCE course, beginning history teachers have a number of real concerns. Some are obvious: will you be able to establish and maintain an orderly classroom environment? Will you be able to face the challenge of surly and potentially hostile 15-year-olds? Surprisingly, for history graduates, another common concern is subject knowledge. Inevitably you will be asked to assess your subject knowledge, either as part of the initial interview process, as part of pre-course preparation or in the first weeks of your PGCE year. This process, usually referred to as auditing, was also used as a tool by the Office for Standards in Education (Ofsted) to decide how well you have been prepared to teach new or unfamiliar material. The auditing of subject knowledge is ongoing and you will inevitably have to review the development of your subject knowledge at regular stages in your PGCE year. This is a valuable activity and should be regarded as another stage in your development as a reflective teacher. When you review and evaluate the ways in which your subject knowledge has improved you need to go beyond updating a checklist of topics which you have either taught, or observed being taught. An audit suggests a process familiar to accountants; it may be an inappropriate term implying as it does that subject knowledge can be quantified in such a simplistic manner.

The problem with audits is that they focus quite specifically on hard subject content. There is an inevitability about this but such a limited view of history reduces the discipline to eras, periods and centuries, and to lists of events, people and places. Good audits go beyond chronicling and have an element of reflection built into them; similarly the focus of a good audit should be linked to setting targets or highlighting areas for future development. The subject knowledge model which beginning history teachers and history tutors have to work with is one which has been imposed largely by Ofsted, who began a series of systematic and rigorous inspections of initial teacher training in the mid-1990s. The inspection framework was applied across the full range of secondary subjects. That different disciplines could view subject knowledge in very different ways was not an issue, and history had a reductionist model of subject knowledge imposed on it. The consequences of this can be seen in Arthur and Phillips (2000). Her Majesty's Inspectorate (HMI) responsible for conducting the first round of history subject inspections, produced three chapters, essentially a series of reflections on their experience of visiting history PGCE courses across England (Baker et al., 2000). Their views on subject knowledge are interesting and reveal an essentially old-fashioned view of history. Consider some of these comments and decide for yourselves which are controversial or uncontroversial:

- Inspection, as well as research evidence indicates that without such (subject) knowledge the quality of teaching and learning in the classroom suffers.
- Inspectors come to a judgement about the adequacy of history trainees' prior qualifications and experience, as well as their intellectual capacity.
- Ideally, candidates would enter training with an overview of British, European and world history.

- Few know much about the medieval and early modern periods.
- Inspectors look carefully to see whether they (trainees) have sufficient experience of learning history.

Such comments are revealing: did the inspectors have a hankering for a golden age of history education in British universities? Is there something inadequate or inferior about history degree courses today where undergraduates might not have to take any number of general survey courses? Are history graduates today more ignorant or less well educated than their predecessors? And just when does a history graduate cease to have the experience of learning history?

In becoming a history teacher you have to develop an understanding of different kinds of historical knowledge and the Ofsted view of subject knowledge is not only limiting; importantly it does not help beginning teachers to see beyond a checklist of dates and personalities. This is where matters can become technical and for a beginning teacher de-contextualized, which means you have no point of reference in your own everyday experience. However, it is important to get to grips with these new ideas as they provide the starting point for much to follow. It will also be important to relate some of these ideas to your graduate understanding of history.

- As a history graduate you have demonstrated that you have developed a sophisticated understanding of history.
- You can break this down into what you might 'know' about particular periods of the past from the modules you followed, or from the dissertation you might have completed.
- You probably have an innate understanding of how history works.
- Through completing numerous essays, or sitting examinations or preparing for seminars, you instinctively know how to tackle a historical problem, to work with the evidence and apply an understanding of historical method to that body of evidence.

Perhaps what HMI really meant when they wrote 'Inspectors look carefully to see whether they (trainees) have sufficient experience of learning history' was, how aware are history graduates of the way that they learnt history?

Going further back in time, try to use your personal experience of learning history at GCSE or at AS level and A2 and think about the process of your historical education. For GCSE you would have followed either the Modern World Syllabus, British Social and Economic History or the Schools Council Syllabus which probably involved a study of medicine through time. This described the content but the syllabus also required you to answer a number of questions which were evidence or source based. Your GCSE course therefore involved working with the syllabus content *and* learning how to 'do' history: the procedure of historical enquiry.

These distinctions are important because a significant part of being a history teacher involves helping pupils to learn how to 'do' history. Think carefully about these ideas:

- learning history
- learning how to do history.

They are very different; you might not have thought too much about the distinctions. Learning history perhaps implies that history involves the facts, the detail; it is about absorbing, becoming familiar with, in short you have developed an expertise in 'knowing' history. As a graduate you therefore must know a lot of history. Learning how to do history is different, it implies there is a process, that history is a systematic organized inquiry with a defined methodology or methodologies. Doing history therefore involves practice or training in disciplinary methods.

This is a useful point at which to consider the nature of history and how teaching history, and being a history teacher adds a different dimension to your historical understanding. Table 1.1. illustrates the relationship between the different elements of subject knowledge: from the factual subject content – the substance of history – to what is described as the 'facility' or the procedural aspects of history. Historical understanding as facility is important: it helps to define history as an inquiry – or process – led discipline and provides us with a systematic methodology to organize the result of historical research. The final element of subject knowledge is pedagogical subject knowledge. At the start of your PGCE year this is the element of your professional understanding which is least developed, for obvious reasons. It is the understanding which history teachers develop over the course of their professional life; it links your graduate understanding of history with an awareness of curriculum requirements and combines this with your understanding of pupils as learners of history. Together these preconditions will help to create a history lesson where the teacher has made a number of decisions about teaching strategies and suitable resources.

You might think that this discussion is becoming even more bogged down in jargon and even less relevant to your development as a history teacher, but you should already have realized that teaching history is not straightforward. This discussion is designed to work with you as history graduates:

- to help you reflect on what you know well
- to raise your awareness of the nature of historical knowledge and historical understanding
- to help you apply your understanding of how history works and in doing so help you to develop a critical and reflective approach to subject knowledge
- to help you to understand the different and specialized historical knowledge that you will come to use as a history teacher.

**Table 1.1** The nature of historical understanding: the relationship between the substantive and procedural elements of history

| **A. Substantive historical understanding as the mental representation of events and societies** | **B. Substantive historical understanding as the representation of the nature and significance of people's lives in the past** | **C. Historical understanding as 'facility' or procedure** | **D. Knowledge and understanding of history pedagogy** |
|---|---|---|---|
| Awareness of structures and processes shaping society | Explain complex relationship between individuals and circumstances | Understanding of historical methodology and techniques. | How students' understanding of history develops |
| Complex interactions between individuals and social groups | Understanding human behaviour motivation | Understanding how and why historical accounts are constructed | Student perceptions and pre-conceptions of history |
| Fundamental shifts and turning points | Role/significance of important personalities | Application of understanding to A and B | Decision-making re teaching strategies |
| Understanding uses analysis of evidence to create coherent perspective | Explaining thoughts and actions in historical context. | Understanding substantive historical concepts, e.g. feudalism, kingship, colonialism. | Measuring students learning and understanding |
| | Placing individual in context | Understanding procedural, or second-order historical concepts, e.g. cause, significance, evidence | |
| Typical organizing concepts:<br>Change<br>Cause and consequence<br>Similarity and difference | Typical organizing concepts:<br>Significance<br>Motive | | |

*Source*: adapted from Booth (2003)

## What should you know?

> I think my degree was a bit lacking looking back on it. It was relatively easy to pick up subject knowledge just because it was so vague. I think that overall you don't need a history degree to teach history as long as your degree is in something similar using thinking skills like geography or philosophy or anything like that. (Anna, a history NQT reflecting on the relationship between their degree and the demands of teaching history in the Secondary School)
>
> For me personally my degree was about doing history – you learn how to write essays and pass exams. (John, comment from a history PGCE discussion board written at the start of the course)

These views, at opposite stages of the PGCE year are interesting and reflect similar attitudes to history. First, that subject knowledge – the 'hard facts' might be less important and that some information is easier to assimilate and then present to pupils. The most significant aspect though is the idea that the disciplinary structures – the procedural elements or 'facility' of understanding history – are more important. Both comments realize that it is the process of doing history which is important as far as understanding is concerned. What separates the two comments 'however' is the element of awareness. Anna, at the end of the PGCE year, was quite confident, the factual subject knowledge demands had not presented an impossible challenge. When these issues were developed in further discussions it was clear that Anna not only had a good understanding about appropriate levels of subject knowledge, but also how the ages and abilities of the students could affect subject content. She believed that it was more important to have a particular mental outlook which could create interesting and challenging activities for students to tackle. By contrast, John understood how to do history – it was about 'writing essays or passing exams' – and, although he had been successfully demonstrating his aptitudes, he was apprehensive and less confident about the history he did not know. Initially, John also found it difficult to explain exactly what 'doing history' meant. When questioned further he was able to both describe and analyse the thinking and reasoning that went in to writing a history essay. The views of Anna and John throw an interesting light on ways that beginning history teachers see their relationship with subject knowledge and this is probably where the Ofsted view of subject knowledge and a more considered understanding of what graduate subject knowledge might look like part company.

Since 2000 the Quality Assurance Agency (QAA – responsible for assessing the quality of subject provision in higher education) has undertaken a process know as benchmarking: setting out in detail what graduates in specific subjects might be expected to have learnt. The history benchmark statements provide a number of curriculum guidelines linking the chronological and geographical range of modules combined with access to a narrower range of specialisms which clearly link to the research interests and expertise of members of staff. More significantly the benchmark statements consider degree learning outcomes and the 'skills and qualities of mind' which a graduate historian ought to be able to demonstrate. The importance of the benchmark statements are that they provide a starting point for beginning history teachers to reflect on their subject knowledge and what it means to be a history graduate.

## Points for reflection

Using the QAA benchmark statements to reflect on your understanding of ICCN history. A link to the benchmark statements can be found on the companion website, www.sagepub.co.uk/secondary.

- An appreciation of the complexity of reconstructing the past, the problematic and varied nature of historical evidence
- A command of comparative perspectives, which may include the ability to compare the histories of different countries, societies, or cultures
- An awareness of continuity and change over extended time spans
- An ability to read, analyse, and reflect critically and contextually upon historical texts

If you were to 'reflect' on the bullet points above it might be interesting to ask for your initial thoughts. The result might be a series of explanations: your interpretations of what you think the statements mean.

For example:

The 'complexity of reconstructing the past' – does this simply mean constructing an accurate account of what happened? Or 'the problematic nature of evidence' – does this refer to the understanding that some evidence is more difficult to understand or that some evidence might be incomplete?



If you were to reflect further on your first thoughts you might consider what reconstructing the past really means. Is it that evidence is mediated by the writer, that it is the historian (or film-maker or novelist) who has created a particular interpretation of the past and is it equally important to understand how and why a particular interpretation has been constructed?

In a similar vein the evidence might be equally 'suspect' or constructed from a particular perspective; this is more than understanding the writer's point of view; it might involve developing a deeper understanding of the period or place that influences the creator or interpreter of the evidence.

As you reflect on the QAA benchmark statements it would be equally useful to look at Table 1.2 which considers how historical understanding might develop in an undergraduate. It is adapted from Alan Booth's *Teaching History at University* (2003). In some respects this is a reflective guide for history teachers working in higher education and Table 1.2 suggests ways in which undergraduates' understanding of history might develop over the course of their degree programme. If you look again at the idea above that reconstructing the past simply involves putting together an accurate account of what happens, this could be described as a 'uni-structural view' of the past and is therefore not particularly sophisticated in terms of advanced thinking. The notion of progression built into Table 1.2 might therefore help you to develop a more critical and reflective view of your own historical understanding.

Hopefully you are beginning to develop a greater awareness of what 'knowing' history involves; your 'epistemological understanding'. It is more than another technical term and can help provide you with a framework or series of reference points which link to your subject and how it might be possible to describe or articulate what understanding or knowing history involves. It is highly probable that you have not had to think about your subject – history – in quite this way before, however this discussion and these new ideas are important. Because the discussion is focused on the context of your graduate understanding it should be easier to comprehend or appreciate the ideas being developed:

- this focus on your understanding of the way history works – your epistemological understanding – *and*
- the requirement for you to think about how you are processing these ideas – your metacognition.

Understanding these ideas is a key to developing a critical and reflective perspective on your eventual classroom practice. This is not so much about developing a philosophic approach to your history teaching but developing a way of thinking about your teaching which enables you to identify or recognize issues and understand how these can be addressed. In short, being a reflective teacher is about becoming a better teacher.

Being a reflective teacher is also about transferring understanding; if you know how understanding in your subject is created and constructed you should be able to apply that knowledge in your own teaching. If you have

**Table 1.2** Progression in historical understanding

| Stage | Description – student understanding | Characteristics |
|---|---|---|
| Pre-structural | History is about learning things about the past | A superficial view of history, sees the subject as received knowledge, believes that there is a single, simple received or correct view |
| Uni-structural | History is about getting the facts and putting them down in an orderly fashion | Sees history as simple sequence of events, has an understanding of evidence as information and that history is created by putting facts together. The result is a series of simple narratives |
| Multi-structural | Understanding is about seeing what historians' views are and how they differ | Understands that historians have different views, that these can be shaped by the way evidence might be selected or that historians hold different views. Understanding history is simply about knowing or listing these different views. A more advanced understanding at this level might indicate similarities and differences. No real appreciation that differences might be explained/ understood by historiographical tradition |
| Relational | Understanding is about comparing and contrasting interpretations, understanding how different historians' views fit together and reaching an independent conclusion | Developing a more sophisticated understanding of history, a more systematic series of connections is created, awareness that there is a process in creating historical understanding which is as significant as the process |
| Extended | Understanding is seeing different perspectives from the past and the present; how views are a product of their time and shaped by changing ideas and ideals | Developing a level of original thinking. Begins to see that history is mediated by the wider world and by the self. Understands that questions raised in historical enquiry have wider implications. Ability to engage in critical reflection and self-reflection on the discipline |

*Source*: adapted from Booth (2003: 24)

developed an awareness of your own thinking – your metacognition – you are also in a position where you can help your pupils to develop their own thinking skills and therefore they, like you, will become better learners.

## DEVELOPING PROFESSIONAL CRAFT KNOWLEDGE

A recurrent theme in this book is developing a critical and reflective approach to history teaching. By beginning with your experience or understanding of what it means to be a history graduate you can begin to develop a particular attitude of mind which you then apply to teaching your subject. What you will do over the course of your PGCE year is begin to develop your 'craft knowledge'. This involves combining your graduate knowledge and understanding with the experience which you will gain from working in the classroom. Your knowledge and understanding of teaching history will develop over your teaching career, you might just think that this was simply experience but *professional craft knowledge* is far more complex.

Trying to pin down what the professional craft knowledge of a history teacher looks like is difficult. Peter John (1991: 11) concluded that 'History Teaching is multi-faceted and complex' and that the 'history teacher is not a passive deliverer of facts'. Perhaps you are already coming to the conclusion that teaching history is not going to be that easy. It is interesting to consider John's article in more detail. In some ways this involves 'An appreciation of the complexity of reconstructing the past' as the article is now some years old and was written some time before the QAA benchmark statements and the changes that have taken place in understanding teaching and learning (history) in higher education. John referred to ideas by Shulman and Schon, who tried to account for the nature and the development of teachers' professional knowledge which Shulman defined as 'the organisation, selection & communication of knowledge in the classroom'.

It is one thing to define professional knowledge but Shulman admitted that how teachers manage to transform their knowledge into effective teaching is not clearly understood. Schon simply describes this as 'Knowledge in Action' but, as you will probably appreciate by now, historical knowledge is very complex. John's article is therefore important in that it was the first attempt to describe what history teachers' professional craft knowledge might look like. There are a number of different element or stages and it would be useful to compare these to the ideas already raised about the nature of 'historical knowledge. (See Table 1.3.)

It might be reasonable to suggest that the stages by which professional craft knowledge grows depends upon experience and is therefore developmental and cumulative. The second element in the formula lies in the ability of the beginning teacher to reflect on their own practice and the practice of others. In some respects professional craft knowledge appears to be exclusive, even mysterious; this might be explained by the distinctions and definitions of different kinds of historical knowledge. Both Shulman and John (working from Shulman's ideas) imply that knowledge is simple and complex. John's definition of 'subject knowledge' might be summarized, albeit crudely, as facts which are accumulated over the years, while pedagogic content knowledge is more

Table 1.3 Defining and describing history teachers' professional craft knowledge

| Knowledge of history | Knowledge of teaching history | Knowledge of 'education' |
|---|---|---|
| History teachers' thinking is knowledge (fact)-driven<br>History teachers' knowledge is organized and structured by tasks they have encountered in the classroom<br>Knowledge is semi-permanent and is influenced by teachers' values/beliefs/attitudes | Pedagogical content knowledge: pivotal knowledge about how to teach history, e.g. approaches to topics, structuring approaches, knowledge of underlying concepts and procedures<br>Knowledge of teaching, strategies – role plays group work, etc. | Knowledge of learning<br>How children learn and specific problems/issues surrounding how pupils learn history<br>The teacher's view/ understanding of the process of learning history<br>What does learning history involve/look like?<br>What are appropriate learning activities?<br>Why some activities are more effective |
| History as events/topics/ personalities: this knowledge is developmental, cumulative, acquisitive | Curriculum knowledge<br>Knowledge of texts<br>Syllabus/curricular expectations/ requirements<br>Resources | Knowledge of the institution<br>Contextual knowledge of school, department, class<br>The pastoral element<br>Institutional knowledge enables the teacher to be an effective member of the school community |
| Knowledge is informed by teachers' understanding of the process of history and historical writing | Organizational knowledge<br>Organizing classes/groups, school visits<br>Technical/professional/managerial aspects | |
| Knowledge is the foundation of and principally responsible for informing planning, expectations, resources, teaching strategies | | |
| Knowledge helps to diagnose/understand pupil misconceptions | | |

*Source*: adapted from John (1991)

complex and more exclusive, the domain of experienced history teachers. In this construction of knowledge the understanding of the new graduate's beginning history teacher education course is less significant; it is only one element of the baggage of historical understanding which has been accumulated over the period of his or her undergraduate studies. John's work is now over 15 years old and therefore takes no account of the cultural shift which has taken place in teaching and learning in higher education since the early 1990s.

> We have Ofsted in at the moment and so are off timetable, merely observing. I watched the Head of History teach today – it was fantastic. Bottom set year seven and he had them eating out of the palm of his hand. It was a truly great lesson to watch – but it made me feel a bit depressed if I'm honest. I just kept thinking 'I wish I could do that!' – it made me realize how much I have to learn. I said as much to him at the end, and he told me to remember that I was watching ten years' worth of experience which made me feel marginally better! (Emma, describing professional craft knowledge)

What is interesting about this comment is the sense that the Head of History appears to possess an ability to work a class, comments such as 'eating out of the palm of his hand' suggests that, like a music hall entertainer, the teacher knows how to work an audience, and it is all down to experience. In some ways this might appear depressing as Emma suggested, and becoming a good history teacher is down to nothing more than experience.

On further reflection Emma produced a more descriptive account of the lesson:

> It was a bottom set y7 class, who I have problems with because they misbehave. The Head of History had no such problems whatsoever – they're utterly terrified of him and do EXACTLY what he says! So he was able to do more 'exciting' things with them. It was a lesson about the Crusades. They'd done an introductory lesson with me the week before so Steve started them off with a game of 'verbal tennis' to get their brains in gear (they work in pairs, asking each other questions to revise what they already know). I can't do this with them because I can't get them to calm down afterwards.
>
> (They sat) in a huddle around the table whilst he left the room to 'get in character'. When they were all seated, he came into the room as a Crusader, waving a Crucifix before him. This had the boys in hysterics. He told them that his name was 'Raymond of Toulouse' and that they could ask him questions about what it was like to be a Crusader. He also had some printed slips of paper with questions on to help the class if they dried up. Basically, they got to quiz him about life as a Crusader and he answered them in a humorous but informative way (e.g. One boy asked 'Do you get a reward for fighting?' and he replied 'God rewards me [stage whisper] but until that time, I take whatever riches I can get!').

So how does this help us to understand professional craft knowledge? Let us try to pin down Emma's understanding.

- Emma understands the nature of the group and her relationship with them; this influences the teaching strategies she feels comfortable with.
- She also appreciates why the Head of History is able to use what might be termed high-risk teaching strategies.

- There is also an awareness that learning is more effective when the students are active and engaged in what they are doing. In this case the pupils were asking the questions.
- Significantly, there is also an understanding of the nature of this group as learners and how the questioning was 'managed' to support less able pupils.

Comparing the two accounts of the lesson is valuable; it demonstrates the importance of critical reflection and the significant role this plays in the development of professional craft knowledge. Both accounts appeared to be largely narrative and they did not appear to develop or move forward; however, a more careful analysis of the second account enables some of the detail to be taken further; for example, Emma's observation that this is a group she has had problems with. This understanding influences Emma when she is planning her lessons with this group; she is likely to make a decision about strategies which will enable her to establish and maintain a more orderly teaching and learning environment.

From these descriptions it might appear that professional craft knowledge is almost exclusively linked to school experience and that the contribution made by your graduate understanding to the development of your professional craft knowledge is more limited. It might be that your graduate historical knowledge is innate, in other words you are calling on this aspect of your understanding in an unconscious or semi-conscious way: it is always there but in the background. To demonstrate how the different elements of your professional craft knowledge work together it would be useful to refer to the following lessons on the accompanying website: www.sagepub.co.uk/secondary.

- Portrait of a good lesson. The Motte and Bailey Castle.
- Portrait of a good lesson. Public Health.

It should be relatively straightforward to identify where, when and how curriculum knowledge and pedagogical knowledge play a significant part in the development of these lessons, but it would be equally useful to make links between the way historical understanding has been outlined in Table 1.1 and the accounts of the lessons. You should be able to identify if the lesson has a focus on:

- Substantive historical understanding as the mental representation of events and societies: A (this refers to column A in Table 1.1)
- Substantive historical understanding as the representation of the nature and significance of people's lives in the past: B

You should also be able to identify how each lesson develops:

- Historical understanding as 'facility' or procedure: C Here it would also be useful to consider which historical concepts are developed and the extent to which they are first- or second-order concepts: substantive C1 or procedural C2.

You might also like to consider where, and at which point in the lesson, the teachers are using their developing understanding of

- The pedagogy of history teaching: D

These lessons are useful because they illustrate the very different subject knowledge demands that teaching history involves. In terms of factual content the lesson on the Motte and Bailey castle was limited. The lesson was one of a sequence which was considering how the Normans imposed their rule on England following the Battle of Hastings.

- The pupils had to know that the Normans constructed a particular kind of castle because it was easy to construct; they had to know what it looked like and how it might have functioned in the eleventh century. (A)
- What makes this lesson difficult to understand is that the preconception which pupils are likely to have of a 'castle' is very different from what a motte and bailey castle looks like. (D)
- The crucial element of the lesson was how to teach a particular concept – that of a motte and bailey castle. (C1)
- What made this lesson successful was not so much the factual content but the teaching strategy. Looking at an image and then attempting to describe and reproduce the image with the rest of the group really required the group to work and think co-operatively. (D)

There were two other elements of the lesson which were important and which again illustrate the balance between subject knowledge and pedagogical knowledge.

The first element focuses on consolidating understanding, pulling threads together. This was done with a simple PowerPoint presentation which used photographs of the remains of a motte and bailey castle today. These demonstrated that the motte and bailey was real and the pupils were able to relate the features of their diagram to the series of ditches and mounds which remain today. They created an impression of the size and scale of the castle and an image over open countryside showed how a castle might dominate the landscape. (C1)

The second element focused on how individual groups had organized the task between them; the students were being asked to think about their thinking and how they had solved a problem. (D)

This very explicit focus is important and if it is made a regular feature of teaching, students will consciously begin to develop a repertoire of thinking skills or problem-solving skills. It was pedagogical knowledge which made this lesson successful: the decisions about the task, the organization of the groups, the need for the groups to think and work together.

The second lesson demanded a great deal more from the teacher in many different ways. The lesson was being delivered to a Year 10 GCSE group and therefore had to address the issue of curriculum knowledge, in this case the specific requirements of the examination syllabus. The lesson was also demanding in terms of subject content: students had to understand the links between rapid urban growth in the nineteenth century and the impact this had on living conditions. (B) Again the focus is on the way that the teacher addressed these issues and used her pedagogical understanding to create a very effective lesson. The historical content of the lesson was relatively straightforward: visual and written resources were readily accessible but the beginning teacher used her pedagogical knowledge to make a number of decisions about the way the lesson was structured. The layout of the room and the props were used to emphasize the idea of overcrowding. Rather than set questions on urban conditions and mortality rates, pupils were given individual character cards to discover what happened to them. (D) Recording information on the large gravestone helped pupils see patterns which linked to rapid urban growth. The students were working with far more historical knowledge in terms of cartoons, engravings and contemporary accounts but they were having to make links and connections using this material. In completing these activities they were also developing an understanding of second-order concepts – in this case the consequence of rapid urban expansion. (C2) The classroom strategies employed demonstrate the eclectic nature of history teaching: the physical use of space is characteristic of a number of exemplars available on Ian Dawson's 'thinking history' website (www.thinkinghistory.co.uk/), and the character cards are devices used in a number of museums, for example the Thackray Medical Museum in Leeds and the In Flanders Fields museum in Ieper. (D)

## SUMMARY

This chapter has introduced you to a number of key issues which will play a significant part in your development as a history teacher, certainly over the months of your PGCE course, and hopefully into your NQT year and beyond. They key idea has been to develop your awareness of what being a critical and a reflective history teacher involves. This is a key idea in teacher education and teacher development. It can be a difficult concept to understand, and is certainly a difficult idea to put into action. This chapter should have given you some ideas about critical reflection and what this process might involve. The focus of the chapter was also on you as a history graduate and as a beginning history teacher; it deliberately made reference to your skills as a history graduate and your abilities to think as a history graduate. It should be a familiar world. Rather than immersing you immediately in the less familiar environment of the history classroom and history teacher education, the intention is to help you to develop an awareness of your own historical thinking. Hopefully, after reading this chapter you may at least have thought about your subject differently; the intention is that you are in a situation where you are aware of three key themes:

- Metacognition
  - Are you able to articulate how you think through a historical problem?
  - Have you moved on from simply answering a historical question or analysing a historical source (and doing it very well) to a situation where you can state with a degree of confidence 'This is what I think about this issue and this is how I have thought through the problem'?
- Epistemology
  - Have you a more developed understanding of what historical knowledge looks like?
  - Can you see that there might be different degrees or levels of historical knowledge or understanding?
  - More significantly, are you able to explain how or why one level of historical understanding is more complex or more sophisticated that the previous level of understanding?
- The professional craft knowledge of the history teacher
  - Do you at least have an understanding of the nature of your own 'graduate subject knowledge'?
  - Can you appreciate how this is a part of the wider aspect of craft knowledge?
  - Are you beginning to develop an understanding that subject knowledge is more than the 'facts' and that there are a number of different elements to subject knowledge?

The discussion in this chapter focused on developing ways of thinking about your subject; if the chapter did nothing more then it might just be a useful exercise but ultimately not related to your ambition to become an effective, critical and reflective teacher of history. You have, unwittingly, been introduced to another valuable thinking technique – modelling. Developing an understanding of metacognition is good for bringing out the philosopher and this might have enabled you to obtain a post at some Renaissance Court. A real awareness of metacognition involves recognition that the techniques are transferable; they can be applied in different situations. You are modelling your thinking and you can apply similar techniques in your teaching; if you understand how you learn you are going to be in a situation where you can help your pupils to learn to learn.

## FURTHER REFLECTION

Some of the first activities you are likely to be involved in during your PGCE year may focus on the history curriculum and the position and status of history as a school subject. It might be useful to apply some of the ideas raised in this chapter to your discussions.

Within a short period of time you are also likely to be observing real teachers, teaching real pupils. You will undoubtedly have a number of observation tasks to undertake but, again, it might be useful to begin to focus at some point on the different kinds of historical knowledge and understanding which experienced teachers rely on. Refer back to the analysis of the Motte and Bailey lesson. Try to write a summary of the lesson and then afterwards try to identify the different elements of subject knowledge.

## Further reading

For developing a perspective on history and history teaching you might like to start with Peter John's 1991 article: 'The Professional Craft Knowledge of the History Teacher'; *Teaching History*, 64 (July): 8–12 This might then help you to understand how history teachers put their professional craft knowledge to use.

Husbands, C., Kitson, A. and Pendry, A. (2003) *Understanding History Teaching: Teaching and Learning about the Past in Secondary Schools* (Buckingham: Open University Press), Chapter 5 'What do history teachers know'.

Alan Booth's (2003) *Teaching History at University* (London: Routledge) is important. Chapter 2 'Learning history for understanding' will help you to understand the nature of the historical knowledge and understanding you bring to your PGCE course.

## Useful websites

Live links to these websites can be found on the companion website.

You should consult the history and the citizenship National Curriculum documents. Focus less on the content – what has to be taught – and more on the aims and the philosophy behind the curriculum.

http://curriculum.qca.org.uk/skills/plts/index.aspx?return=http%3A//curriculum.qca.org.uk/skills/index.aspx

http://curriculum.qca.org.uk/subjects/history/index.aspx?return=http%3A//curriculum.qca.org.uk/subjects/index.aspx

http://curriculum.qca.org.uk/subjects/citizenship/keystage3/index.aspx?return=http%3A//curriculum.qca.org.uk/subjects/index.aspx

The QCA subject benchmark statements are useful to develop an understanding of the attributes and attitudes of mind a history graduate should have developed by the end of their degree programme. This link takes you to the 'subjects' area. You might like to compare the attributes of different but linked degree programmes. www.qaa.ac.uk/academicinfrastructure/benchmark/honours/default.asp

# 2 YOU AND YOUR CURRICULUM: A PUBLIC PERSPECTIVE

**This chapter considers the following issues:**

- developing a sense of ownership – you and your views of the history National Curriculum
- understanding issues relating to content
- how the curriculum has developed and who drives change
- understanding the relevance of a community of practice to you as a history teacher
- teaching key concepts
- narrative frameworks – how the key concepts work together
- understanding significance.

If the previous chapter introduced you to the idea of metacognition – thinking about your thinking – this chapter requires you to adopt a more philosophical approach to your reflections. The focus is firmly on the history you are expected to teach but the issues the discussion raises, demonstrates that over the course of your professional life what you will have to teach will be subject to continuous change. At this stage you might think that the changing demands made on you will reflect changes in the historical content you are expected to deliver but if the changes of the past 15 to 20 years are typical, then changes to the history curriculum are more driven by pedagogical considerations. As a future history teacher, and presumably someone who has both an interest in and a real concern for history, it follows that you have a professional opinion about both the content of the curriculum and how it is taught. The first part of this chapter therefore focuses on the impact that the introduction of the National Curriculum has had on the way history was taught.

It is highly probable that the first days of your PGCE course will ask you to consider the role of history in the curriculum and the justification for teaching the subject. These activities are more than introductory and you should see them as providing you with a series of signposts for your future career as a history teacher. You need to be quite clear about your reasons for teaching history and the kind of history teacher you want to become. This is not about whether you want to be 'the people's friend', 'Mr or Miss Firm but Fair' or 'the terror of the lower IV remove'. The focus should be on you having a clear understanding about the role history might or will play in your classrooms and the schools you teach in. Habits and attitudes which you foster and develop over your PGCE year and into your NQT year will influence the way your career as head of department or faculty will grow. The most recent changes in the National Curriculum which are being implemented from 2008 are significant. Of course, every politician will claim that their curriculum changes are different, are going to change schools like no other reforms. These are usually accompanied by groans from put-upon-teachers. These changes are likely to be important for you as a history teacher because there is a deliberate emphasis on the 'useful' or the utilitarian and a move away from the emphasis upon acquiring subject knowledge simply for it own sake. The introductory discussion in the previous chapter focused on Mick Waters's vision for the curriculum and it is important that you keep your eye on this bigger picture. Where history will play its part in this new curriculum is in terms of:

- civic participation
- responsible citizens.

As a new history teacher you should be clear about the role your subject plays in meeting the aims and aspirations of the curriculum. This does not mean those of the Qualifications and Curriculum Authority (QCA) or the latest politician to arrive at the latest manifestation of the Ministry of Education but the aims and aspirations of your school and the students who are being taught history by you. History always has appeared to occupy an uncertain position in the curriculum and it is important to be aware of the opportunities to define and secure the role, not necessarily the position, of history in the new curriculum. This is why it is important to understand not just what has happened with the history curriculum since the inception of the National Curriculum in 1991, but to understand the part that 'history teachers' played in defining the nature of history in the national curriculum.

## THE 'COMMUNITY OF PRACTICE' AND THE IMPACT OF THE NATIONAL CURRICULUM

By 'community of practice' we mean the history teachers, local authority advisers, history teacher educators and researchers, and a range of other professionals with an interest in how history is taught in schools. The introduction of the history

National Curriculum probably aroused more heated discussion than any other curriculum area, but the debate was on two different levels. On a political level there was a real concern about the actual content. At another level there was a professional discourse which, while concerned about content, was more focused on how history was going to be taught. On a personal level I feel that subsequent revisions have been steered more by pedagogical considerations and that the community of practice now has a more significant role in initiating change. If I am right, this is one more reason why you need to be concerned, not only about the content of the curriculum but also about how history is taught.

As well as introducing you to the idea of metacognition, the previous chapter suggested that developing an awareness of how you learnt history and your understanding of the way history is constructed, demonstrates the relevance of epistemology. History is clearly more than just content. What separates history from, say, the *Anglo-Saxon Chronicles*, is a systematic and methodological approach to the past. Crudely it might be phrased as an attempt to understand and explain rather than simply recount the past – or a past. To develop a more informed understanding of the history National Curriculum therefore requires you to know far more than the titles and the related content of the Study Units. You need to develop a conscious understanding of the conceptual ideas and processes which underpin the curriculum. The history National Curriculum is therefore far more than a list of topics to be taught, it is itself an epistemological construction.

In the opening paragraph it was suggested that discussion about the history National Curriculum takes place at two different levels – the public and the professional. The public perception of the curriculum is that it is simply a list of topics that have to be taught and that there is therefore an officially approved list of details which might include famous people and significant events. The danger with such an approach is that one person's significant event or important personality might be another person's instrument of oppression, subversion or political indoctrination. Each time the history curriculum has come up for review, predictable headlines appear in the right-wing press complaining that national heroes like Nelson or Drake are being written out of the curriculum in favour of the archetypal obscure anti-hero who is everything but a dead, white, English male, whose dubious reputation probably rests on fighting the British Empire. The *Daily Mail* regularly sends its readers into apoplectic outrage claiming that Winston Churchill is out of the latest version of the history curriculum, which is a bit rich coming from a paper which claimed in 1938 that Britain had no interests in Czechoslovakia! In a favourite and much quoted view the former history HMI, John Slater, referred to this 'English' curriculum in the following terms: 'British, or rather Southern English, Celts looked in to starve, emigrate or rebel, the North to invent looms or work in mills; abroad was of interest once it was part of the Empire; foreigners were either, sensibly allies, or rightly defeated.' (1989: 1)

**Table 2.1** Opening topic for French pupils in their final year at college

| | |
|---|---|
| The First World War and its consequences (4–5 hours) | • Chronological account of the military phases of the conflict<br>• The nature and effects of total war on the economy, society and culture<br>• The hardships of the soldiers and the civilian population<br>• The cost of the war including the Russian Revolution and the wave of revolutions which followed |

It might be interesting to contrast our view of a national curriculum with the French 'programme of instruction', to give you some idea of what central direction is really like. Table 2.1 shows the opening topic for French pupils in their final year at college: the equivalent of our Year 10.

The entire programme for history is an endless list of topics covering French and world history from prehistory to the fall of the Berlin Wall and beyond. French pupils have a number of documents to study. We all 'do' documents these days so perhaps this is an element of commonality. If you were following a history (and geography) teacher education course in France you would have to buy the following text: *Enseigner L'Histoire au College avec Les Documents Patrimoniaux* (*Teaching History in College – Set Documents*). The designation of certain documents as *'patrimoniaux'* invests them with a certain seal of official approval. These documents are not just set texts but are key documents which are part of the heritage of France, something which every French child, and adult, should know. They are also more than documents; some are paintings, some films and, while they are overwhelmingly French, they also reflect the times. For the first World War the key document is the film *All Quiet on the Western Front*. For more contemporary history the key document is a photograph of Buzz Aldrin on the Moon in July 1969. The book closes with an account of the fall of the Berlin Wall. These documents are cultural artefacts which might be considered to have an iconic status, not just in France but could justifiably be claimed to have a relevance to humanity. Trust the French to be philosophical. On a personal and a practical note I was visiting the new memorial museum in Oradour sur Glane on the outskirts of Limoges a couple of years ago and I heard a young French visitor remark to his father, as they passed by contrasting images of de Gaulle and Pétain: *'Ah, le discours du Marechal Pétain et l'appel du General de Gaulle'* just as they appear in *Les Documents Patrimoniaux* – perhaps proof that the French system is effective.

The idea that there is a collection of essential documents – a historical canon – which every pupil is introduced to is 'interesting'. However, the teacher's guide is more significant for what it reveals about the nature and status of these documents and, following from this, how these documents are used in the classroom. As the documents have a semi-official status there is also a right way to use the documents and they highlight particular issues above and beyond the mere history: the universal nature of the Declaration of the Rights of Man and Citizen for example, the idea of human rights is a legacy of the French Revolution. The documents are uncompromising: the Declaration of Rights of Man and Citizen are there in full, in this case in the language of the Enlightenment – no simple cut down versions, no beginner's guide and no differentiation for French pupils. The documents, however significant or important, are part of the programme of instruction. They are not there to provide an insight into differing interpretations or to introduce French pupils to the idea of source analysis – on occasions these documents might illustrate something iconic about a time or event but primarily they instruct.

## Points for reflection

- It would be worthwhile contrasting the underlying philosophies evident in the account of Slater on page 28 with those of the French programme of instruction for history. Why do the English appear to enjoy an element of self-parody while the French appear to have a clear sense of mission about the place and purpose of history in the school curriculum?
- Should teachers in secondary schools in the UK have a similar list of key documents which reflect either an accepted canon or the idea that some of these documents could be described as 'patrimonial'?
- From the understanding you have developed of epistemology in the previous chapter, what observations or conclusions might you draw from the French programme of instruction and the way that historical understanding is measured in France?

Points for reflection

This French interlude is interesting if only to demonstrate what can and does happen in a system where there is a tradition of central direction and control. This can be traced back to the Third Republic where education had a clearly defined civic purpose – and an anti-clerical intent. In some ways the English elementary system performed a similar role but the outcome might have been different: education serving the needs of Queen, Empire and God – who was also rumoured to be an Englishman. The strong civic purpose endured in France and continuing Republican evangelical zeal has ensured that the historical education of young people has changed very little since 1945. More significantly there has, up to a point, been a general acceptance of the content of the history curriculum. Where controversy has existed it has tended to mirror concerns in French society itself about the way that the defeat and occupation of 1940 and the Vichy regime have been depicted.

In the UK we also have national myths and national heroes but we are always more than ready to debunk them. Presenting Dunkirk as something less than a British victory, or suggesting that the Royal Navy played a more significant role than the Royal Air Force (RAF) in 1940 tends not to provoke the kind of national soul searching that the attempt to broadcast the documentary film, *The Sorrow and the Pity,* did in France in 1969. Instead, here in the UK we tend to specialize in the feigned moral outrage of the conservative press whenever the history National Curriculum is about to change. This does not mean that the nature and direction of change in the history curriculum has been uncontroversial; it is just important to realize how these changes have taken place. There are two different arenas – the professional and the political. At times they coexist quite peacefully. During the late 1980s and throughout the 1990s when the history National Curriculum was taking shape for the first time any semblance of détente was shattered. Proponents of different historical schools adopted progressive or traditionalist standpoints and aligned themselves with conservative or liberal ideas about the nature and purpose of school history. The flavour of this acrimonious period is best captured in Rob Phillips's *History Teaching, Nationhood and the State* (1998). It is a highly readable analysis of the debates surrounding the creation of the history National Curriculum and his insider information provides a unique insight into the thinking of the then Conservative government.

*History Teaching, Nationhood and the State* was published in 1998 and almost 10 years on it might be appropriate to consider the wider perspective and examine the longer-term consequences of the introduction of the history National Curriculum. At the time, there was real concern that issues identified by the professional community of history teachers would be set aside in favour of a history curriculum which was narrow in terms of content – dead, white, British males – and in terms of assessment – the regurgitation of lists of dates of kings, queens, Acts of Parliament and British military victories. In this sense the discussions surrounding the nature and future direction of the history curriculum were hotly contested. As might be expected, the discussions generated a great deal of heat in the usual places – the media and Parliament – but the discourse among the community of history teachers focused on different issues.

To understand this idea of a developing community of practice it would be useful to look at the situation in the years immediately before the introduction of the history National Curriculum. The publication of *History in the Primary and Secondary Years* by Her Majesty's Inspectorate (HMI) in 1985 provided a valuable snapshot of the range of good practice that existed in the world of history teaching. The report also identified a number of issues which might inform individual history department's decisions about constructing a suitable curriculum:

- making the content relevant and balanced teaching British, European and world history
- balancing the competing and complementary demands of content delivery with those of developing pupils' historical skills and levels of conceptual understanding
- addressing the issue of progression: ensuring that the demands made of pupils are incremental and that pupils' knowledge and understanding increases year on year.

Overall the situation in the mid-1980s might best be described as encouraging, or showing promise. This was markedly different from the situation at the end of the 1960s, characterized by a series of gloomy predictions which claimed that history was in danger. What had happened between 1970 and 1985 was largely down to the history teaching community itself. Consciously, or accidentally, history teaching developed a distinctive pedagogy which informed understanding about the nature of the discipline and increased understanding about how pupils develop an understanding of history. Throughout the 1970s there was a sea change in the way that school history was perceived. In 1971 the *Educational Objectives for the Study of History* (Coltham and Fines, 1971) introduced the idea of objective- or outcome-led history teaching. A year later the Schools Council History Project helped teachers to articulate ideas about the role and purpose of history in the school curriculum and introduced the idea that teaching and learning history was about developing conceptual understanding and an awareness of the processes or methodologies involved in the study of history. These curriculum developments went alongside a growing body of research evidence which focused on pupils' acquisition and development of historical understanding.

The importance of these developments is twofold. The presence of a developing and influential community of practice has had a lasting and growing impact on history teaching at a number of levels. The community of history teaching has developed and retained a sense of independence and confidence, and has provided both a sense of direction and the impetus for further innovation. In the mid-1980s when the public examination system at 16+ was reformed it is significant that the nature and direction of the changes which resulted in the emergence of the history GCSE was informed both by research evidence and the experience of the history teaching community. Discussions surrounding the introduction of the GCSE focused less on content and more on the nature of history as a school discipline, the significant outcome being the GCSE assessment criteria which identified the historical concepts which pupils needed to understand such as causation, the historical processes which they would have to master such as evaluating historical evidence, as well as the ability to evaluate, select and deploy historical knowledge.

The battle for the history National Curriculum in the late 1980s and early 1990s was both different and interesting The arguments might be summarized as skills versus content but the divisions were perhaps more significant. Both sides viewed the aspirations of the other faction as detrimental to the future of history teaching. If the traditionalists got their way, there might be a risk that the political right would define the content of the history curriculum in a very narrow manner. If, on the other hand, the progressives were to win the day, there was a perception that the achievements and the heroes of British history would be overlooked.

The Mark 1 curriculum was inevitably a compromise (see Table 2.2) but from the outset there were significant concerns about some aspects of the curriculum. In 1991 the history National Curriculum covered both Key Stage 3 (KS3) and Key Stage 4 (KS4); as a head of department at the time I remember being profoundly depressed at the thought of having to teach the proposed outlines for GCSE history: they were a backward step, they did not take into account some of the teacher developments that the earlier GCSE reforms had set in motion; above all the content was profoundly dull. In autumn 1991 the most immediate concern was the KS3 curriculum and with it the challenge of managing a vast statutory content and the demands of a new and complex assessment regime. In January 1992 after only one term of trying to come to terms with teaching the National Curriculum it was announced that 'the SAT [standard assessment task] would consist of two written papers, provide opportunities for extended writing, cover all the attainment targets and the programmes of study at KS3' (Phillips, 1998: 118). From Table 2.2 it is immediately apparent that the demands of the history SAT would impose a terrific burden on history teachers and pupils alike. The 'threat' to assess pupils at the end of Year 9, partly based on work undertaken at the beginning of Year 7, effectively meant that history teachers were already teaching with an eye on the test. To make matters worse the day-to-day assessment requirements of the National Curriculum were having a detrimental impact upon the way that the curriculum was being taught In-service courses, meant to help teachers manage the new curriculum, had an insane but inevitable focus upon assessment. In my part of the world, twilight in-service training (INSET) focused on such issues as: How to teach and assess AT1(c) Level 4/5 lessons – *Knowledge and Understanding of History: different features of a historical period – show how different features of a historical period relate to each other.* History teachers were not so much teaching history as creating a new language.

In spring 1993 the entire curriculum was set to be reviewed by Sir Ron Dearing. This was largely brought about as a result of widespread dissatisfaction among primary teachers who threatened a boycott of SATs. The history curriculum at this time had been taught in secondary schools for less than 18 months. The review of the history curriculum produced some interesting results despite fears that the History Subject Committee on the School Examination and Assessment Council (SEAC) had been packed with traditionalists. The working party had been charged with making the curriculum more manageable: essentially this meant reducing the content but also making assessment more manageable (see Table 2.2). Cutting content was relatively

**Table 2.2** An evolutionary guide to the history National Curriculum

| Mark 1: Baker's olde original | Mark 2: The Dearing Review | Mark 3: Curriculum 2000 | Mark 4: Inclusion and diversity |
|---|---|---|---|
| **Content** | | | |
| *5 core Units:*<br>The Roman Empire<br>Medieval realms 1066–1500<br>The making of the UK: 1500–1750<br>Expansion of trade and industry 1750–1900<br>The era of the Second World War<br>*3 Supplementary Units:*<br>A British Study Unit pre-1920 – depth or thematic study<br>A European turning point<br>A study of a non-European society | *Distinction between Core and supplementary Units removed. Requirement to follow 6 Study Units*<br>Medieval realms 1066–1500<br>The making of the UK 1500–1750<br>Britain 1750–1900<br>The twentieth-century world<br>AND<br>An era or turning point in<br>European history pre-1914<br>A past non-European society<br>The content remained carefully defined, history departments were required to teach clearly defined themes, e.g. 'relations of the monarchy with the Church, barons and people, including Magna Carta (1215)' but the specific detail was less prescriptive and provided a list of examples, e.g. 'Thomas Beckett & Henry II, changes in the law and the legal system, the Peasants' Revolt (1381), the Wars of the Roses'. In reality, few schools opted for changes in the legal system, few had time to study the Wars of the Roses | *6 Study Units: 3 UK history, 1 European history, 2 world history*<br>Britain 1066–1500<br>Britain 1500–1750<br>Britain 1750–1900<br>A European study before 1914<br>A world study before 1900<br>A world study after 1900<br>Publication of Curriculum 2000 coincided with the launch by the QCA of the Schemes of Work These suggested ways of creating a coherent framework for the KS3 history curriculum<br>Perhaps more significant was the identification of key or focus questions for pupil inquiry | *The choice of content should ensure that all pupils can identify and understand the major events, changes and developments in British, European and world history.*<br>*Aspects of British history including:*<br>Development of political power from the Middle Ages to the twentieth century<br>Changing relationships through time of peoples of England, Ireland, Scotland and Wales<br>The impact through time of the movement and settlement of diverse people<br>Ways in which lives, beliefs, ideas and attitudes have changed over time<br>The development of trade, colonization, industrialization, technology and the British Empire. Its impact on different people in Britain and overseas – and the nature and effects of the slave trade |

| Mark 1: Baker's olde original | Mark 2: The Dearing Review | Mark 3: Curriculum 2000 | Mark 4: Inclusion and diversity |
|---|---|---|---|
| **Assessment frameworks** | | | |
| *3 Attainment Targets:*<br>AT 1. Knowledge and Understanding (strands a, b and c)<br>Change and continuity<br>Causes and consequences<br>Understanding key features of past situations<br>AT 2. Interpretations of history<br>AT 3. The use of historical sources With each of the 3 Attainment Targets there was a 10 level scale describing different Levels of attainment<br><br>Altogether there were 45 separate Statements of Attainment in the history Attainment Target. There were even attempts to make subdivisions within individual levels. There were ludicrous ideas that pupils might just be 'visiting' a level, they would then move on to be 'secure' before finally 'achieving' a level | *1 Attainment Target*<br>The move from a 10-level series of Attainment Targets to a series of level descriptors was the most significant change. The history Attainment Target attempted to describe 'typical' pupil achievement across a range of indicators. There were 8 levels of performance reflecting the fact that history was no longer compulsory after KS3. Assessment against Attainment Target levels became a case of best fit, i.e. the descriptions which might best describe a pupil's performance<br><br>From this point on there was a significant break with the Mark 1 curriculum and other subjects in the KS3 curriculum. The physical separation of the Attainment Target from the programmes of study in the document effectively removed the link between lesson and learning objectives and ended key stage summative assessment | *1 Attainment Target*<br>Little significant change. There is some editorial 'tidying up' and rephrasing which reflects the experience of teaching KS3 history since the Dearing Report | *1 Attainment Target*<br>Again little significant change. A new emphasis on thinking and learning and the application of knowledge as this extract demonstrates:<br>'They do this through increasing independent and critical enquiry, generating and investigating questions.' |

*(Continued)*

Table 2.2 (Continued)

| Mark 1: Baker's olde original | Mark 2: The Dearing Review | Mark 3: Curriculum 2000 | Mark 4: Inclusion and diversity |
|---|---|---|---|
| **Conceptual frameworks** | | | |
| Conceptual frameworks for the study of history were embedded in the Attainment Target. These were limited to:<br>Change and continuity<br>Causes and consequences and Interpretations of history.<br>This 'atomized' the conceptual structure creating a situation where historical concepts were reduced to a series of banal statements, e.g. 'distinguish between different kinds of change (L5) and show an understanding that change and progress are not the same (L6). This had an inevitable impact on the way that lessons were taught so that teachers spoke about teaching an AT1a level 5 lesson. | *Key elements*<br>In the curriculum document, the key elements followed on from the list of Study Units and specified content<br>In terms of the key elements the draft proposals felt that all they were doing was identifying more clearly the knowledge, understanding and skills which had to be taught. Most of the focus was on the reduction in content and the simplification of the assessment process<br>In both the draft proposals and the curriculum document the key elements appear as a list of additional aspects of history which 'Pupils should be taught,' e.g. '2b to describe, analyse and explain reasons for and results of the historical events, situations and changes in the periods studied'<br>In practice the key elements were increasingly used to provide a framework for learning objectives both for individual lessons and sequences of lessons | *Knowledge skills and understanding (KSUs)*<br>A conceptual framework for the study of history at KS3 moves to the centre of the programme of study. There is a significant distinction between what pupils 'should be taught': the 5 KSUs which appear in bold text<br>After the KSUs the Curriculum 2000 guidance then refers to breadth of study which provides a very brief outline of the content in terms of '3 British, a European and two world studies'<br>In terms of specific content this is provided as a series of examples for each Study Unit and appears in grey type. The official explanation: 'Schools are not required by law to teach the content in grey type'<br>History departments therefore have a significant degree of freedom to create their own programmes of study | *Key concepts and key processes*<br>After a short paragraph concerning general curriculum aims followed by a series of statements about the importance of history, the next section of the QCA history document focuses on the key concepts which 'underpin the study of history'<br>These are significant because: 'Pupils need to understand these concepts in order to deepen and broaden their knowledge, skills and understanding'<br>This represents a shift from the Dearing situation where the key elements simply identified the knowledge, etc.<br>The key concepts are central to developing historical understanding and provide a framework for the study of history<br>The similarity between the key concepts and the QAA History benchmark statements is probably unintentional but nevertheless significant |

straightforward but was always going to prove controversial. However, the most significant change was the appearance of key elements. Commentators tend to see history in terms of content – what is or is not taught. The structures and processes are more complex – perhaps because they belong in the professional domain and there was relatively little comment on the appearance of the key elements.

Reading successive curriculum documents is instructive and like the appearance and position of Soviet leaders above the Kremlin on May Day we can make a number of assumptions about what is more or less significant: for example on page 1 of the draft proposals (May 1994) is the comment 'The examples printed in italics are non-statutory'. There are also some differences in the ordering of items between the *Draft Proposals* and the final document. In the first two Study Units on page 11 of the draft the only non-statutory guidance referred to are the Peasants' Revolt and the Wars of the Roses. In the final document there are far more examples in italics. Finally, the location of the key elements changes between the draft and the final document. In the draft proposals there is a brief explanation of the number and nature of the KS3 Study Units followed by a description of the key elements. In the final document there is a more detailed rationale provided for each of the six Study Units. These details might be less or more significant but the key elements mark a change of direction in terms of thinking about the history National Curriculum. Table 2.2 shows how the key elements have developed in subsequent versions of the curriculum.

With each successive revision the relationship between historical content and the conceptual structures changes so it is possible to argue that the curriculum model which will exist from September 2008 is based more on an understanding (or a recognition) of the nature of history as a discipline and is less defined by the content or the subject matter. This does not mean that we have a content-free curriculum. It might be that the latest document represents a consensus and that, within broad guidelines, there is recognition that there might after all be an entitlement curriculum for history. This last statement might be hard to justify and appears to be suggesting that everyone is completely happy with both the content and with the way that history is being taught. It might be more accurate to state that there is sufficient flexibility within the most recent proposals for individual departments to construct a history curriculum which is most suited to the needs of their pupils.

The period between 1994 and the review which resulted in the introduction of Curriculum 2000 saw the flowering of a far more diverse community of practice which is more confident and has taken history teaching in a number of different directions. The overall effect has transformed the relationship between the current central body responsible for the management and development of the National Curriculum – the QCA – and history teachers. Dialogue is more evident, and individual teachers and history departments have opportunities to demonstrate their own understanding of good practice. More significantly, the history teaching community has realized that there are more opportunities to be inventive. The perceived status of history as 'less important' compared with the core subjects, a view reinforced by the absence of national

tests at the end of KS3, allows history departments a degree of curricular freedom. Before the introduction of Curriculum 2000, Michael Riley's (2000) article in *Teaching History, 'Into the Key Stage 3 history garden'*, demonstrated how the proposed curriculum changes offered opportunities to develop different and imaginative curriculum models. This article can be accessed through the companion website, www.sagepub.co.uk/secondary. You or your institution will have to have a membership to the Historical Association to access the full article online. It is from Issue 99 of *Teaching History*.

Even before Curriculum 2000 the history community of practice had a reputation for being imaginative. In subsequent years curriculum development and innovation has leapt ahead. The Schools History Project July Conference has become a significant annual event which serves as a forum for the exchange of ideas – 'All your CEDP needs in one weekend' is the marketing line. Similarly the Historical Association and in particular the journal, *Teaching History*, have become key players in expanding an informed community of practice and driving forward changes in the way history teaching is developing. Finally the web-based History Teachers' Discussion Forum provides another voice for history teachers. Initially focused on promoting the role of ICT in history teaching, it now provides a more extensive, if at times an anarchic, forum for the exchange of ideas and opinions about history teaching. Its anarchy is one of its endearing characteristics and demonstrates just how com-

mitted and independent history teachers can be.

The most recent concerns focus on the status of history in the school curriculum. In 1991, history was to be a compulsory subject in secondary schools from 11 to 16. Dearing saw the curriculum divided into core and foundation subjects. As a foundation subject, history became optional at the end of Key Stage 3; therefore pupils in the UK are now free to end their historical education at 14 – which puts us in the same league as Albania. Immediately history is seen as less important by pupils and school managers alike, which piles on the pressure for history departments. The results have been interesting; in some schools history is undoubtedly struggling to survive but elsewhere we have witnessed a Darwinian response. History as a curriculum area has been revitalized and evolved to become one of the best taught subjects in the KS3 and KS4 curriculum, second only to art and design (Ofsted, 2005). Much to the delight of some curriculum managers and to the chagrin of some of the more instrumental, history also proves to be a popular option at GCSE. The introduction of free-market principles has, in a number of schools, seen history take on the 'ologies' and the modular studies and beat them hands down both in terms of numbers opting for the subject and good GCSE results at the end of Year 11. These developments might paint an over-optimistic picture as history is still perceived to be facing a precarious existence in the curriculum.

The most recent Ofsted report (2007), *History in the Balance*?, highlights a number of issues which do not just focus on the way the subject is taught or comment upon the effectiveness of that teaching. Instead, there is a consideration of the problems history departments face and how many of these problems are beyond the control of individual teachers and departments. The limited amount of time given over to the subject inevitably has an impact upon the way history can be taught. In some schools history has become part of a humanities curriculum and might be taught in a six-or eight-week rotation. Other schools are introducing a two-year Key Stage 3 which inevitably means that, for some pupils, their historical education might cease at the end of Year 8 – which makes us worse than Albania. The way that history departments have responded to these pressures has resulted in a very diverse and different Key Stage 3 curriculum. If you think that a national curriculum implies standardized content, this could not be further from the truth. In schools where history is popular, deliberate decisions are made about the kind of topics that might be included to fire pupils' enthusiasm. The overall picture is difficult to quantify but the criticisms of the History Practitioners' Advisory Team (HPAT) report, The Way Forward for School History 11–16 contains both valid criticisms of the fragmentation of the current curriculum and some interesting ideas about the way the curriculum might be developed. A link to this report can be found on the companion website, www.sagepub.co.uk/secondary.

## Points for reflection

- One of the ideas raised in this section is that of an entitlement curriculum, that is, those pupils in English – or Welsh, Scottish or Irish – schools have a basic right to learn about the events which have shaped and influenced the communities they live in. If you were to draw up an entitlement curriculum how would you justify the inclusion of the content?
- Are there any elements of world history which you feel it would be important to include in an entitlement curriculum? Again it would be useful to consider your justification for including particular topics.
- How do you respond to these contrasting ideas:
  - Curriculum reform can only be successful if teachers feel that they have ownership.
  - An elected government has the right to impose any curriculum it likes on the nation's schools.

The HPAT report is an interesting reflection on the current state of the history curriculum. The report's concerns could well inform your initial observations once you begin to work in your partner department.

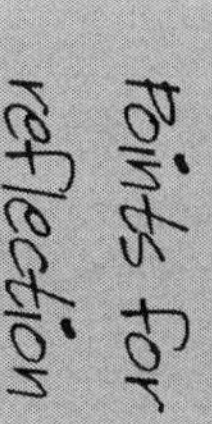

## TEACHING THE KEY CONCEPTS AND KEY PROCESSES

Within the new curriculum framework there is, at the time of writing, very little guidance about how exactly you might approach particular topics. In terms of you beginning to plan lessons you might assume that this is not too much of a problem. It all seems quite straightforward; you are going to teach about the Norman Conquest, ergo the pupils need to know about the events of 1064–1066. This does not appear to fit in with the notion of the history curriculum as a knowledge- or epistemological-based construction. Clearly you need to consider how you are going to involve the key concepts and the key processes. Again the guidance in the curriculum document is not particularly helpful as it simply states: 'There are a number of key concepts that underpin the study of history. Pupils need to understand these concepts in order to deepen and broaden their knowledge, skills and understanding' (QCA 2007: 112).

If you look in detail at the key concepts the direction's there after a fashion:

> Change and Continuity: Identifying and explaining change and continuity within and across periods of history. (QCA, 2007: 112)

It might appear that to address the key concept simply involves teaching a lesson, say, on the consequences of the Industrial Revolution – How did Britain change as a result of rapid industrialization? If you begin to consider this issue you may begin to appreciate how complicated it might be. Consider some of these issues:

- Did the Industrial Revolution affect all parts of Britain in the same way?
- Were there some good and some not so good consequences?
- What did people think about the changes?
- What were the most immediate changes?
- Did some of the changes take longer to make themselves felt?

These might be thought to be relatively straightforward historical questions but the key concept requires more than making a series of lists: as a teacher you would be expected to help pupils explain reasons for the changes and to develop an analysis of the changes. Again this is not straightforward; much depends on how pupils perceive these issues, for example, a cartoon which makes reference to Churchill's Iron Curtain Speech shows industrial recovery underway in the East. Follow the link on the companion website to this cartoon.

An adult interpretation might equate factory chimneys with wealth and economic recovery. When I used to discuss this image with pupils their first impression was that East Germany was a worse place to live than where they lived because it was polluted and built up with factories.

To make your teaching effective you need to have a clear understanding in your own mind of what a particular concept involves. You then need to develop an awareness of how pupils might understand the concept and why their understanding of the concept might prove problematic. We would not expect you to develop this understanding yourself. Earlier in this chapter we made reference to communities of practice, and one of the elements of this community of practice is the body of research evidence which has accumulated over the years. A good reference for understanding some of the issues relating to pupils' understanding of change can be found in *How Children Learn: History in the Classroom* (Donovan and Bransford, 2005: 43–6) – following up this reference will enable you to appreciate the importance of the research base. You should be able to understand:

- pupils' perceptions of an idea
- how and why their perceptions are shaped in particular ways
- how this might inform your teaching
- what you need to do to make pupils' understanding more sophisticated.

The curriculum document itself reinforces the argument that we have, wittingly or unwittingly, developed an epistemological curriculum. The curriculum aims are quite complex and involve far more than simply teaching a list of prescribed topics.

The key activities involve pupils

- asking questions
- finding out
- investigating
- developing an understanding of the nature of historical study
- substantiating arguments
- making judgements.

The key concepts, then, are not simply taught, it is not a case of 'today we are going to do diversity' – the guidelines in the curriculum document emphasize that pupils have to deepen and broaden their understanding of key concepts. To be able to do this successfully you need to be clear in your own mind what understanding these concepts involves. Take a concept like chronology. Even chronology is complex:

1. Understanding and using chronological conventions appropriately.
2. Developing a sense of period through describing and analysing relationships between the characteristic features of a period or society.
3. Building a chronological framework of periods and applying understanding to place new knowledge in its historical context.

Chronology is a key organizing tool for developing pupils' understanding of history and as a 'concept' within the history curriculum. It has become both more complex and more significant compared to the statement about chronology which appeared in the previous curriculum document. In Curriculum 2000 it was virtually limited to point 1 above; however, describing the key features of a period was there – just in a different context. This change serves to demonstrate a number of key issues which reinforce the idea of the curriculum as an epistemological model.

Table 2.3 should help you to understand why these changes have been implemented since Curriculum 2000 and how this related to a general awareness that some weaknesses in pupils' historical understanding was related to chronological (mis)understanding. This was far more than pupils not knowing names or dates and links more directly to problems pupils were having constructing narrative accounts. Once you begin teaching it will be natural to think about some of these key concepts in isolation, something along the lines of 'Today, class, I am mostly doing chronology' but you need to look at the guidance in detail. Chronology is important for helping pupils to construct an accurate map of the past but is also 'essential in constructing narratives and explanations'.

This approach to developing conceptual understanding is more significant in view of some problems highlighted in the Ofsted *History in the Balance* report (2007).

> Young people's knowledge is often very patchy and specific; they are unable to sufficiently link discrete historical events to answer big questions, form overviews and demonstrate strong conceptual understanding. They often do not know about key historical events, people and ideas.
>
> Young people's sense of chronology is relatively weak and they are generally unable to reflect on themes and issues or relate a longer narrative or story of the history of Britain, Europe or elsewhere over an extended period of time. (Ofsted, 2007: 13–14)

The explanatory notes (QCA, 2007: 112) reveal that this issue, which has already been identified as chronological understanding, is 'essential in constructing historical narratives and explanations'. There are also further clues in the curriculum document which should help you to understand how chronology links to other key concepts: change and continuity, and cause and consequence. If you refer back to Table 1.1 in the previous chapter you will see that these pairs of ideas are aspects of substantive historical understanding and are key to developing historical understanding. It is quite easy to see how they are related to chronology and how each of the key concepts links to another. The relationship between chronology and causation is important and there is a significant difference between what 'you': as beginning history

**Table 2.3** Why chronology has become a more significant organizing concept in the history National Curriculum

| **Identifying the issues** | **Thinking things through** | **Implications for your teaching** |
| --- | --- | --- |
| Problem<br>• Pupils' 'general' historical understanding<br>• Difficulties with developing a coherent road map of the past<br>• Pupils fail to see a series of bigger pictures<br>• Pupils unable to make connections | A recent problem?<br>• Previously, was history just about learning names and dates?<br>• Why is this a problem now?<br>• Draw on a range of evidence: research, inspection, professional reflection<br>• History a more demanding curriculum area | • An understanding of pupil perceptions is one starting point.<br>• How do pupils understand historical time?<br>• How do pupils use this understanding to construct a more intelligent view of the past? |
| Which might be a result of:<br>• Fragmentary nature of curriculum<br>• Teaching some episodes in detail<br>• Isolated sequences of history detached from each other<br>• Linking periods together is less successful | Research<br>• Understanding how children construct models of the past<br>• Awareness of chronological misconceptions/problems for historical understanding and historical explanation<br>• Chronological understanding underpins analysis and ability to construct narrative | • Why might pupils' chronological understanding change from Year 7 to Year 10?<br>• Does research help to inform these understandings?<br>• How should research inform your teaching? |
| Which could be caused by:<br>• Lack of curriculum time<br>• Decision-making and choices – what is and is not included<br>• Strong sequences of lessons which do not necessarily connect<br>• Some activities or topics taught in isolation | Professional reflection<br>• Issues raised and discussed in professional forums<br>• Links to own teaching practice<br>• Responding to changes in nature of history teaching – developing sustained narratives<br>• Linking concepts in analytical framework – chronological understanding and causation | • What is the overall aim of using chronology as an organizing concept – the bigger picture?<br>• Once you start teaching go back to these issues. Ask yourself: 'Where and how is the research informing my teaching?'<br>• What issues remain beyond or outside your control? |

teacher, should appreciate and understand about the links between chronological awareness and causation. You see 'events' in terms of linked or related developments and can understand how circumstances might affect subsequent events. Similarly you are able to understand the consequences of events. Your well-developed chronological frameworks provide an additional layer of meaning and can help you to organize or make sense of that complex series of relationships which we call history. Students of all ages will not possess such a complete road map of the past. There are, naturally huge gaps in their knowledge. Their conceptual awareness or understanding is similarly imperfect. Shemilt (2000) explores some of these shortcomings of history teaching and provides a useful understanding of the different ways in which a student's historical understanding is not fully developed. Rather than a road map of the past young people might be working with a medieval map of the world where continents are not only imperfectly formed but there are also signposts which contain metaphorical warnings: 'here be dragons'.

## Points for reflection

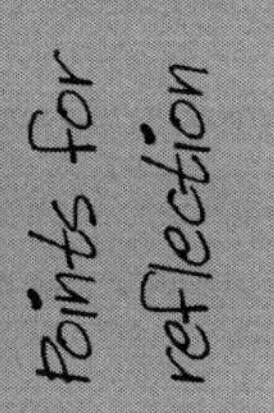


This time the reflection is different. The purpose here is to focus your thoughts on what you might have to teach. You should read Alan Kelly's article Dichronic Dancing on Ian Dawson's Thinking History website, a link to which can be found on the companion website, www.sagepub.co.uk/secondary

> 'There is an expectation in the requirements that younger pupils should have some kind of 'map of the past', but the presumption seems to be that this will somehow 'emerge' from a 'coverage' of relevant 'content'.

- Kelly's 4 stages of development are intended to address the problem identified above. How might (or how should) your understanding of these 'stages' help you to teach history more effectively?
- How well developed is your Diachronic Understanding?

## DIVERSE AND SIGNIFICANT INTERPRETATIONS

The final discussion in this chapter focuses on the remaining key concepts: significance and interpretation. They are in some ways very distinctive concepts and they can be quite difficult to teach. Over recent years they have also developed a quite distinct pedagogy.

## Diversity

Diversity makes its first appearance in the new curriculum but it seems strange to magic a new concept out of thin air. Just as chronological understanding has been given a greater prominence in developing and understanding of historical narrative and the bigger picture, so diversity has been reshaped. In the old KSUs or the key elements there was always an area which considered the diverse nature of societies and the different attitudes, values and beliefs of groups and individuals. In some ways this idea of understanding different perspectives was an attempt to make empathy more respectable. Diversity, or understanding diversity, is now one of the key curriculum aims – not just for history – and it is perhaps in this area that the history curriculum can carve out an important place for itself. It is in some ways a highly political 'concept' but in the light of the July bombings and the debate about social cohesion, diversity has an important place in the curriculum. These themes are followed up in more detail in Chapter 10 'A diverse and controversial subject'.

## Significance

In some ways it could be useful to go back to your undergraduate or graduate work and develop a definition based on this understanding. In all probability you will have tackled an essay along these lines: 'How significant was factor X in the development of … OR as a cause of …' As you can see this could well be another way of writing an assignment based on causation. The way that you might develop your answer would be to consider a range of likely factors, discuss the views of various historians who have had ideas about the particular period and then argue for and against one particular factor – probably summoning up a range of evidence to support your ideas.

In teaching terms the temptation might be to provide a number of cause cards and ask pupils to undertake a 'diamond or pyramid sort' where a hierarchy of events of causes is created; those at the top being more important, and so on. The result is that pupils then are able to decide which is the most significant cause or factor. The curriculum document (QCA, 2007: 112) is a little brief on this: 'Significance. a. Considering the significance of events, people and developments in their historical context and in the present day.' This does not give much away, apart from the last phrase – in the present day. The explanatory notes do, however provide more clues:

- considering why judgements about the significance of historical events, issues and people have changed over time.
- identifying the criteria and values used to attribute significance
- statements about significance are interpretations that may be based on contestable judgements
- judgements about significance are often related to the value systems of the period in which the interpretation was produced.

Significance is clearly a far more 'significant' concept than might be thought and again reflects thinking on the nature of the history taught in the curriculum. Martin Hunt (2000) revitalized discussions about the nature of significance in *Issues in History Teaching*. Significance, he argued, was as much about demonstrating to pupils that history was important and relevant to their everyday lives. It is about connecting – helping pupils see beyond the bored or apathetic 'So what?'

What follows is an illustration of the way that the history teaching community can refine and define a particular concept. Articles in *Teaching History*, by Rob Phillips 'Historical significance: the forgotten "Key Element"?' (2002) and by Christine Counsell 'Looking through a Josephine-Butler-shaped window: focusing pupils' thinking on historical significance' (2004), demonstrate how different this conceptual idea might be. As a consequence teaching about significance has been transformed and is arguably both challenging and rewarding, leading to opportunities to devise work which is highly original and imaginative. In one way significance is a concept which can be used to pull ideas together, to enable pupils to develop an overview of an event, a personality or even to assess the key features of a longer period of time. This links to ideas raised by Shemilt (Stearns et al., 2000), who felt that one of the problems of teaching history is the difficulty pupils have making sense of narrative frameworks. The bullet points in the explanatory notes (QCA, 2007: 112) require some hard thinking on the part of pupils. By formulating criteria and considering why these might change over time requires them to contrast and compare events and attitudes from a range of shifting perspectives. This is far more demanding than completing a diamond sorting activity. Again you can argue that if 'significance' is taught well pupils should begin to understand, first, that there might be more than one valid narrative framework and, second, how these multiple perspectives might be created.

If teaching about significance sounds challenging there are a number of different ways in which pupils might be able to demonstrate their learning. You might want to consider these focus questions:

- How should we remember ....................................? (fill in your own event, century or personality)
- Why should we remember ....................................? (again just fill in the blank)

Exploring the idea of significance raises the idea that a particular assessment of an event or personality might be an interpretation or a construction. The key issue is to understand how and why an interpretation was constructed. Understanding that historical accounts are interpretations also requires an understanding or an awareness of the circumstances prevailing in society which favour one particular view. An obvious mistake that beginning teachers make is to assume that interpretation is all about reading and understanding evidence. Sounds confusing? It is.

In your teaching you will be expected, at some point, to use and interpret sources but this is not necessarily interpretation of history. Similarly when you are teaching interpretations of history it will involve (among other things) a careful examination of evidence: considering issues such as intent and audience. To some extent interpretation of history is also an introduction to historiography – usually the most unpopular element of any undergraduate's history course!

There are more misconceptions surrounding this conception than any other in the history curriculum – so much so that in summer 2004 HMI organized a conference to explore 'Interpretations of History'. Again the context and the nature of the conference is important. The Office for Standards in Education had flagged up that this was an element of the KS3 history curriculum which was not taught particularly well, that there was a degree of uncertainty about what interpretations involved or demanded. Indeed, the opening statement at the conference makes it clear that this uncertainty is not just confined to teachers but to Ofsted inspectors as well. The conference once again demonstrates how the history community of practice works; this was not an attempt to impose a party line but to explore how best this area of the curriculum might be taught by sharing ideas and expertise. Again the comment about the report carrying no authority is 'offered only as an addition to a continuing debate'.

One of the best ways to understand what interpretations of history might involve is to establish clearly what it does not involve. The report highlights in a very useful way what it considers to be 'light or non-existent interpretations' (QCA, 2004: 4). This illustrates a veritable genre of history lessons which in their own way might be good history – it is just that they do not make the grade as interpretations of history. What we are talking about here are the: Haig/Cromwell/Napoleon/Lenin, hero or villain? exercises. Take Haig (Douglas not William): as part of a unit of work on the Western Front or the First World War pupils might be asked to assess the role of Field Marshall Haig – was he a callous butcher who cared nothing for the suffering of the ordinary soldiers who fought in the trenches or was he the leader who enabled the British Army to win the Great War? One way that this is taught is to present a range of primary and secondary sources for and against. The exercise resembles a court case and pupils are expected to come to conclusions about Douglas Haig. One variation to this activity might be to present pupils with different views of Haig so that one half of the class comes up with one view of Haig and the other half reaches different conclusions.

So why is this not an interpretation? It is difficult to see how this is an interpretation of history. The focus is more on how the evidence surrounding Haig can be used to provide differing assessments of his capabilities as a military leader. If we wanted to turn this into an interpretations activity it would have to be reshaped significantly. First you would need to place the 'Butcher Haig' view into a different context. From the 1960s onwards a particular view of the General Staff and Haig entered the popular consciousness. Part of this was down to the play *Oh, What a Lovely War!*, to the book *Lions Led by Donkeys* and also by the screening of the BBC documentary series, *The Great War*. Throw into the mix increasing anxiety about nuclear war and it is possible to argue that the view we have of Haig is a product of the 1960s. This view is so pervasive that it entered public perceptions and was instrumental in shaping the *Blackadder* interpretation of the Western Front. The key issue about this as an interpretation of history is trying to understand how and why the butchers and bunglers view of military leadership was a product of the 1960s.

Like the idea of exploring significance with pupils, interpretations of history is challenging and, hopefully, the discussion illustrates the importance of clarity of purpose. Again with this aspect of the key concepts it is possible to see that it links into the same agenda: the desire or the intention that one of the outcomes of teaching history to pupils is that they are able to develop a coherent series of narrative constructions. That they will be able to see and appreciate the bigger picture, know how the parts of the bigger picture fit together and, perhaps, begin to understand that it might be possible to paint different 'big pictures' of the same, or similar, narratives.

## THE KEY PROCESSES

The final aspect of the curriculum are the key processes. These reinforce the view that the history curriculum is becoming increasingly sophisticated and recognizes or reflects a view of school history as an academic discipline with its organizational or conceptual ideas and a systematic organized method of inquiry. The key processes are

- historical inquiry
- using evidence
- communicating about the past.

These processes are central to students' work in history and should help you, as beginning teachers, to plan activities with more focus and precision. The role of the key processes are also explored further in subsequent chapters. In terms of the whole curriculum review, these processes link in quite explicit ways to thinking skills and to literacy. In this respect then, the key processes might be thought of as being generic but they also need to be viewed within a disciplinary framework.

### Communicating about the past

This key process focuses on the ability of students to 'communicate' their understanding. At one level it provides a mechanism whereby history teachers are able to discover what their students know: it might be a conventional essay or some form of written work; on the other hand students could demonstrate their understanding by creating a PowerPoint presentation or taking part in a role play. As the explanatory notes (QCA, 2007: 14) indicate, communicating is about writing, speaking and listening: history developing or contributing to the development of students' literacy skills and possibly developing their ability to use ICT to communicate ideas. In a history-specific sense this key process also recognizes that 'doing history' requires you to follow disciplinary conventions. The explanation develops like Russian dolls:

- Ideas like chronology can help to impose a structure on historical communication.
- Communicating an understanding of history involves constructing arguments and explanations.
- Argument and explanation depend upon conventions and impose structure on the history.
- Evidence is an integral element of argument and explanation and the use of evidence is further bound by disciplinary conventions.

On the other hand, these ideas might more resemble a circle of *Jungle Book* elephants trunk to tail as it is difficult to say exactly where the process begins.

## Historical enquiry

This again is a general skill which, in terms of the whole curriculum review, promotes thinking and learning and tries to foster a sense of independence in students. This generic element also focuses on ways of working – as groups or teams which help to develop patterns of working might well be part of the world of work. There is also an expectation that students will reflect critically on historical questions or issues: effectively this writes thinking skills into the history curriculum and developing students' metacognitive awareness. Chapter 1 focused on ways in which you might be able to develop you own critical thinking; if it is part of the curriculum for young learners, you are going to be at an advantage if you understand thinking and metacognition from your own perspective.

There is also a history-specific element to this idea of inquiry. For a start it emphasizes that history is far more than re-creating stories from the past. It involves trying to answer questions; it demonstrates that history serves to satisfy basic human curiosity. To be successful curious learners, students need to be able to ask appropriate questions and this requires a rigorous approach to the discipline.

## Using evidence

Evidence might be thought of as the 'key' key process; it is after all at the heart of the discipline. At one level using evidence can be the enjoyable part of history. It is the element of the subject where teachers often claim that students have the opportunity to work like real historians simply because they are working with real evidence. It is also the part of history that can be exceptionally dull and tedious – 'death by a thousand sources' is a frequent comment. It is also an aspect of history teaching that has come in for criticism from history teachers themselves: the use of evidence in GCSE examinations forces students into stultifying stereotypical answers and the way sources are presented in some textbooks is very poor.

The use of evidence in the history curriculum has also been a focus of academic investigation. Project CHATA examined the development of students' understanding of second-order concepts – causation and evidence – and the findings are important for you as beginning history teachers (Lee and Ashby, 2000). As history graduates you have developed a sophisticated understanding of evidence and its significance in the construction of historical accounts. Again the way you have constructed this understanding has probably been unconscious, you have over time developed an innate awareness of evidence – both as a physical entity and as an abstract idea. For example you will have used evidence to develop an understanding of the effects of industrialization on mill workers in the mid-nineteenth century by reading the reports of the Parliamentary Commission into factory conditions. In a seminar you would be able to develop a line of argument or reasoning along the following lines: 'the evidence tends to suggest that …' .

The way that evidence is used, or has been used, in the history classroom can have an effect on students' perceptions of the past. You may be able to remember some of the simplistic views about bias and reliability or the comparative merits of primary (eye witness) evidence and secondary (written after the event) evidence. Explaining evidence in these ways to students has an effect on the way that they view the past, and Lee and Ashby's work provides that useful insight.

This has been a brief introduction to the key processes but they are significant aspects of the history curriculum and turn up frequently in subsequent chapters. Chapter 3 looks in more detail at the way the key concepts and processes provide focus and direction for students work. In Chapter 4 the links between the National Literacy Strategy and communicating about the past are explored. Active history and thinking skills in Chapter 5 link to the key process 'Historical enquiry'. These are the more obvious links, and as you read through subsequent chapters you will inevitably be able to make further links and connections with these key concepts and key processes.

## AN EPISTEMOLOGICAL CURRICULUM?

The aim of this chapter has been to provide you with an overview of the curriculum you will be expected to teach. It is important that you, like your pupils, have an understanding of the bigger curriculum picture. When this curriculum was first introduced there were justifiable concerns about the political direction and nature of the history curriculum and it will be a matter of opinion about which faction, if any, emerged as the winner in the 'great history debate'. The direction that history teaching has taken post-Dearing is interesting, to say the least. It might be argued that history teachers are pragmatic by nature and just get on and teach history. I have tried to argue that the community of practice which existed before 1991 had a degree of confidence and was already mapping out where it wanted to go. Ideas about assessment criteria and assessment objectives that had been brought to the fore in the discussions surrounding the introduction of GCSE perhaps demonstrated that there was a level of acceptance of a more focused approach to teaching and learning. The transmutation of Attainment Targets to key elements in the space of two years – and their most recent incarnation as key concepts and key skills – demonstrates that the history curriculum is as much about *how* we teach history as *what* history we teach.

The public forum, as always, has been more concerned about the 'what', rather than trying to understand the issues surrounding the 'how'. If we accept this view it is possible to argue that, since Dearing, curriculum reform has largely been in the hands of a proactive community of practice. It might be possible to offer different explanations or interpretations to account for this proactive approach but I would like to suggest that this is down to a fierce commitment to history both as an academic discipline and as a subject in the school curriculum. I also like to think that historians have a naturally subversive streak and they are ready to take advantage of, or to create, opportunities to enhance the standing of their subject. The curriculum changes which will be implemented from 2008 present a number of different challenges which history teachers need to be aware of. As a community we have confidence in our discipline but the challenge for the future lies in making the connections between the subject and its relevance to students as successful learners and responsible citizens. As an organized discipline with a recognized series of methodologies, history naturally promotes a particular kind of learning. This is a key transferable skill and it is important that you are one able to articulate this idea in a convincing manner. It is not enough to simply parrot 'history teaches thinking skills', or 'history teaches important transferable skills'; you need to be far more specific. In terms of civic participation and responsible citizens you need to be able to articulate exactly how history contributes to these outcomes. Again you need to be more hard-edged; the woolly and liberal ideals which vaguely believe that you can understand the present through studying the past need more attitude. You might like to consider your view of responsible citizenship; how does medieval history make its contribution? Is it just about teaching the history of Parliament, of King John and Magna Carta? These perhaps are the new questions to which the history community now needs to turn its attention. In the years following the introduction of the National Curriculum we succeeded in defining and developing our subject. It is perhaps time to redefine the value and purpose of our subject in a similar fashion.

In arguing that the curriculum model which has evolved is an epistemological model I hoped to be able to emphasize the importance of the *how* rather than the *what* we teach. The key concepts provide an organizational framework for the study of history and understanding their quite specific requirements should help you to develop your understanding of history teaching. As always, you need to relate this to your own understanding of the subject and to the way you made sense of the subject as an undergraduate. You might have done modules on the Tudors or any other period of history but I am certain that your course handbooks would have framed the content in a challenging, intriguing or thought-provoking way. Similarly, lectures, seminars and assignments would have had a specific intent. It could be a useful activity to revisit some of these and try to link individual sessions to some of the key concepts in the history curriculum. Finally, I hope that the nature of these discussions also demonstrates that, while we talk about an epistemological curriculum model, you have realized that at the heart of this is the subject matter of history itself. No matter how good your analytical skills or your conceptual understanding, if you do not have a sound understanding of the narrative frameworks you are not going to be a convincing teacher in the history classroom.

**What the Research Says: Where to now?**

This chapter has also tried to demonstrate how recent and relevant research can inform our understanding of effective history teaching.

There are a number of links on the companion website to Ofsted reports and *Teaching History* articles. These should be your starting point to develop further your professional understanding.

Understanding how the history curriculum is put together is an important first step towards becoming a reflective history teacher. In your own mind you need to have a deep and informed understanding of the conceptual structures embedded in the curriculum and how you will use these ideas to give your lessons direction. To make your teaching effective, however, you need to develop an understanding of the ways in which students view these conceptual ideas.

Shemilt in Stearns et al., (2000) is a 'must read' as it provides you with an idea of the gaps in children's understanding of the past. Some of these gaps do relate to the way that they are, or have been taught, but are also explained by their reasoning.

Further articles on chronology can be followed up on Ian Dawson's Thinking History website, a link to which can be found on the companion website – go to Teaching Issues/Chronology

In Stearns et al.'s (2000) *Knowing, teaching and learning history,* the chapter by Lee and Ashby on the Project Chata findings provides some useful insights into the ways students think about evidence.

Chapter 2 of *How Students Learn: History in the Classroom* also by Peter Lee, takes a systematic look at key concepts and looks at students' ideas and understandings related to these.

It is important that you have your own understanding of these key processes and key concepts but it is as important to have an understanding of how student's perceptions of these concepts might be different from your ideas.

## *Further reading*

Arthur, J. and Phillips, R. (2000) *Issues in History Teaching* (London: Routledge). Two key chapters: M. Hunt's 'Teaching historical significance' and C. Counsell's 'Historical knowledge and historical skills: a distracting dichotomy'.

Donovan, M.S. and Bransford, J.D. (eds) (2005) *How Students Learn: History in the Classroom*. Committee on How People Learn: A Targeted Report for Teachers. National Research Council. Washington, DC: National Academies Press.

## *Useful websites*

Live links to these websites can be found on the companion website.

The latest Ofsted report (2007), *History in the Balance,* is likely to be a key document: www.ofsted.gov.uk/publications/070043. This link takes you to the link for the *Diversity & Citizenship* report by Sir Keith Ajegbo: http://publications.teachernet.gov.uk/default.aspx?PageFunction=productdetails&PageMode=publications&ProductId=DFES-00045-2007.

# 3 PLANNING TO TEACH AND LEARN

**This chapter considers the following issues:**

- the significance of planning
- how to develop your own awareness of decision-making in the classroom and some of the factors which impact on your decision-making.
- the nature and significance of learning objectives and learning outcomes, how these relate to key concepts and key processes and how they provide structure for your lessons
- the link between learning objectives and the nature of student tasks
- the role of focus and enquiry questions in short- and medium-term planning and how to use enquiry questions to develop coherent sequences of lessons
- longer-term planning across a key stage and the role of the QCA schemes of work
- an analysis of the way in which learning objective and student activities link together in a lesson.

The chapter focuses on the Home Guard lesson with Year 8.

Planning any lesson is a complex task. It has always been at the heart of learning to teach but might have been regarded as an activity largely for beginners. A frequent comment from trainees goes along the lines of 'but my mentor doesn't seem to do much planning'. James Calderhead's work in the 1980s looked at issues relating to teachers' planning and observed that experienced teachers did a great deal of informal planning which could take a variety of forms from brief notes which were little more than memory joggers:

> Experienced teachers have various 'plans in memory' as a result of their previous experiences and may rarely need to design an activity from scratch. Planning may

> revolve largely around thinking about how a similar lesson 'went down' on a previous occasion, and making a few appropriate adjustments to the mental plan. In addition, some activities have become a routine part of classroom life. (Calderhead, 1984: 72)

Since this was written, the classroom climate has changed; the creation of Ofsted in the early 1990s saw classroom teachers at least paying lip service to the idea of producing formal, written lesson plans. More significantly, in the attempt to improve the standards of teaching and learning it has been recognized that effective planning plays a large part in improving learning as this extract from Assessment for Learning makes clear:

> A teacher's planning should provide opportunities for both learner and teacher to obtain and use information about progress towards learning goals. It also has to be flexible to respond to initial and emerging ideas and skills. Planning should include strategies to ensure that learners understand the goals they are pursuing and the criteria that will be applied in assessing their work. How learners will receive feedback, how they will take part in assessing their learning and how they will be helped to make further progress should also be planned. (Assessment Reform Group, 2002: 2)

As a beginning teacher this might appear daunting. The principles of planning might therefore be summed up as follows:

- Lessons should have a clear purpose
- The learning objectives being shared with students so that they know
  - what they are going to learn
  - how they are going to learn
  - what they should know, understand or be able to do at the end of the lesson.

### What will you have to plan?

As a beginning teacher planning can be a puzzling and complex series of activities. Over the course of your PGCE year and into your NQT year, you will have to plan at a number of different levels.

- It is likely that the first step in planning will involve planning a single activity in a lesson. It could be that your mentor asks you to plan something for her/him to teach, alternatively you could be co-planning and co-teaching with your mentor. If this is the case, you might be asked to plan the lesson opening, or an activity based around a document or an image.

*(Continued)*

*(Continued)*

- As your confidence develops you will then be expected to begin planning individual lessons. Again it is probable that your mentor will ask you to plan a single lesson around one topic.
- By the time you are beginning your first full-time teaching placement you could well be given the history department's scheme of work and told to plan a series of lessons based on one of the modules in the Scheme of Work. Alternatively you might be told that you have to teach The English Civil War up to the Restoration of Charles II and that you have eight weeks and 16 lessons to cover this topic. This would be referred to as medium-term planning. You would need to address the subject knowledge and ensure that your lessons cover a range of the key concepts and key processes. You might also be working with a GCSE group and you would have to become familiar with the syllabus content, the examination assessment objectives and the particular requirements of the examination paper or the course work element
- As an NQT you could well be given responsibility for developing the programme of study for a particular year group. You would have to ensure that there was an element of coherence between the different modules. You might have to take account of approaches and themes in other years. It would also be appropriate to consider the resources available and any particular interests or areas of expertise you could call on. You might even be asked to build in a field work element into the programme of study.

## PLANNING AS DECISION-MAKING

Planning for a beginning teacher involves far more than simply selecting a series of objectives and outcomes. Planning a lesson involves the teacher making a whole series of interrelated decisions. In trying to understand what this process involves it would be useful to work from an example of this process.

In the first chapter one of the good lessons which was described focused on public health in towns in the nineteenth century. It would be well worth reading through this again, but this time with an eye to the planning that went on in the lesson. Read the first paragraph of the commentary on the public health lesson on the companion website. It describes how the physical layout of the room and the additional resources are used as aids to learning in the lesson. The activity required a great deal of effort, imagination and creativity. However if you were asked to describe the aims of the lesson you should immediately be able to link this to overcrowding in towns, poor water supply and the possible impact that this had on the health of the inhabitants. The point of this discussion is to help you to see that planning is far more than just describing the history you are going to teach. There are other important factors that you have to take into account. In the case of the lesson on public health in towns, K's plan had to consider the questions listed in Table 3.1.

**Table 3.1** Lesson planning: asking questions

| Questions | Significance |
|---|---|
| Links to previous and subsequent lessons? | Any lesson connects to previous learning and sets the stage for subsequent lessons |
| Content? | The requirements of the GCSE Schools History Project examination syllabus – ensuring that key content was covered and the key conceptual issues made clear to the pupils |
| Resources? | From locating suitable resources, to adapting or developing images or documents. Production of work or information sheets. Whiteboard/video/props |
| Teaching space? | How the physical teaching space is going to be used |
| Teaching strategies? | Making decisions: will students work individually, in pairs, in groups? |
| Learning objectives? | What will the pupils have to learn, understand or have done by the end of the lesson? |
| How will I know learning has taken place? | How will the pupils be able to demonstrate what they have learnt or understood? |

There are no set answers to these questions, in fact they are more like a list of variable factors which teachers have to take into account when planning any lesson. To make matters even more difficult there is another layer of complexity which focuses on teachers' decision-making. Again when planning the lesson, K made a number of decisions which further helped to shape the lesson. These decisions might have been based on some of the following factors:

- Knowing the students in the group, the activity was described as high risk. This means there is potential for things to go wrong.
- The complexity of the tasks – might there be easier ways to get the same points across?
- Could the point of the learning be lost in all the moving about?
- What is the end product – will it ensure coverage of the syllabus?
- Will the students be confident about what they have learned?
- The lesson was in the afternoon – are the group better learners in the morning?
- The lesson is being observed by mentor and supervisor. Will this affect the behaviour of the group?

Add to this the individual needs of some pupils and whole-school policies and you might have to factor in the extra support for pupils with special educational needs (SEN) or pupils who have English as an additional language (EAL). You might also have to consider how this lesson contributes to the school literacy policies, and perhaps this sequence of lessons has something to do with citizenship.

Under these circumstances you might justifiably think that planning is going to loom large in your professional life, certainly over the course of your PGCE year and then into your NQT year and beyond. The good news is that planning does become easier; the bad news is that planning lessons and sequences of lesson can be a difficult skill to master but at some point in your PGCE year you will become aware that you have made that significant breakthrough.

- When you begin planning you may feel that it is very much a mechanical chore.
- You will have to complete a planning template and list the subject content and learning objectives and learning outcomes.
- You will have to outline the teaching and learning sequences.
- It is highly likely that you will have to address a list of other aspects indicating that you have considered learning styles, citizenship, literacy and numeracy.

You will realize that you have made that breakthrough when the lesson plan template represents your thinking processes; where you are articulating what you want the lesson to achieve and what you want the students to learn. By this stage you probably feel that the lesson plan is in your head and the plan is simply a way of recording your ideas. The key to making this move lies in the way you conceptualize or visualize planning. If you refer back to the first chapter the opening discussion focused on the idea of metacognition – you thinking about your thinking. The focus of these opening paragraphs was on your ability to reflect on the way that you learnt history. Thinking about your thinking should become second nature over the course of your PGCE year and, if you consciously develop a reflective disposition, you should begin to understand the purpose of lesson planning. If we go back to K's 'checklist' you might begin to appreciate where the element of reflection – metacognition – plays a part in lesson planning. Putting a lesson together, however, is metacognitively complex and to get some idea just how complex this is it would be useful to refer back to Chapter 1 and the discussion on the professional craft knowledge of history teachers. When you originally read this section you might have found it baffling, because your contextual understanding of schools was limited. As you begin to come to terms with the planning process it should start to make more sense; Table 1.3 categorizes the different aspects of a history teacher's professional craft knowledge and it would be valuable to try to highlight the aspects of professional craft knowledge that planning a lesson might involve.

Points for reflection

## Points for reflection

Look again at K's lesson which focused on public health in towns in the nineteenth century. How might the following issues influence the way you planned the activity:

- content
- group
- resources
- strategies
- outcomes/end product.

Refer back to Table 1.3 in Chapter 1 and the description of K's lesson. Lesson planning was described as metacognitively complex. Does understanding the professional craft knowledge of the history teacher help you to understand some of the thinking that went into K's lesson planning?

## SHORT-TERM PLANNING THE INDIVIDUAL LESSON: OBJECTIVES AND OUTCOMES

The discussion so far has focused on the difficulties and hardships you are likely to face when planning lessons. Time to be more positive and consider how you begin to develop your ability to put a lesson together. You need to be clear in your own mind about a number of key terms, the first of these are *learning objectives* and then *learning outcomes*. It is important to develop a sound understanding of what these concepts mean *and* how they relate to each other. The best way to develop your understanding of these key terms is to watch them being explained to a class. If you watch Clip 1, the introduction to the Home Guard lesson (0 mins to 4 mins 30 secs), you will see Peter Duffy from North Liverpool Academy explain these terms to a Year 8 lower-ability group. To develop your understanding further you could also watch the other lesson introductions. In this lesson Peter Duffy begins by outlining what will be happening in the lesson and explicitly describes the learning objectives and the learning outcomes:

- *Objectives* link to the series of historical tasks.
- *Outcomes* relate to the work individual students undertake.

**Developing a key understanding 1**

It is important to really understand this idea of *objective-led learning*. Are you able to:

1. Construct your own definition of learning objectives?
2. Explain what the learning objectives for this lesson are?
3. Construct your own definition of learning outcomes?
4. Explain what the learning outcomes are for this lesson?

**Table 3.2** Linking objectives with key concepts and key processes

| Learning objectives | Link to National Curriculum key concepts and key processes |
|---|---|
| Identify the key features of the Home Guard | Key concept: chronological understanding<br>Developing a sense of period through describing the relationships between the characteristic features of periods |
| Analyse historical sources | Key process:<br>Using a range of historical sources, including textual, visual and oral sources<br>Evaluating the sources used in order to reach reasoned conclusions |
| Use historical sources to evaluate how effective the Home Guard were | Key concept: chronological understanding.<br>Developing a sense of period through analysing the relationships between the characteristic features of periods and societies |
| By completing the worksheets based on an analysis of the sources and by reporting back to the whole class at the end of the lesson each group was also communicating their understanding and knowledge about the past. | |

The next step is to understand where these conventions come from. In the previous chapter, on the National Curriculum, reference was made to the key concepts and key processes in the history curriculum. On the QCA website, a link to which can be found on the companion website, www. sagepub.co.uk/ secondary you should be able to make links between Peter Duffy's learning objectives and the key concepts and the key processes as shown in Table 3.2.

Hopefully Table 3.2 will help to demonstrate how the different planning threads can be pulled together. The key issue is that you can make the link between learning objectives, which outline the nature of the historical tasks pupils will undertake in a lesson, and the key concepts and the key processes – the conceptual and procedural elements of the National Curriculum. Figure 3.1 explores the relationship between key concepts and key processes and demonstrates how the two areas of the curriculum are used to provide direction and

structure when planning lessons. It would be useful go to the website and read the analysis which accompanies the next lesson extract. Clip 2 (21 mins) takes you to the next section of the Home Guard lesson to discover how the key processes have been used to give the lesson direction. Figure 3.1 outlines how the key concepts focus on the history itself. You might like to think about this as the lesson content. What might not be so straightforward for you to appreciate is that the 'work' that the students are completing is just as significant. At this stage of your classroom experience you might be inclined to think that the students are just '*doing*' history, they are perhaps simply '*answering questions*'.

The 'doing' history is in effect a key process; in this case the students are '*communicating their understanding*'. Again if you go to Clip 3 (29 mins 40 secs) you will be able to see this key process in action.

**Key concepts: what you do**

- Provide an organizational structure for history.
- Provide a direction for historical enquiry.
- Describe what students should know and understand.

1. Chronological understanding
2. Cultural, ethnic and religious diversity
3. Change and continuity
4. Cause and consequence
5. Significance
6. Interpretation

Any activity should use at least one of these concepts as a focus for teaching and learning. In some lessons it would make sense to combine two or more of these concepts to provide greater coherence. For example a comparative study of Empires: key concept: change and continuity might also involve describing and analysing characteristic features: key concept: Chronological understanding.

The use of these concepts also provides a framework for assessment. The Home Guard lesson focused on the key concept: Chronological understanding 1.1b: developing a sense of period through describing and analysing the relationships between characteristic features.

**Key processes: how you do it**

- These might be described as history skills.
- The processes are the methodological structures which enable history to be created.
- They do not describe what students should know or understand but what they should be able to do.

1. Historical enquiry
2. Using evidence
3. Communicating about the past

**Using evidence** could be described as the only history-specific skill or process. Using evidence is part of the discipline of history and there are rules and conventions about the nature, value and types of evidence and how evidence supports and develops a line of enquiry.

**Historical enquiry** could be viewed as a general thinking skill. It provides direction for a line of investigation. A historical enquiry should promote thinking and questioning in a disciplined way and should also consider the value of smart or intriguing questions to give an enquiry extra bite.

**Communicating about the past** might also be considered to be a general skill. The key issue is explanation and presentation, the key attribute the structure and organization of the explanation. This process places great demands on students. Again there are disciplinary conventions which shape the way explanations use evidence. Key ideas are structure and coherence. The literacy demands on students can be significant but the wording of the curriculum here recognizes that understanding can be communicated in a variety of ways.

**Figure 3.1** Understanding key concepts and key processes

**Developing a key understanding 2**

It is important to really understand how the key concepts and key processes in the history National Curriculum provide structure for your lesson plans. Can you

1. Explain how these features of the curriculum help your planning?
2. Understand these in terms of 'what you do' and 'how you do it'? (Figure 3.1)

## WHAT COMES FIRST: CONTENT, CONCEPTS OR QUESTIONS?

The focus or emphasis so far on learning objectives and the link with the key concepts and key processes in the National Curriculum might appear to be counter-intuitive. You might reasonably be thinking that you wanted to become a history teacher not a concepts and processes teacher. The history content appears to be secondary to the planning frameworks and this is often another cause for concern with beginning history teachers. When you first begin to put lesson plans together there is a natural inclination to consider the facts – *how will we get the facts across*? This view of history considers historical understanding – knowing history as the accumulation of facts and learning – as the successful memorizing of facts. Such a view of history can have an impact on the way beginning teachers approach lesson preparation, where plans resemble film scripts complete with stage directions. Much better to realize early on that lesson plans are about organizing and structuring students' learning, and not about how the teacher will get across a series of facts. If you begin to look at the progress of Peter Duffy's lesson about the Home Guard it should become obvious that it is driven by the history. From the lesson plan it is clear that the lesson is part of a sequence of lessons which are investigating life on the home front in Britain during the Second World War. From the start there is a substantial body of knowledge involved in understanding the nature of the war on the home front. The next clue is in the opening question – the focus question for this particular enquiry. There is nothing accidental or fortunate about this question. It is phrased in such a way that it intrigues or interests students – of any age. A relevant historical question which would be suitable for an undergraduate dissertation might simply ask 'How effective was the Home Guard?' Such a dissertation might ideally collect and evaluate oral evidence drawn from a locality to illustrate national issues. Posing the question in terms of 'Real Army Granddads' Army' is less intimidating than 'Evaluate the Effectiveness of the Home Guard in the period 1940–1945'. The use of intriguing focus or key questions is important in providing direction for a lesson; the learning objectives might be thought of as a little cumbersome but the focus question neatly sums up the approach of the enquiry. More importantly, suggesting two alternative propositions about the Home Guard is good for developing an understanding of the way that history works and enables the teacher to demonstrate, or the pupils to discover, that people sometimes have different views and opinions about an event or the role of a historical character, and that developing an informed understanding might involve balancing conflicting ideas or views. This approach is clearly better than writing a number of paragraphs about the Home Guard which have a series of sub-headings: *When the Home Guard was formed, Why the Home Guard was formed, What the Home Guard did*, and so on.

### Points for reflection

The link between focus questions and good history teaching is not accidental. It would be worth your while examining in detail a number of school history textbooks to develop your own awareness of the way that focus questions are used to develop historical enquiry.

- Look at the date of publication and try to compare texts from the early to mid-1990s with more recent texts.
- Look at the titles of individual chapters.
- Look at the length of individual chapters.
- Look at the way evidence or source material is used.
- Look at the style and nature of the questions.



## PULLING IDEAS TOGETHER

The discussion so far has covered a great deal of ground and it is probably appropriate to try and review the main issues so far. In terms of your own metacognitive development the key issue which has been raised is that of the professional knowledge of a history teacher.

- As a history graduate your professional knowledge was relatively uncomplicated – you developed an understanding of different periods or genres of history and the conceptual structures and the process which support historical enquiry.
- As a history PGCE trainee you are beginning to understand how your professional academic knowledge relates to:
  - the historical content
  - the conceptual structures in the history National Curriculum
  - the process of studying history.

- As a beginning history teacher you develop your awareness of how the concepts and processes shape the nature of the tasks that students undertake.
- You further develop the ability to articulate your thinking about tasks to students so that they begin to understand the aims and purposes of the history they are doing.
- You are then able to frame your historical thinking as key questions which indicate to students the nature and the purposes of the work they are being asked to do.

The purpose of this discussion so far has been to help you understand *how* it is possible to create well-focused learning objectives. However, it is also necessary to understand *why* it is important to develop the ability to frame well focused learning objectives.

Peter Duffy's Year 8 are not only told what the learning objectives are – the aims or purposes of the lesson are also explained. Important ideas like analysis are explored and, finally, the learning outcomes are shared so that the pupils have an idea of exactly what will be required during the course of the lesson. Having precise, focused objectives helps explain to the students what they will be learning and how they are going to learn. This is an important part of Peter Duffy's practice and you will be able to observe him sharing the learning objectives in all the filmed lessons.

## Points for reflection

Click on the link on the companion website which opens up relevant PowerPoint slides from the *Assessment for Learning* element of the National Strategy; there are just four slides which focus on planning.

- When you have read these slides it might be helpful to draft your own guidelines, perhaps using the heading: 'Planning is good when …'
- Now open the link to Peter Duffy's lesson plan for the Home Guard lesson. In what ways does this lesson plan replicate some of the ideas in your checklist?
- The lesson plan also contains other information: how and why do you think this information is valuable.
- The focus in this section has been on the Home Guard lesson. To develop your understanding of these initial aspects of planning it would be useful for you to observe more closely the Year 7 lesson which focuses on the murder of Thomas Beckett. Make a note of the learning objectives outlined in the opening sequence. How do these relate to the key concepts and processes in the National Curriculum?

## FROM FOCUS QUESTIONS TO ENQUIRY QUESTIONS: WHAT IS MEDIUM-TERM PLANNING?

This might not be the style of question to inspire you but hopefully it does explain the direction of the next discussion. An essential article which develops the idea of key focus or enquiry questions is 'Into the Key Stage 3 history garden' by Michael Riley (2000). A link to this article is available through the companion website. It comes from Issue 99 of *Teaching History*, published by the Historical Association, and you or your institution will need to be a member of the H.A. to access this article online. This was published at the time history teachers were considering how the curriculum review for 2000 might impact on their departments. The article recognized that Curriculum 2000 offered a great deal of flexibility in terms of how the KS3 history curriculum could be developed in the light of changing and improved practice. One of the main features of these improvements was the way that questions were being used creatively and imaginatively to shape and lead pupils' thinking and learning in history: hence the article's subtitle, 'Choosing and planting your enquiry questions'. For Riley good questions are at the heart of good teaching and he asked history teachers if their enquiry questions would:

- capture the interest and imagination of your pupils
- place an aspect of historical thinking, concept or process at the forefront of the pupils' minds
- result in a tangible, lively, substantial enjoyable 'outcome activity' (that is, at the end of the lesson sequence) through which pupils can genuinely answer the enquiry question?

This discussion began by looking at Peter Duffy's focus question about the Home Guard. If you read Michael Riley's article carefully you will begin to understand how focus questions can be more significant and can lead the focus or direction for a sequence of lessons, thus moving your understanding of planning issues from a single lesson to a sequence of lessons – what is usually referred to as *medium-term planning*. The Home Guard lesson involved the pupils in three main activities: the card sort, a whole-class analysis of a source and the carousel activity which focused on understanding and analysing sources where the students worked in groups. The overall aim of the lesson was to make some decisions based around the puzzle: Real Army or Granddads' Army? In the same way, planning a sequence of lessons might involve pupils resolving a similar conflict. It is, however, more difficult to ensure that an enquiry question which spans a series of lessons retains its coherence and its focus. It is all too easy for pupils (and beginning teachers) to lose sight of the longer-term goal. The lesson about the Home Guard is therefore just a single lesson in a sequence where pupils examine in more detail the nature of the civilian experience of war between 1939 and 1945. If you had to plan a sequence of lessons your initial thought might be simply to jot down a series of headings which might highlight the important topics to cover:

- Evacuation
- Blitz
- Role of women
- Home Guard
- Rationing.

You might then begin to think of an overarching theme. This could be informed by Angus Calder's *The People's War*, which has as its focus both the experience of war on the people of Britain and its longer-term impact after 1945. Consider how these following similar questions are subtly different and how these differences would affect the nature of the enquiry:

- Was Britain a different (or a better) place to live in 1945 compared with 1935?
- How was Britain a different (or a better) place to live in 1945 compared with 1935?

It might appear that both questions would cover the same ground but from your understanding of the Home Guard lesson you should be able to work out that the *Was* question offers more possibilities or opportunities. Both questions involve looking at the material differences pre- and post-war and the different attitudes of people pre- and post-war. The *Was* question, however, suggests that there might be some debate about this. What has happened here is that the broad historical framework for an enquiry has been established. This ensures that there is a coherent theme running through any sequence of lessons and that there is a clear conceptual framework which runs through this sequence of lessons (Figure 3.2).

Setting up this sequence of lessons hopefully demonstrates how the process of medium-term planning can work. The impression might have been created that all that is required is a 'smart' question but 'smart' is one of those words that have a different meaning in a different context. Working from a question tends to channel thinking in a particular way; you end up looking for material to fit the question. Again, working from the history helps you to develop a coherent and considered sequence of lessons. The example above has an element of integrity and is based in good history and should result in good classroom history.

The framing of the question demonstrates how one word can make all the difference. Consider if the enquiry had used either the word HOW –

- students' work would be directed in a certain way.
- requires students to make a list of changes.

or the word WAS –

- suggests that there is an element of uncertainty.
- enables students to develop a series of dialogues,
- allows evidence to be used in ways that suggest history can sometimes be a matter of opinion.
- enables students to undertake work that might involve making choices to decide which view or which event might be more valid or more significant.

The key point here is that the enquiry offers opportunities to consider not just what happened, but how historians and others view the changes or the significance of a period or of particular events. Point and counterpoint discussion and analysis can often form the basis of good classroom history.

**Question: Was Britain a different (or a better) place to live in 1945 compared to 1935?**

**Theme:** Examination of a series of arguments which considers evidence for and against material improvement in 'life' between 1935 and 1945.

**Key conceptual ideas:**

- Change and continuity between 1935 and 1945
- War as an agent of social, scientific, technological change
- Change and progress are not necessarily continuous, identical or linear
- Significance: making historical judgements

**Key proccesses**

- Historical enquiry
- Evaluating evidence
- Communicating understanding

**The People's War historical content**

- 1939–45 a significant social upheaval
- Election of a Labour government and the introduction of the Welfare State
- Austerity
- Changed social relationships, deference to class was less pronounced, the era of the common man
- Science and technology changed significantly in the wake of war
- Advances in medical science
- War fundamentally changed international relations
- The depths of inhumanity, the bombing of Hiroshima and Nagasaki hint at a terrifying future
- Coming to a decision

**Translating historical content into a Scheme of Work**

Constraints: Time – number of available lessons. Resources: texts/film/web

Developing a structure for enquiry, e.g.

Housing:

| Before war | Impact of War | Post-war |
|---|---|---|
| Slums/depression | Scale of bomb damage | Reconstruction |

Such a framework provides a pattern for a sustained enquiry. Within each area there is an opportunity to consider ideas like a shared/common experience, significant exceptions, changing attitudes, values, expectations and beliefs. Nature of change and variations in pace of change.

**Figure 3.2** Medium-term planning: developing a coherent series of lessons

To develop a sequence of lessons based around the effects of the Second World War you need to begin with a good enquiry question. For the sequence of lessons to be successful it would also require each individual lesson to have an equally strong focus. It should be apparent how each part contributes to the whole. You should be able to see that with the sequences of lessons, or topics, suggested it is not about developing the lessons chronologically, starting in 1939 and ending in 1945 but picking up on the key issues or themes which contribute to the whole. You could make a case for an evaluation of the role of science and technology in wartime along the lines of:

- Science: Dr Jekyll or Professor Hyde – saviour or scourge of humanity?

In the short term this considers the part played by science, in the longer term students would use the conclusions reached in this lesson to develop a wider and more considered overview to answer that overarching enquiry – were people better off pre-war or post-war. Creating these kinds of enquiries requires good history, a strong conceptual focus and a sense of coherence where each lesson develops and contributes to the whole.

Michael Riley's article also demonstrates how important the precise wording of an enquiry question can be and how subtle changes can shift the direction, nature or focus of a lesson sequence. Riley's discussion focuses on enquiry questions which could direct a series of lesson on the social history of the Middle Ages – the development of towns and the contrast with rural life. Riley links good questions with words and phrases like 'buzzing', 'intellectual curiosity', 'historically rigorous', 'intriguing' and suggests that questions should also give students an 'understanding of how history works' (2000: 12). Quite a challenge!

## Points for reflection

Read Riley's (2000) article from Issue 99 of *Teaching History,* a link to which can be found on the companion website. Riley suggests that the following questions are more or less – and some decidedly less – satisfactory. Which of these questions would intrigue? Which questions would fail to make the grade?

- Did towns make people free?
- In what ways did medieval towns matter to people who did not live in them?
- What was life like in medieval towns?
- What were the turning points in the development of medieval towns?
- How did people live in medieval towns?

It is one thing to recognize a good question, another to decide the answer the question demands in terms of an enquiry question for a short sequence of lessons. Riley's discussion is valuable here because it should help you to understand how phrasing and wording change the focus or direction of an enquiry.

You might also like to consider the Dodgy Questions activity which focuses on the Treaty of Versailles (Riley, 2000: 11). This is designed to extend your thinking about what constitutes a strong and a weak enquiry question.

## QCA SCHEMES OF WORK AND PLANNING ACROSS A KEY STAGE

One of the key issues in Chapter 2 focused around the idea of a community of practice, the idea that the world of history teaching comprises teachers, advisers, researchers, teacher educators, examiners and textbook writers. This community of practice operates in different arenas at different levels but one area where they were able to work with a significant common purpose was in the development of the QCA Schemes of Work. The KS3 Schemes of Work are likely to change with the introduction of the new history curriculum from September 2008 but it is highly likely that the Curriculum 2000 version of the Schemes of Work is still out there: perhaps informing your partner school's KS3 programme. Writing the Schemes of Work was an 'interesting' process. The individual units were written by a number of different authors, each writing to an approximate framework. The significant difference between the Schemes of Work and earlier illustrative material was that the former did represent the collective ideas from across the community of practice rather than an official view imposed from above. However there were perceived problems with the original draft of the Schemes of Work; they were too diverse, resulting in some editorial tidying up on behalf of the QCA (diversity was not a historical concept in 2000). However, the individual units did reflect the idea of focus questions and might be thought to illustrate how the history teaching community of practice has a real influence on the direction that history teaching takes. It would be interesting to take Michael Riley's checklist for focus questions and consider if the questions in the Schemes of Work deserve the epithet 'buzzing' or if the end result is a 'tangible, lively, substantial enjoyable outcome activity' (Riley, 2000: 12). The questions serve a purpose but are decidedly pedestrian, and at times resemble a pedestrian with bad feet. Heather Richardson, then working for the QCA, wrote an Introduction to the Schemes of Work (Richardson, 2000) which appeared in the same *Teaching History* issue as Michael Riley's 'Into the Key Stage 3 history garden'. There is a useful diagram which demonstrates how a department could construct their own departmental scheme of work for the QCA units. The diagram also demonstrates ideas of coherence and continuity between KS2 and KS3 and between the different units within KS3. Despite emphasizing the flexibility and the ability to tailor the curriculum to the needs of individual schools' and pupils' needs the diagram presents a fairly predictable view of what a Key Stage 3 history curriculum might look like. It is interesting to compare the QCA view of the history curriculum and the more thematic ideas presented in the Key Stage 3 garden

The Schemes of Work, which can be found on the Standards website, a link to which can be found on the companion website, provide one insight into how longer-term planning objectives might be met. The website itself is well organized in the way that it allows you to dissect the entire Scheme of Work from a variety of different perspectives. It is possible, therefore, to consider how the different history units link to other curriculum areas: not only to the obvious areas of citizenship or literacy but less obvious connections such as art and design. This area alone is worth evaluating. Once in your placement schools, it will be worth considering the extent to which your partner department makes use of the KS3 Schemes of Work and the extent to which it has informed longer-term departmental planning. It is important to have in mind the relaxed 'official view' about the Schemes of Work:

> the schemes of work are not statutory. Schools may use as much or as little of the schemes as they find helpful. Teachers may wish to use them to develop or refine their own scheme of work by amending or adding materials as appropriate to meet the needs of the children in their school. (www.standards.dfes.gov.uk/schemes2/secondary_history/?view=get)

While 'Teach yourself plumbing' might give you some basic instructions about changing a tap washer it would hardly be a suitable guide for installing a new central heating system. So it is with the Schemes of Work; they are an interesting starting point and provide some useful insights into the way the KS3 history National Curriculum can be translated into a coherent programme of study.

## THERE AND BACK AGAIN: USING LEARNING OBJECTIVES AND OUTCOMES TO DRIVE THE LESSON FORWARD

This chapter began by looking at individual lessons and the way that learning objectives and learning outcomes provide a structure and a direction for a lesson. This extended outwards to examine issues relating to planning sequences of lessons and, finally, to consider longer-term planning across a key stage. Like the Hobbit, the planning journey has gone to the distant shores of long-term planning; time to return back again to the closer and more immediate world of planning lessons and activities within a lesson. Having had the benefit of a traditional grammar school education, I have fond memories of history lessons which were probably endured rather than enjoyed. Beginning a General Certificate of Education (GCE) modern world history course at the start of the fourth form (Year 10) I suddenly found I was 'doing the Franco-Prussian War in 1870'. How we had got there from the previous years lessons on Napoleon, I do not know. Franco at that time was still the ruler of Spain and Prussia had briefly figured at the Battle of Waterloo. This was very confusing but it did not appear to matter. We had to listen for a long time, then we had to make notes about the causes of the Franco–Prussian War from one textbook and learn the notes for the next lesson when we would have an essay question to answer. I still remember odd details about the Hohenzollern Candidature, the Ems Telegram and the French Army being ready to the last gaiter button. This was the first lesson in September and the pattern repeated itself for the following 20 months.

Learning GCE history was difficult because there appeared to be no point or purpose – other than passing the examination. It was difficult to see the point of the lessons or where the lessons were going. This next series of discussions focuses on the part learning objectives play in your lessons. You have already seen that they are a valuable planning device providing structure and direction for your lesson. They can also be written on the whiteboard or displayed on the interactive whiteboard (IWB) and referred to at the start, and maybe at the end, of a lesson. The next point for reflection is more extensive, its purpose is to help you focus on the way that learning objectives play an active part in a lesson.

## Points for Reflection

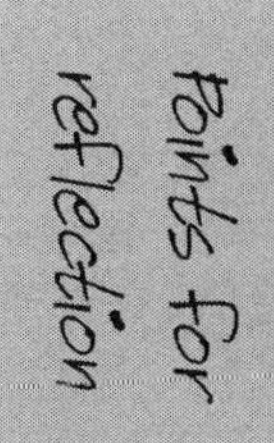

One of the essential elements of your PGCE programme is lesson evaluation. This can be difficult but might be though of as another example of metacognition.

As you watch the next part of this lesson, (6 mins 45 secs) you will be observing what the teacher does and what the students do. The lesson notes that accompany Clip 5 provide you with this information.

Watch the first 10 minutes of the lesson, up to the point where the students complete the card sort activity. Peter Duffy leads this lesson from the front, but pay particular attention to the way he breaks this opening sequence into different sections. Also make a note of the role the students play in this part of the lesson. To develop your powers of observation and reflection, and a more evaluative frame of mind, ask yourself a series of questions:

- How long is the teacher talking to the students?
- What is the nature of the talk?
- How are students actively involved?
- How would you describe the 'tone' of the teacher's talk?
- How does the teacher introduce the topic ?
- How does the teacher establish that the students understand the learning objectives?
- Can you describe what the students do when they are 'doing a card sort'?
- How does the teacher 'teach' when the pupils are doing the card sort?

The key issues with this focused observation were to consider:

- the role of learning objectives
- the nature of teacher talk
- establishing levels of understanding
- making decisions about student activities
- the role of the teacher in pair and group work.

---

This points for reflection has looked at the opening sequence of the Home Guard lesson for a number of reasons:

- to consider activities within a lesson and how a teacher manages the opening activities in a lesson
- to help you to develop a more critical and analytical framework by directing your thoughts to specific incidents in the lesson
- to demonstrate the dynamic part that learning objectives and learning outcomes play in a lesson.

Learning objectives and outcomes are not just abstractions. Peter Duffy's every-day practice demonstrates that they play a significant part in a lesson. The opening sequence you have just observed demonstrates how the objectives link to and frame individual activities within a lesson. The plenary at the end of the card sort was more than a classroom routine it was there to consolidate and reinforce learning. As Peter Duffy was working with pairs and individuals he was also checking levels of understanding; were the class beginning to under-stand that in some respects the Home Guard was less effective, in others it could have been a useful component of Britain's civil defence. In other words the opening activity linked to the first learning objective 'Identify the key features of the Home Guard'.

The links between learning objectives and activities within a lesson are demonstrated in Figure 3.3. This is an example of a planning template which enables trainees to account for the sequence of activities within a lesson. Sometimes planning documents use simple lesson timings to record sequences of activities but this variant is designed to focus trainees' attention on students' learning. This demonstrates in a dynamic way how the lesson moves from teacher to student activities. This template can be used dynamically ideally there should be more written in the right-hand column, the crucial factor is that the student activity column describes the work that students are required to undertake or complete. Each 'block' of student work should also relate to a particular learning objective.

This discussion has focused on the link between learning objectives and lesson activities. The nature of the individual activities is part of the decision-making process that was referred to at the start of this chapter and it would be valuable to consider the factors that are likely to influence the decision-making process. The main lesson activity focused on working with sources. In a more conventional lesson the students might have worked from a question sheet which required them to analyse a source and then answer questions. This might have involved more class teaching with the teacher leading from the front. A variation on this idea might have students working by themselves on the worksheets, with less explanation from the teacher.

As you watch Clip 6 (33 mins 40 secs) you will see the students working in groups. You need to try and understand why the teacher made this decision. It would be valuable to focus on the way the teacher works closely with the different groups.

The final part of the lesson demonstrates how teachers might have to make decisions as the lesson progresses. This can involve a number of issues:

- recognizing that students are making progress at a different pace than anticipated
- recognizing that the pace of the lesson might need speeding up or slowing down
- responding to an unexpected event in the lesson.

Timings in these circumstances can be either less than accurate or less than helpful. As a skilled teacher, Peter Duffy could have moved the lesson on at various points – particularly when the groups were working with the different pieces of evidence. Clip 7 (48 mins 30 secs) considers the final stages of the lesson and you might like to consider whether the teacher needed a longer period of time at the end of the lesson to explore students learning. Instead the decision was taken to spend more time with the evidence activity, which allowed the teacher time to explore how groups and individuals were making progress with the task. There was time to pursue lines of questioning to help students work out for themselves the significance of particular sources. This is another example of experienced teachers' decision-making – the ability to compromise with a plan, to be flexible and to recognize how to make the most of classroom opportunities.

This template shows how lesson moves from left to right, from teacher activity to student activity. The time element is shown by movement down the page creating a zigzag line. Blocks of activity should be separate. It should be possible to link student activity with learning objectives.

| *Teacher activity* | *Student activity* |
| --- | --- |
| Introduce focus of lesson.<br>Learning objectives and learning outcomes.<br>Explain meaning of analyse and judgement. | Activities should link to learning objectives. |
| | Pair work. Students work on card sort identifying some of the key features of the Home Guard. This will help them to make judgements about information does it show Home Guard as effective or ineffective – Real Army or Dad's Army? **L.Obj 1** |
| Mini-plenary – consolidating understanding.<br>Q&A session based on card sort. Selected students asked to give their views.<br>Ask students to sum up impressions so far.<br>Introduce reading activity – analysing a source. | |
| | Whole-class reading task. Evidence can contain conflicting information/ideas.<br>Develop understanding of<br>On the one hand<br>On the other… **L. Obj 2** |
| Introduce Carousel task<br><br>Teacher support/work with groups.<br>Ensure progress and orderly move to new tables. | In groups students read/look at/watch sources and decide:<br>• What source says about Home Guard<br>• What does source think of Home Guard?<br>• Why is source important/reliable?<br>Groups work with evidence for between 5 and 8 minutes. **L. Obj 2 and 3** |
| After third session provide groups with flip-chart paper and explain about making judgement re Home Guard. | |
| | Students weigh evidence and decide if Home Guard was Real Army or Dad's Army.<br>Present ideas to rest of class in closing plenary.<br>**L. Obj 3** |
| Final plenary use group presentations to refer back to learning objectives. | |

**Figure 3.3** The dynamics of a lesson plan

## SUMMARY

Planning is time-consuming but has a certain inevitability about it, like death and taxes. Beginning teachers find two aspects daunting. The first is the time taken to put a plan together; initially this can take far longer than the lesson itself. It might be instructive to make a note of the time it takes you to put your first plan together, and compare this with the time it takes you later in your PGCE year. The second daunting element is originality. Can you, should you, do something creative, imaginative and exciting every lesson. Probably not but there is help out there – from your colleagues, from your mentor, from *Teaching History* or from the History Teacher Discussion Forum – but do not forget your own practice. History teachers should be eclectic, picking up ideas from anywhere. The key starting point should be the history.

- What do you have to teach?
- Who do you have to teach?
- What do they need to know?
- How are they going to learn?

This chapter has raised some of the important issues relating to planning history lesson. To develop lessons successfully, you need to ensure that you are doing more than 'telling them about how the French Revolution started'. Understanding objective-led learning is one key to becoming a confident and competent lesson planner. One way to develop this capability is to be able to articulate your own thinking. They (the students) are not going to 'do' a topic you want them to know or to understand and you need to be able to articulate how they are going to develop their understanding. Once again it comes down to metacognition and understanding the kind of knowledge you are developing as a teacher – your growing professional craft knowledge.

**What the research says**

The Assessment Research Group have illustrated the significant link between effective planning and effective learning and this has had a significant influence on the Assessment for Learning strand of the National Strategy. If you go to the website companion, www.sagepub.co.uk/secondary and follow the link to and download 'Assessment for Learning: Beyond the Black Box' you should be able to identify the characteristics of good planning and be able to understand the contribution planning makes to effective learning. You might like to 'apply' these ideas to the lesson you have been analysing in this chapter.

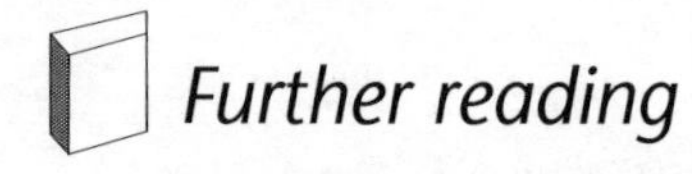

## Further reading

Calderhead, J. (1984) *Teachers' Classroom Decision Making*. Eastbourne: Holt, Rinehart and Winston.

Riley, M. (2000) 'Into the Key Stage 3 history garden: choosing and planting your enquiry questions', *Teaching History*, 99: 8–13.

## Useful websites

Live links to these websites can be found on the companion website.

The QCA website for National Curriculum key concepts and key processes. It would be useful to investigate key skills and processes for other subjects and compare them with those for history: http://curriculum.qca.org.uk/subjects.

History teachers' discussion forum useful, relevant discussions relating to a wealth of planning issues. www.schoolhistory.co.uk/forum/index.php?showforum=1&prune_day=100&sort_by=Z-A&sort_key=last_post&topicfilter=all&st=15.

What kind of history should school history be? Chris Culpin's Medlicott Medal Lecture on the History Association (HA) website: www.history.org.uk/Secondary.asp.

# 4 THE ELEMENTS OF TEACHING AND LEARNING HISTORY

*This chapter considers the following issues:*

- the importance of starter activities which are coherent, link to the purpose of the lesson and which are immediately engaging and thought-provoking
- understanding how children learn and how this can help to make your teaching and students' learning more effective
- the role of questioning and developing your understanding of the nature of questions
- the importance of effective plenaries which help students to understand not only what they have learned but also how they have learned.

This chapter explores some of the issues raised in the planning chapter and considers the idea of history's different contribution to the National Strategy. Although only concerned with KS3 the issues discussed have relevance to all aspects of history teaching. In the KS3 National Strategy guidance notes, 'About the starter activities' (2001: 4) it states:

> In the KS3 lesson starter, the aim is to ensure that every pupil is fully engaged with each of the tasks or activities, whether working as an individual, part of a group or with the rest of the class. Most lesson starters will include several short activities that maintain pupils' interest while focusing explicitly on the teacher's chosen objective. A well-balanced starter will allow time for pupils to work without teacher intervention for some of the time, but will also include some direct and specific input from the teacher in order to move the learning on, influence the direction that the learning takes, differentiate the level of challenge to meet pupils' individual needs and ensure that the main teaching points are conveyed clearly.

When introducing this topic early in the start of the PGCE year the following PowerPoint slide was used to introduce the topic:

**Beginning to plan your lessons**

You need to make a written note of the session aims for today

- This session will give you some pointers about ways in which you should begin lessons.
- The session also demonstrates the importance of good opening activities to intrigue pupils and engage them with their learning.
- By developing an awareness of the importance of good lesson openings you will be addressing QTT Standards.
- You will also begin to develop your understanding of the role of the KS3 Strategy in raising pupil achievement.

After the group had made a note of the session aims, they were asked to decode the following message with a prize for the first correct solution:

Eisenhower SHAEF May 31 1944.

673728466 68375673

46927466 46646368 337363368 8766 7388533 9328437 9 2777622437

4663 5825 464 77333

The code always takes some time to decipher and demonstrates why the experts at Bletchley Park who eventually cracked Enigma were mathematicians rather than historians. Initial attempts produce lists of numbers and letters A = 1 and so on. The atmosphere is always interesting at this point and the element of competition increases the tension. The first members of the group to work the message out were usually female and the solution has more to do with lateral thinking than logic. After a few minutes first one mobile phone appeared and then another: the solution – predictive texting.

Talking through this opening sequence of activities is used to develop an initial understanding of evaluation and reflection:

- What was engaging about the code exercise?
- Why did they copy down the session aims when copies of all presentations are available on the intranet?

Understanding the appeal of the code task was uncomplicated – it was a challenge, there was an element of intrigue and they had been fooled into thinking this was a genuine historical activity – the name and date convinced them of that. As to why they had copied the session aims, they realized that they were gullible and at this stage would do anything without thinking or questioning. More significantly, when asked what they thought the session would be like, they assumed that they would be at the receiving end of a fairly formal lecture which would give then some useful information about planning lessons. This anecdotal example is in some ways quite simplistic: it is effective in so far as it highlights expectations when a teaching session begins in a predictably routine and particularly dreary manner. The opening paragraph of this chapter took you through the literary equivalent. By way of a contrast the code exercise illustrates the motivating effect of an engaging and intriguing start to a teaching session. Lesson starters can and do come in all shapes and sizes this example might justly be regarded as nothing more than a neat stunt. It did engage and did provide a focus for evaluation, but I am not sure how it really contributed to understanding the real nature and purpose of lesson starters.

Rob Phillips's 'Making history curious: using initial stimulus material (ISM) to promote enquiry, thinking and literacy', (2001) demonstrated a more coherent approach to arousing the interest of students. This article appeared at roughly the same time as the KS3 National Strategy, as it then was, began to promote the idea of the lesson starter. It is worth comparing the article with the quote taken from the National Strategy at the start of this chapter because it illustrates an important point that is developed elsewhere in this chapter. The article is primarily a report of an action research project undertaken with history PGCE trainees at Swansea University and, as such, demonstrates how research informs classroom practice. There are a number of examples of the way that initial stimulus materials can be developed, and in this respect it is a useful guide providing sound practical advice. However this article is not just a series of handy tips but demonstrates how this approach has real rigour.

The first example develops a suitable ISM for teaching a series of lessons about the English Civil War: in exploring ideas with the Swansea PGCE group a print showing the execution of Charles I is used. The print, which is provided on the companion website, www.sagepub.co.uk/secondary, provides opportunities for students to explore the image but, more significantly, the pupils are

able to develop a series of questions which they want answering and which provide a sense of direction for subsequent lessons. This kind of work also helps to develop questioning skills: it becomes clear that 'When was Charles I executed?' is not as good a question as 'How did Charles I end up getting his head cut off?'

The print of the execution of Charles I used as an ISM, or a starter, occupied a significant part of the lesson but then this was the beginning of a sequence of lessons looking at the origins of the Civil War. There is a real qualitative difference between the nature and the purpose of 'lesson starters' which are suggested in the National Strategy and the idea of ISMs suggested by Rob Phillips. Until quite recently the National Strategy has been viewed as something akin to the revealed word with the status of sanctified doctrine: 'at every lesson beginning there shall be the writing down of lesson objectives and there shall be conducted a word search to quieten the multitude, thereupon the lesson can begin'. Such a mechanistic approach can be effective but it is not necessarily connecting the lesson beginning to real learning.

Finally in this discussion, it would be useful to observe and then evaluate the beginning of a lesson. If you observe the opening of the Year 8 lesson on Thomas Beckett, on the companion website, www.sagepub.co.uk/secondary, try to work out why the beginning of this lesson was effective and try to decide for yourself if this was simply a lesson starter or an example of an effective ISM. The actual sequence only lasts two minutes but in that time a great deal had been achieved:

- The lesson began even before the pupils entered the room – lights down, suitable music playing helped to establish an atmosphere.
- The 'body' on the ground: students had to walk around or step over the outline of the body.
- The group were in their places waiting for the lesson to begin within a minute of entering the room.
- The deliberately serious tone of the teacher helped to convey something about the nature of the lesson.
- The effectiveness of this was conveyed in the response of the group, as was highlighted by the teacher.
- Even before Peter Duffy had mentioned Thomas Beckett the class had an idea that they would be working on a murder investigation.

## ENDINGS, PLENARIES AND CONSOLIDATING LEARNING

Just as the National Strategy has sensible ideas about how lessons should begin, there are ideas about how lessons should end. There is an impression created by certain television programmes which depict life in schools that a typical lesson ends with the teacher in full flight, the bell goes and there is a

'January sales' rush for the door. The *Grange Hill* ending is, hopefully, mythical but there is a world of difference between an effective end to a lesson and an orderly end to a lesson. An orderly end to a lesson is a reflection of management and might include the collecting in of books and other resources, homework written down in planners, and rows or groups dismissed as they fall quiet. An effective end to a lesson will have considered how the learning can be summed up and consolidated – this is the National Strategy plenary. If you refer back to the Home Guard lesson on the companion website you will be able to see that consolidating learning is not something that just happens at the end of the lesson.

- After 10 minutes Peter Duffy brought the class together and worked through the 'answers' to the card sort activity.
- At 21 minutes there is a brief summary of the information which can be drawn out from the source on the interactive whiteboard. In both these episodes in the lesson there is a formal, structured consolidation of learning.
- Each 'micro-plenary' also links to one of the learning objectives; in terms of assessing understanding or being able to measure learning these points in the lesson are important.
- At the end of the lesson the final activity involves groups feeding back to the rest of the class what they feel are the significant points about the Home Guard.

It is worth examining one of the lesson endings in more detail. The lesson with Year 7 focused on the murder of Thomas Beckett and the closing activity lasted for approximately 5 minutes from 32 minutes to the end of the lesson. Peter Duffy works with three examples of pupils' work. The work the students are completing relates to the final learning objective – *making a historical judgemen*t. While the group were working, Peter Duffy was looking at the group's responses and selected three different conclusions.

The plenary here consisted of:

- an analysis of the responses considering the strong points and demonstrating the strength of each contribution
- an explanation of the strengths of each answer was good and how they matched the levels that pupils are expected to work to.

The importance of this activity was not so much in the act of reading out 'answers', but exploring what each student had written. The purpose of this plenary was to share assessment criteria with the rest of the class and help them to understand how to develop their ability to argue historically – that key process communicating about the past where they are learning how to present a structured and substantiated argument.

A plenary can also be used to help students develop an awareness of how they work and how they think. Metacognition is good not just for beginning teachers but for all learners. If students can be helped to articulate how they have arrived at an answer or solved a problem they are, hopefully, going to be able to transfer this ability in other learning situations. Learning to learn is a significant aspect of a thinking skills approach to teaching and learning and these issues are explored more fully in the next chapter.

Just as lesson starters can be trivial settling tasks, so plenaries can be equally ineffective if they appear to be tacked onto the lesson in the closing minutes. By now you should be developing an understanding of what it means to learn history. If you look back at Peter Duffy's learning objectives they were phrased in terms of

- explain
- analyse
- make a judgement.

A plenary ought to address these objectives, so you need to decide if a game of bingo or a web version of hangman really tests learning or at best what facts the class can collectively guess or remember. A link on the companion website takes you to a history teachers' discussion forum where Steve Illingworth discusses a range of strategies for developing that elusive but effective plenary. Just as a good starter begins to engages students with their learning, so an effective plenary should provide them with an opportunity to reflect on their learning. After reading through Steve Illingworth's ideas you might like to attempt to classify the range or type of plenary using the criteria below.

- Reflect on the subject: students are asked to assess what they feel they have discovered or understood.
- Reflect on their progress: students are asked to consider where they were at the start of the lesson and how the lesson has made a difference to their knowledge or understanding.
- Reflect on their learning: students are asked to think about how they solved a problem or worked out an answer.
- Reflect on barriers to learning: students are asked to consider what was difficult about the topic, or why they found it difficult to understand.
- Reflect on future progress: students are asked to set targets for what they want to learn or find out in subsequent lessons.

Points for reflection

## Points for reflection

Developing your criteria for a good beginning to a lesson. Once you have read this opening discussion it would be valuable to read Rob Phillips's (2001) article on initial stimulus materials. A link on the companion website takes you to the document *ISM v Lesson Starters* a collection of ideas taken from The School History Discussion Forum.

- You should be developing an understanding of the value and purpose of ISMs. If you read through the list of ideas in the document, are you able to suggest if this is a good ISM or a lesson starter?
- What criteria could you draw up to define an effective ISM?
- Based on your criteria for an effective ISM, can you draw up criteria for effective plenaries.

## UNDERSTANDING LEARNING

This discussion focuses on ideas about how people learn, how different methods of learning might be more appropriate for each individual and how this can inform the way that you plan and teach a lesson. The previous sentence did not mention theories about children, pupils or students learning: understanding how learning can be more effective is universal – it applies to you as well as the students you will be teaching. One theme running through the chapters has been metacognition – thinking about your own thinking, articulating how you were able to work through a problem. The discussions so far have had a historical context – asking you to reflect on the way you think as a historian. The next step is to develop an understanding of ideas about learning and how they can inform your teaching: this is part of the realm of cognitive psychology. The process of teacher education is in some ways cyclical: new ideas appear to become fashionable, they may fade but in a few years they are dusted off and rediscovered or recycled. A frequent element of teacher education courses in the 1960s (it is always useful to have a decade to scapegoat) was educational psychology, but by the late 1980s and early 1990s such approaches to teacher education were dismissed as too theoretical. The development of National Strategies specifically designed to improve the quality of learning in schools rediscovered learning theories and decided that they might actually be relevant. Some of the training materials, however, reduced quite complex ideas to levels of absurd simplicity.

In terms of pupils learning history the influence of cognitive psychologists has been significant. Jean Piaget's view of cognitive development suggests that there are particular stages that children go through. From the age of 11 children develop the ability to think in what Piaget (in Husbands, 1996: 15) termed 'the formal operational thought'. Simply and briefly, he believed that children from this age were developing an ability to think in more abstract terms, to reason logically and to draw conclusions. There would appear to be a correspondence between this type of thinking and historical thinking, but there is a sting in the tail. Developing the ability to think in abstractions develops gradually and approximately from the age of 11. The key word is 'develop'. Children cannot be taught to think in abstractions – they develop an ability. It is about maturation rather than learning, just as with a good bottle of Bordeaux.

This is not simply an abstract theory. In terms of developing historical understanding, of thinking historically, the outlook is gloomy. History teachers might just have to stand around kicking their collective heels until the next developmental stage begins. Fortunately, experience suggests otherwise and a significant strand of research into children's historical thinking has provided a different view of how children perceive, learn and understand history. One impetus which provides an alternative explanation for cognitive development comes from the work of social constructivists, in particular Jerome Bruner and Lev Vygotsky. Trying to define this in a single sentence is difficult. The significant difference is that social constructivists believe that cognitive development is a social process – in other words, learning involves interacting and communicating, initially with parents but then others; friends, classmates, teachers. Understanding is built or developed and moves from one step to another; again learners can be helped to construct their own understanding, and the process of helping them to build a new understanding is referred to as scaffolding. Vygotsky, a Russian cognitive psychologist, explained how the idea of scaffolding learning might work. He suggested that there was a zone of proximal development – a gap in understanding. Bridging this gap involves moving a learner from where they are to where they have the potential to go. To be a social constructivist is to believe that intelligence is not innate or fixed and everyone has the potential to learn. Vygotsky was possibly one of the few people to die of natural causes in the Soviet Union in the mid-1930s. Given the circumstances of the time, it is worthwhile considering the extent to which his ideas represented Stalinist orthodoxy at the time – if only to irritate educationalists.

Before considering how these ideas relate to your classroom, it might be worthwhile returning to a teaching sequence. The Home Guard lesson can help to illustrate some of these abstract ideas; time for some concrete examples. From 29 mins 30 secs to 31 mins 30 secs. Peter Duffy is working with a group looking at the recruiting poster. He looks at the answers two of the students have written on their worksheets and develops a dialogue with the rest of the group. The use of skilful questioning develops a deeper understanding and the use of gestures and prompts encourages others in the group to add further ideas. The students have developed a level of understanding for themselves but the teacher helps them to go that bit further. This is what could be meant by social constructivism, the teacher uses his specialist understanding – his professional craft knowledge – to involve the rest of the group to develop a deeper understanding.

This brief insight into ideas about cognitive development provides you with some valuable pointers. When planning the lesson, or when thinking about his teaching approaches, Peter Duffy did not consciously sit down and decide that he was going to develop a social constructivist approach in his lesson. Decisions about teaching strategies become instinctive, part of his professional craft knowledge, but as a beginning teacher it may be more important, or useful, to be more self-conscious of the way you approach your teaching.

- It helps you to develop a professional methodology or approach to teaching.
- It provides you with a professional language which enables you to articulate what it is that you are doing in the classroom.
- It provides you with a useful insight into the way that students might be learning.

You might have begun thinking that these theories about teaching and learning are just theories. If you can now understand how ideas about cognitive development are there in front of you in the history classroom, you can begin to develop a more informed understanding about teaching and learning.

On a wider note, the impact that ideas about cognitive development have had on history teaching are significant and they help to inform everyday practice. Understanding how children view and understand evidence and historical accounts is complex. As a beginning teacher it might be difficult to appreciate just how differently a young person makes sense of the past. In terms of something as simple as evidence, they might simply view it as information which tells us something about the past. They might take an absolutist view – that an account must be true if it comes from the past. The added complication of reconciling different accounts of the past might suggest that one account is correct, the other incorrect; a more nuanced view might believe that one account is more correct than the other. A more developed understanding of evidence might encourage an element of scepticism as young people recognize that evidence might be partial or created from a particular perspective and the search for the one true objective account becomes important. If there can be such a range of ideas about the nature of evidence, there is an equally diverse range of understandings when young people try to understand the attitudes and beliefs of people in the past. Students might begin with a completely uncomprehending attitude – why on earth did people do that or believe that? This has been referred to as the Divi Past or a deficit past – 'they did things like that in them days because they were not as clever as us today', 'Milk used to come in bottles because they didn't have cardboard' (Lee, in Donovan and Bransford, 2005: 45). This view explains students' ideas about trial by ordeal in the Middle Ages (Husbands, 1996: 78). Or reactions to Hitler – 'he was a madman, they should have locked him up' (Lee, in Donovan and Bransford, 2005: 34). This view of historical understanding might even help teachers to understand the summaries written by one of the groups in the Home Guard lesson. They believed that the Home Guard was less effective because they were using guns from the nineteenth century – they might believe this because nineteenth-century guns were older and not as good as later guns. The real reason for the ineffectiveness of the Home Guard had more to do with the speed with which they were recruited and so were ill-equipped and untrained. Unless the group ideas are explored in more detail this is just a hypothesis but it might serve to demonstrate the value of research in helping to understand students' thinking. The hierarchy of understanding people's beliefs which is outlined in Husbands (1996) is valuable in what it reveals about the ways students perceive the past. It is evidence which helps teachers understand how and why students perceive the past, and might be used in a practical way to move students' thinking on. In other words, students' responses are not necessarily random; the nature of their replies may provide a useful insight into how they are thinking. It is not so much about correcting students' misconceptions – as the QTT standards would have you do – but understanding their views or perceptions and having an awareness of where they are coming from. Again in practical terms you could be developing a series of questions about the changing attitudes of a German Jewish family in the 1930s. These families faced many dilemmas and their views and opinions changed in response to the political climate. Victor Klemperer's diaries (1998; 1999) provide a valuable insight into his thinking and into the thinking of elements of the Jewish community in Dresden. He was initially very pessimistic in 1933, but hoped to weather the storm. He later tried to use his academic contacts abroad, only to find that it was too late. His diaries record his changing values and attitudes, and those of his Jewish friends in this period. A typical response from pupils might venture that Klemperer was foolish, that he and his wife should have left as soon as possible because Hitler was going to start a war and kill all the Jews. If you are aware that there is going to be a range of responses or ways that students might interpret actions in the past, it might be possible to anticipate some of these and be prepared to deal with them. The alternative is just to be bewildered by the range of ideas and responses that students come up with.

There is a substantial body of research evidence available which provides an invaluable insight into young people's historical thinking and which can help you to develop a more informed understanding about what is happening in the history classroom. This research has real practical value; if you know how students are constructing their understanding of history it can help you to make their learning more effective – how you need to approach a topic to make their understanding more advanced. This is not about teaching more facts, but about developing a deeper level of conceptual understanding or a more sophisticated understanding of the value of evidence. Throughout a student's historical education they will be using evidence; they will be required to understand the reasons for the Norman Invasion or the origins of the Second World War. Your teaching will need to take into account their developing understanding of evidence, and concepts like cause and consequence. This links to important ideas about progression which will be considered more closely in a later chapter.

Points for reflection

## Points for reflection

This activity is designed to help you understand the following:

1. How research into children's historical thinking can help you to understand perceptions and misconceptions.
2. How students at different stages or levels of understanding might explain Victor Klemperer's failure to leave Germany before 1939.

Before you begin to consider how students might try to understand why Victor Klemperer did not leave Germany in the period before 1939, it would be worthwhile trying to develop your own explanation based on the facts below and your own knowledge and understanding of the period.

*Important 'facts' about Victor Klemperer*

- Klemperer was a Social Democrat and therefore a natural opponent of Hitler.
- Klemperer was an atheist and fought with distinction on the Western Front in the First World War and regarded himself as a good German patriot.
- His wife was an Aryan
- As a front-line veteran he had, for a while, protected status.
- Working in a university, Klemperer was a civil servant.
- His friends constantly guessed wrong and optimistically predicted the end of the Nazi Regime at any moment.
- Klemperer and his wife had just bought and moved into a new house.
- He was nearing retirement, he was always worried about money and was never certain if his pension would be stopped by the Nazis.
- He had contacts in foreign universities but as the 1930s drew on it became harder and harder for academics to find a country willing to accept them.
- After *Krystallnacht* all Jews leaving Germany were subject to punitive exit taxes and were unable to take anything with them above a few hundred Reichmarks.

The stages described below come from Ashby and Lee (1987).

| | |
|---|---|
| The Divi past (Level 1) | Students find it difficult to understand or account for actions in the past. This is explained by the belief that people in the past were not as intelligent or as advanced. |
| Everyday empathy (Level 3) | Students explain the past as something generalized – everybody believed or acted in a particular way. They base their explanations or understanding on their own commonsense view. |

| | |
|---|---|
| Contextual empathy (Level 5) | Students might try to construct an explanation by considering a wider context. They are able to distinguish between what the historian knows and how and why the viewpoint of someone in the past could be different. They may try to explain actions in terms of what was known or understood at the time. |

## MI AND VAK

One area of your teaching where you will be confronted with the idea of research informing practice will be in the field of multiple intelligences (MI). If you look carefully at Peter Duffy's lesson plans you will see that the plans address different learning styles. Opportunities are built into the teaching and learning activities which appear under the heading VAK.

Howard Gardner is an American psychologist who suggested the idea of multiple intelligences in his book *Frames of Mind*. Gardner felt that IQ tests only measure a particular kind of intelligence; he came to see intelligence as the capacity to solve problems or to fashion products that are valued in one or more cultural settings. Gardner originally suggested that there are seven types of intelligence:

1. Visual/spatial intelligence
2. Musical intelligence
3. Verbal/linguistic intelligence
4. Logical/mathematical intelligence
5. Interpersonal intelligence
6. Intrapersonal intelligence
7. Bodily/kinaesthetic intelligence.

In the National Strategy these have been reduced to three: visual, auditory and kinaesthetic, hence VAK. A simple Google search for VAK produced over 11 million entries. Clearly, multiple intelligences, or at least the National Strategy version, is big (educational) business and it is more than just schools who have their own understanding of VAK. There are a number of 'tests' available online where you can work out your own learning style. A link on

the companion website takes you to the West Midlands National Grid for Learning. The way that schools have involved themselves with multiple intelligences is interesting. Some have become enthusiastic 'born-again' evangelists in the way that they have signed up to the idea of multiple intelligences. It tends to be a managerial whole-school approach which insists that all lesson plans demonstrate how they are going to cater for the different learning styles of their students. These schools see VAK learning as one of the ways of ensuring that standards of teaching and learning are improved. As with all 'four legs good, two legs better' absolutist approaches the reality is more subtle and success might have more to do with more thoughtful planning and planning for a variety of tasks or activities in a lesson. Howard Gardner's own writing is accessible and relevant for history teaching. Reviewing MI theory 20 years later he wrote:

> In particular, I focused on the importance of achieving understanding in the major disciplines – science, mathematics, history, and the arts. For various reasons, achieving such understanding is quite challenging. Efforts to cover too much material doom the achievement of understanding. We are most likely to enhance understanding if we probe deeply in a small number of topics. (Gardner, 2003: 8)

In terms of history teaching what Gardner writes might be particularly relevant to this discussion. The key is having an awareness of how a discipline might be taught or learnt more effectively. John White produced an accessible critique of MI theories being more concerned about the evangelical approach referred to above:

> The educational world, including government agencies as well as schools, has gone for MI in a big way. But for the most part it seems to have taken over the ideas without questioning their credentials. MI theory comes to schools 'shrink-wrapped', as one teacher put it to me. This is understandable, since schools do not have the time to investigate all the ideas that come their way that look as if they have some mileage in the classroom. (White, 2004: 2)

White's lecture is a well-crafted critique and is an equally accessible counterweight to ideas about MI. This does not mean you have to read Gardner and then read White and make up you mind and decide whether you are an evangelist or an agnostic. In the previous chapter, reference was made to historians being eclectic, taking resources, ideas and teaching strategies from anywhere and using them if they are perceived to improve the quality of teaching and students' learning. Taking such a pragmatic view, there is empirical evidence of a kind to suggest that there might be something to MI. White himself acknowledges that the theory might be flaky but 'the use to which teachers put it seems to produce the goods – to give children more self-confidence and desire to learn' (White, 2004: 19).

For a beginning history teacher, one of the most useful sites for ideas and resources is Ian Dawson's www.thinkinghistory.co.uk, which has been mentioned in earlier chapters. This website is closely linked to the Schools History Project (SHP) and the ideas and activities reflect the SHP philosophy. Discussion and ideas on the site focus on making history active and making students think. Many of the techniques employed might well have links to ideas about MI and they contain well-worked examples of teaching strategies which meet shrink-wrapped VAK

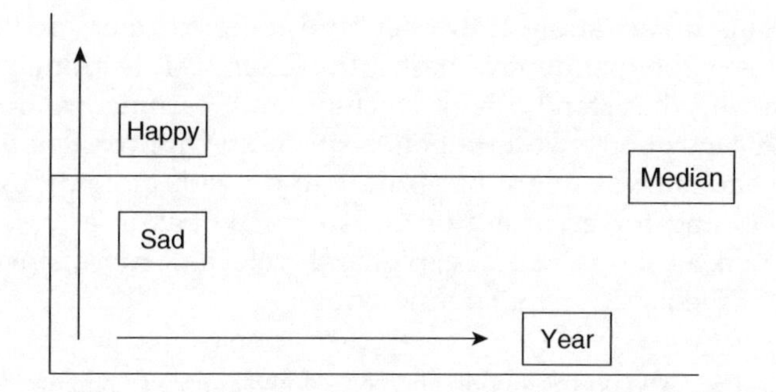


**Figure 4.1** A living graph template

requirements. Another link on the companion website (www.sagepub.co.uk/secondary) takes you to an activity called 'Germs Have Feelings Too'. The key to this activity is a lifeline or living graph which provides students with an opportunity to place ideas above or below a Median line (see Figure 4.1).

This technique can be used in a variety of settings. It plots change over time on the horizontal axis, and the state of euphoria, or otherwise, on the vertical axis. Close to the Median line is just happy or slightly sad. The shrink-wrapped VAK enthusiast would recognize that this is a good kinaesthetic activity because the learner will be placing ideas or cards in a physical space. A more clued-up history teacher will tell you that this device is good for reinforcing chronological understanding at one level but can help to develop reasoning and argument. Placing ideas close to, or a long distance from, the Median line requires an element of justification, for example, is the degree of happiness or sadness absolute or is it relative to the event immediately before, or something else?

Peter Duffy uses a combination of these thinking-skills ideas throughout his teaching. The GCSE lesson on Vietnam (found on the companion website) tries to help his pupils to understand, as part of a coursework study of the Vietnam War why various nations were interested in Vietnam. Ian Dawson refers to these techniques as 'Physical Maps' where the space in a classroom is used to represent location and distance, geographical details which play a significant part in a historical situation, but frequently the geographical significance may be unfamilair to students. Peter Duffy refers to his activity as a 'human map re-cap'. Again the physical use of space is important and provides students with a number of visual and or physical clues. Such activities can help to make learning more memorable and help students recall details and ideas in later lessons; an open question such as 'remember when we did the human map recap?' can provide that key link to previous learning. The human map activity might help students to understand why China and the USSR were interested in Vietnam, because of the proximity. America's interest is less easy to understand, but the physical distance between the USA and Vietnam prompts a different line of questioning.

If you fast-forward to 22 mins 30 secs you will be able to observe the students working on the next task, which involves them trying to understand and explain why the Superpowers became involved in Vietnam. The resources here are used as props to help the students develop their understanding of causation and to support and structure their explanations. The nature of the resources are important; they could quite easily have been in the form of sources A–F on a worksheet but take the form of laminated cards. Again in VAK terms this might be thought to be suitable for kinaesthetic learners but if you look at the cards themselves you can see that they use a variety of visual signals. History not only employs a sophisticated technical language but uses metaphors and analogies in quite an unconsidered way. As history graduates, you are probably not aware of these and use them unthinkingly – assuming that everyone else will understand – just like you do. How might a 14-year-old visualize the concept of an arms race or an 11-year-old a ruler? If a chemist refers to reactive metals or halides you might have a vague idea what they are taking about – a chemist could see these as chemical symbols on the Periodic Table, their location on the table providing further clues about their properties and qualities. This section of the lesson provides some valuable ideas about using graphical or visual clues as aids to student learning. Pupil learning or understanding in this part of the lesson demonstrates the power of explanation and the role of visual props in developing an explanation. In terms of your own understanding what you might want to take from this short teaching sequence is not that you have to go away and dogmatically prepare a series of VAK resources for each class you will teach. You should be open to ideas (as the Standards demand), but understanding the principles which may lie behind an idea like multiple intelligences and knowing how these ideas might help you to develop a wider range of teaching strategies to enable and to support your students' learning is more important.

## QUESTIONING AND THINKING SKILLS

Questioning is one of the basic skills you will need to master as a history teacher. A useful observation activity that many PGCE trainees are often asked to undertake focuses on the questioning that takes place in a single lesson.

The question sheet on the companion website records some of these observations. They simply record the type of questioning that takes place in a history classroom. These observations were made within a few weeks of beginning autumn term placements and were used as the raw material for a university-based session on questioning. These raw responses were used to develop a deeper understanding of the role, purpose and nature of questioning. The key issues were:

- How do teachers use questions at the start of a lesson or teaching sequence?
- How are subsequent or supplementary questions developed?

- How do teachers respond to students' answers?
- How do teachers make use of students' responses?

Questioning and developing historical understanding go together; developing an effective questioning technique is often one of the key elements of becoming an effective teacher, so it is worthwhile considering the nature of questioning and historical questions in particular. In the planning chapter you saw how important focus or enquiry questions are to good history teaching. The idea was developed that taking time to craft good questions is worth the effort because it results in good, focused history. It follows that the questions you are going to ask in class also need to be considered carefully. As you watch your mentor teach, you will notice that their questioning appears faultless. They begin with a fairly simple opening question which might relate to the previous lesson, or the focus of the current lesson; it might just be a straightforward 'who can tell me about ...?' The next question might ask a student to develop his or her ideas more fully, or might ask 'why do you think ... ?' or 'how did you work that out?' What develops is a dialogue where the teacher almost effortlessly asks more questions. Initial planning by beginning teachers is frequently heavy on content, rich in factual detail, but often light on process. The terse comment 'Q&A session' in plans is typical. There is an almost innate belief that question and answer (Q&A) sessions run themselves. In some of your initial lesson evaluations it would be valuable to focus quite specifically on these Q&A sessions:

- Have they direction?
- Do they help to structure and develop students' understanding?
- Are they as fluent as you intended?

To help you develop the art of questioning it could be valuable to develop a systematic approach to Q&A sessions:

- What is the purpose of the Q&A session?
- In what direction do you want the questions to go?
- How many steps or stages might be needed to get there?
- Can you anticipate any wrong answers?
- How do you get the direction of questioning back on track?

To answer these questions you need to understand that the different key concepts and key processes in the National Curriculum focus on different ideas. They therefore have their own conventions: for example, if you are teaching a lesson about the causes of the Second World War you do not come straight out with the $64,000 question – 'OK, who can tell me what caused the Second World War?' If you were to ask this question you might get a one word answer: 'Hitler' or you might get a more subtle answer – 'Germany invaded Poland'. Such a view is understandable but it does not make for good history;

understanding the causes of the war therefore involves an understanding of the complex web of issues which would link the German reaction to the Treaty of Versailles to Hitler's own personal role in events to the interests of other European nations – big and small.

A key text for understanding the conventions of asking historical questions and framing those important tasks is Tim Lomas's *Teaching and Assessing Historical Understanding* (1993) – unfortunately now out of print but should be in most university libraries. Lomas systematically considers the different concepts and processes, examines particular problems related to teaching these concepts and, finally, suggests a series of useful questions related to causation or significance. Lomas also considers how you can make questioning more progressive or more challenging so it is possible to understand how the questions about causes which you ask 12-year-olds can be made more challenging for 16-year-olds. It is an indispensable guide for developing your understanding of questioning. In the chapter on assessment the link between setting clear and precise questions which test a student's level of understanding will be explored more fully.

Developing an informed understanding of the complex nature of questioning again brings us back to the National Strategy and the rediscovery of previously neglected ideas associated with questioning. Bloom's taxonomy is back on the menu and is used to heighten awareness of the nature of different types of questions and the different intellectual demands they make of students. Bloom was another cognitive psychologist, who suggested a framework or hierarchy which was originally used to categorize learning objectives; in the National Strategy it is linked more to a hierarchy of questions. His classification is therefore doubly useful and can be an aid to planning activities as well as thinking about questions. The foundation of his taxonomy was based on the idea that not all learning objectives or questions are equal. For example, learning a list of dates, while important, is not the same as the ability to analyse or evaluate. There are any number of guides on the web – as with VAK a simple Google search throws up 745,000 entries. Table 4.1 is a useful summary which will allow you to see how tasks and questions can be made more complex and how the different activities present different levels of challenge.

## LITERACY THE COMMON DENOMINATOR

The final element of this examination of the components of a history lesson focuses on the links between history and literacy. If you were to give serious consideration to the ways that history is presented, communicated or conveyed, it should be obvious that it is a discipline that is intimately linked to language. History is an academic discipline but for generations it is a means of cultural transference, a way of preserving collective memory. In pre-literate societies there is a strong oral tradition that both records and preserves collective memory. If you were to reflect on your own historical education, it has involved a great deal of reading – and probably as much writing. It is near impossible, and

**Table 4.1** Hierarchy of thinking skills

| Skill | Pupils should be able to: |
|---|---|
| Information-processing | 1. Locate, collect and recall relevant information<br>2. Interpret information to show understanding of relevant concepts and ideas<br>3. Analyse information, e.g. sort, classify, sequence, compare and contrast<br>4. Understand relationships, e.g. part/whole relationships |
| Enquiry | 1. Ask relevant questions<br>2. Pose and define problems<br>3. Plan what to do and how to research<br>4. Predict outcomes, test conclusions and improve ideas |
| Reasoning | 1. Give reasons for opinions<br>2. Draw inferences and make deductions<br>3. Use precise language to explain what they think<br>4. Make judgements and decisions informed by reasons or evidence |
| Creative thinking | 1. Generate and extend ideas<br>2. Suggest possible hypotheses<br>3. Be imaginative in their thinking<br>4. Look for alternative innovative outcomes |
| Evaluation | 1. Evaluate information they are given<br>2. Judge the value of what they read, hear and do<br>3. Develop criteria for judging the value of their own and others' work or ideas<br>4. Have confidence in their own judgements |

even undesirable, to detach one from the other. It also might help you to understand why history can be such a difficult subject to understand. In Chapter 2 the focus on the National Curriculum involved an analysis of a series of concepts. If you were to compare the history Attainment Target with the science Attainment Target you would notice an immediate difference. Attainment in science is measured by demonstrating knowledge, for example when sunlight shines on a leaf a process called photosynthesis takes place, carbon dioxide from the atmosphere is taken into the leaves and works with a chemical called chlorophyll which converts sunlight into energy. A by-product of this process is oxygen which is released into the atmosphere. In history a student has to understand how and why interpretations of history are constructed and why these interpretations might differ according to the time when they were constructed.

The fact that one of the key processes in history involves students communicating their understanding shows how significant listening and speaking, reading and writing are in developing historical understanding. However, history is not just about communicating – it has a focus on what might be termed disciplinary conventions. In communicating understanding there is an expectation that students will use the language of the subject which relates, for example, to chronology – not just AD and BC but more particular concepts such as Tudor or early modern or inter-war. The key concepts are part of this subject-specific vocabulary. Communicating historical understanding is therefore difficult and complex. To make matters even more difficult for students there are other expectations: history is more than an account; it may involve the construction of argument. Again there are quite specific conventions relating to coherence and structure but also about the use of evidence to substantiate an argument.

Literacy in history and understanding the links between and with the Literacy Strategy involves far more than simply correcting spelling, punctuation and grammar. The Literacy Strategy document is a useful and important guide. Some of the important issues in the guide highlight the role of particular approaches to teaching literature and the different components – listening, speaking, writing. Careful reading of the guide is important, for example it will make you aware of expectations: what activities, ideas or terms might a student in Year 7 or Year 9 be familiar with. In this way it is possible to ensure that the demands you are making of students in history correspond with those made in English.

Working with the key process 'communication about the past' you also need to develop your understanding of the demands this imposes on you as a history teacher. On first reading the expectations relating to communicating about the past, it is inevitable that you think 'writing an essay' or writing answers to a set of questions. Strategies for developing students' abilities to structure their historical writing are explored more fully in the next chapter but the exercise below may provide you with an indication of the problems which you might well face.

## Points for reflection

Follow the link on the website to Sam's essay, which will take you to a web-based activity which explores the connections between history and literacy.

The activity is designed to give you a practical insight into the symbiotic relationship between history and language. In particular:

- the importance of literacy as an essential component of historical understanding and as an aid to historical understanding
- the importance of structure and support in developing students' ability to communicate effectively
- the role of the history teacher as a teacher of English, in developing and structuring historical understanding.

After completing this activity you should be able to write your own history and language manifesto based on these bullet points.

The hidden theme of this chapter has probably been 'history does it better'. It is highly likely that when you are being interviewed for your first job you could be asked a question about the National Strategy or Assessment for Learning; you might be able to parrot a few phrases about MI or VAK or Bloom's taxonomy which might get head teachers nodding enthusiastically. However, if you want to demonstrate that your ideas about teaching and learning are based on a deeper understanding of these principles, you need to be able to impress your potential head of department. History teaching is a research-informed profession. Being a reflective history teacher means that you have not just understanding of how students learn history and why the same students find history difficult to learn, but the decisions you make will, to some extent, be informed by this growing body of professional and academic literature. The purpose of the chapter has been to make you aware of some of the significant ideas about learning and hopefully demonstrate how these are able to inform the way you teach.

There has been a strong focus in this chapter on the links between research and teaching history. The chapter has examined the way that national strategies are an important element of the school improvement agenda which aims to raise standards in secondary schools. Like history teaching itself, however, it has been the intention to show how good history practice goes beyond some of the simplicities which have become part of the 'one size fits all' National Strategy. Ideas about effective history teaching are often based on solid research evidence. Part of becoming a reflective history teacher involves developing an understanding of this research base. It is all too easy to dismiss theory as being too difficult to grasp, or not really relevant to 9C on a wet Wednesday afternoon. Being an effective teacher involves more than deploying exciting teaching strategies or fun activities. Knowing why a particular teaching approach works, or understanding how students perceive and understand the past, is important. It makes the difference between a teacher and a reflective teacher who understands how to make learning in the history classroom effective.

**What the research says**

There are some useful links in the body of this chapter which will enable you to follow up some of the current ideas from cognitive psychology which underpin and inform aspects of the National Strategy. Gardner is a very effective communicator and some of his online articles are particularly informative. It might be particularly valuable to examine some of the more nuanced ideas of his relating to multiple intelligence and relate them to the bargain basement VAK-uous version which finds its way into schools.

It is also important to develop an informed understanding of the work of Dickinson, Lee, Shemilt and Ashby on how children interpret and make sense of history. The most useful and accessible source can be found in Donovan and Bransford (2005). Also useful is Ashby and Lee (1987).

Two articles by Lee and Shemilt in *Teaching History* are also important: Lee and Shemilt (2003) and (2005).

## Further reading

Rob Phillips's article (2001) 'Making history curious: using initial stimulus material (ISM) to promote enquiry, thinking and literacy', *Teaching History*, 105: 19–25 is a starting point. To see how this is used in practice you might like to read and compare the prologue and Chapter 1 of John Guy's biography of Mary Stuart, *My Heart is My Own* (HarperCollins, 2004). The Prologue describes the last hours of Mary Queen of Scots – not just the botched execution but also the fierce stand-up row she had with a Protestant clergyman on the scaffold. By contrast Chapter 1 opens with the birth of Mary. It is worth applying Rob Phillips's ideas to the Prologue and to Chapter 1.

## Useful websites

Live links to these websites can be found on the companion website.

You might want to check out your own preferred learning style at: www.bgfl.org/bgfl/custom/resources_ftp/client_ftp/ks3/ict/multiple_int/index.htm.

You might also come across something called Brain Gym – these *Guardian* articles demonstrate how sometimes we need to develop a more sceptical approach to bad science: www.guardian.co.uk/life/badscience/story/0,,1733683,00.html and www.guardian.co.uk/science/2006/mar/25/badscience.uknews.

# 5 MANAGING TEACHING AND LEARNING

**This chapter considers the following issues:**

- developing effective teaching and learning strategies in the classroom
- active history, and how active history can be used to promote effective learning
- thinking skills, and how the focus on thinking skills requires a more considered approach to teaching and learning history
- learning to learn or leading to learn, developing an informed and critical understanding of the history exemplification materials

The chapter includes three case studies where experienced history teachers outline thinking skills activities.

A question which PGCE interviewees are often asked is: 'why do you want to be a history teacher?' One answer crops up again and again: 'because I had an inspirational teacher when I was at school or at university'. This is probably true but applicants to PGCE history courses are the result of a long weeding-out process and they represent a minority of the school and university population. It is probably fair to say that one PGCE applicant's source of inspiration might be another's cure for insomnia. Taking a more objective view there might well be something in the view that history is one of the subjects that is particularly well taught in the secondary school. History departments operating in a free-market economy have to fight hard for their customers at the end of Year 9. Yet a subject that is perceived to be difficult and whose utility is questioned can still, in some schools, wipe the floor with the opposition. A head teacher at a partner school famously confided to the head of history that he wished he could bottle what the history department did and prescribe it to the rest of the school. This may only serve to demonstrate that history teachers are both indiscreet and highly effective propagandists, but there is something to this, and the aim of this chapter is to put flesh on the bones of the previous chapter. The National Strategy has attempted to codify effective teaching and learning. Chapter 4 considered how some of these 'new' ideas, in reality old ideas made new through the medium of PowerPoint, were supported by research. The real issue, however, was to show you how good history teaching and learning is academically rigorous and supported by a growing body of research evidence.

## ACTIVE HISTORY

One of the key words which history teachers might use to describe either their teaching style or the type of history that they like to teach is 'active'. This can mean different things to different people. Some might just think that it means noise and disturbance. That students work in groups and talk louder and louder until the teacher has to shout even louder. For active, then, read anarchic. The reliable social barometer that is a Google search throws up something like 68,000 entries for active history, however, if you follow the link on the companion website to School History you may begin to develop an understanding of what active history might be. There is an undeniable commitment to developing activities which are enjoyable and engage young people with their learning. It is also obvious that there is a real commitment to the subject from the teachers themselves. School history does not just represent the frenetic activity of a single history teacher but is also a forum where ideas and resources are exchanged. If you look at the front page of School History carefully you will see links to other history department websites. It is worthwhile following these to gain some idea of the number of history departments which, in one way or another claim that they are, or engage in, active history. Chapter 2 introduced the idea of a community of practice; this is one place where this idea is highly visible. It might be valuable to step back from the hyperactivity and try to develop a more considered understanding of this much used idea.

## LEARNING THROUGH DOING

It might be possible to sum up the idea of active learning and active history in a few words: 'what you do is what you learn' or 'to do is to learn'. These ideas might read like lyrics by Rumsfeld and Descartes and sung by Sinatra but there is something about this idea that is appealing. If you return to the card sort activity in the Home Guard lesson (from 7 minutes). This is active learning at a very simple level. The active element lies in the decisions students are making

about the information. If you consider the thinking that is going on you might be able to understand how active learning, first, is not as complex as you might have thought and, second, is relatively easy to organize. So what are the students doing that is active?

- They have to read for meaning or understanding.
- They have to be aware of two different sets of criteria.
- They have to make a judgement about the information and how it corresponds to the criteria.
- They have to physically move the card to one side or another, which reinforces their understanding.
- If this is a paired or group activity, they might have to share ideas or explain their decision to others.
- They might also have to justify or explain their choice to the teacher.

What is the inactive alternative? That they have to copy the information for themselves from a text or a worksheet, or they might have to answer some questions. You might be thinking, in an active sort of way, that this was how you learnt history but then that may just be your preferred learning style. If we think about what might be going on with this kind of activity, perhaps we can demonstrate why this is not active and may not be that effective.

- First, copying – you could copy notes in Latin or Greek; just because your work is accurate it does not mean that you are competent in Latin or Greek.
- If you are answering comprehension-type questions there are very often clues in the question which match the text – a technique known as phrase-spotting. By phrase-spotting you could get 10 out of 10 but, again, it does not follow that you will have learnt anything.

Active learning then involves the student in a very direct way with their own thinking. It is a process which involves stages or steps.

- The students have to process information. This may involve reading, listening, speaking or perhaps even writing.
- The students are developing their own understanding where these new or different ideas are internalized.
- They might then have to demonstrate their understanding, applying this new understanding in a new or a different situation.
- This might involve the learner having to explain, account for, work out, or suggest a solution.

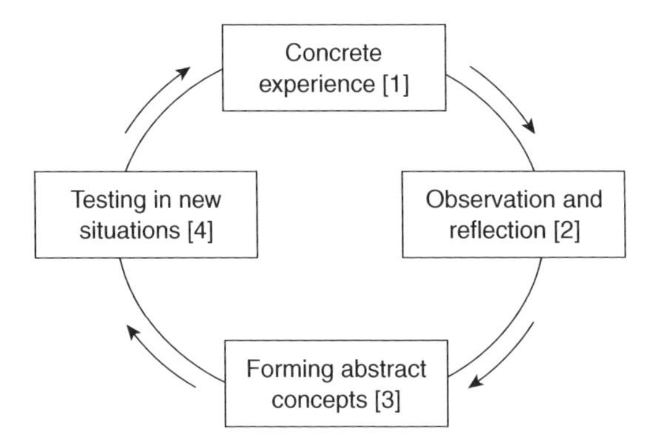


**Figure 5.1** Kolb's learning cycle

This process is part of a learning cycle which was suggested by another American psychologist, David Kolb (Figure 5.1). His experiential learning model has four elements:

- concrete experience
- observation of and reflection on that experience
- formation of abstract concepts based upon the reflection
- testing by applying in new setting.

This is a useful model and is equally relevant to your own developing experience in the history classroom. Reflection and evaluation are part of the process of becoming not just an effective learner, but an effective teacher as well. Hopefully, this is another practical demonstration that ideas about learning are relevant. Developing your understanding of these ideas will help you to become a more effective teacher.

## THE MURDER OF THOMAS BECKETT: OBSERVING, REFLECTING AND LEARNING

This lesson employs a number of active learning strategies and it might be worthwhile analysing in some detail where the active learning is taking place and why active learning is effective. Observing a lesson is a valuable part of your professional development. What you are watching is a model, the analysis focuses on what happens in the lesson but the purpose of the observation is not to help you to replicate what Peter Duffy is doing with his Year 7 group. The analysis of the lesson is designed to help you to develop a reflective perspective. You need to be considering how these ideas and strategies are transferable, how can you apply the thinking and the learning in your classroom. This involves more than thinking 'I could do this with the Treaty of Versailles or the execution of Charles I'. You also need to be aware of the historical processes which are taking place and how these active history ideas help develop historical thinking.

1. The opening two minutes – good use of ISMs or even a very short introductory activity can set the mood. It makes the students curious and helps them to think – or think about thinking in a particular way.
2. 4 minutes to 9 minutes. There are two different active elements in this teaching sequence. The students' interacting with text – they have to read, use criteria to decide and then use colours to highlight – which helps to reinforce understanding. The second active element involves using different props which the students wear at the same time as feeding back their ideas or answers to the rest of the class.

This was obviously a 'fun' element of the lesson but it does serve a useful purpose. It reinforces learning: the physical prompts make ideas more memorable and help the students to internalize their understanding. It is worth thinking further about the text element of this activity. Yes it does help understanding but it also has the potential to make the learning even more active. At one level the students are deciding which character said what. In terms of the historical thinking which is going on, and the potential to develop historical thinking, this text activity is important. Highlighting text enables the learner to sort, to organize, to order and to categorize. It might be difficult to undertake all these activities in this one lesson but you are *reflecting on the potential* of this type of activity *to be used or developed in a different situation*.

The next active sequence involves a technique often used in drama teaching, freeze frames. The purpose of this activity is highlighted on the whiteboard at 11 minutes and this links to a quite specific learning objective; 'to explain the sequence of events that led up to the death of Thomas Beckett. If you advance the sequence to 14 mins 45 secs you can observe the freeze-frame activity in operation. The activity lasts for over 10 minutes. You may not need to look at every presentation but you should focus on the discussion that follows the presentations. The active learning here is at two different levels.

- First, each group has been given a particular episode to depict. This involves the group members deciding what are the key aspects of the information which they have to 'act'. They are developing a deep understanding of their own particular episode.
- All the groups also develop an understanding of the bigger picture, they have to guess or explain what they think is happening. The type of learning taking place here might be called reinforcement; it confirms what the group already know but in a more memorable manner.

One concern that history teachers have is how to build lasting knowledge, how to ensure that the building blocks are understood. In some ways this is a chronological sequence; it is also trying to understand a chain of events. If students have that good understanding, it lays the foundations for more complex thinking which might involve a consideration of motive or an analysis of causes.

## Points for reflection

After watching the first active sequence of the Beckett lesson it was suggested that the type of activity lent itself to a particular kind of historical thinking.

If you consider that this activity was modelling a particular approach that you might like to apply in your own teaching, consider the following issues:

- Assuming that this type of activity could be used to encourage thinking about causes and consequences, what explaining or thinking would you want learners to engage in. Clearly you want them to do more than simply act out an episode.
- This device could also be used to consider attitudes, values and beliefs. What thinking or explaining would you want learners to explore here.

## MODELLING: APPLY ACTIVE TEACHING AND LEARNING IDEAS IN YOUR TEACHING

Modelling is one of the key skills which you will develop over the course of your teaching career. The analysis of the Thomas Beckett lesson highlighted the nature of the learning that was taking place, however, the discussion is quite explicit in the way that it suggested that these kinds of activities were models which could be adapted in other teaching and learning sequences. The key to understanding modelling lies in reflection. One of the ways to demonstrate this idea is to consider some tried and tested strategies which history teachers use in a variety of settings. It is almost inevitable that you will see one or more of these activities taking place during your PGCE year.

### Card sorting

This simple but effective strategy can be used in a number of different settings. A variation on this is using cards to prioritize information to decide which ideas or explanations might be more important. If you have access to the British Educational and Communication and Technology Agency (BECTa) word processing software referred to in Chapter 11, you will see that the Year 8 activity focuses on the causes of the English Civil War. The word-processing activity involves sorting and categorizing causes of the war into three main categories: religious, political and economic. It is also possible to reorder these ideas to facilitate the consideration of longer-term causes and short-term triggers. Using an idea know as Diamond Nines, it would be possible to take the causes and prioritize them to create the obvious diamond shape, with the most important cause or trigger at the apex of the diagram. See Figure 5.2.

This 'evidence' has been edited and provides information of the political economic causes of the Civil War. In a Diamond Nine activity students would have to decide which event went at the apex of the diagram. They might for example decide that 1642 was the most significant. In some ways this is the final straw – the trigger. Another might decide that the problems dated back to the reign of Elizabeth I and therefore there was an element of inevitability about the clash between Monarch and Parliament.

The possibilities for active thinking in this variation of a card sort are significant and would give you the opportunity to develop far more complex ideas about the web of causation. The purpose of the activity is not just to produce a definitive list of causes but to provoke discussion about the way that causes link, that they are not separate and distinct events. It is possible to develop students' abilities to hypothesize – was the Civil War still likely to happen if Factor or Event X is removed from the diagram? Returning to Kolb's learning cycle (Figure 5.1) you could argue that sorting the cards into the diamond only takes the student to

| | | |
|---|---|---|
| In 1629, Charles decided to rule without Parliament. He did so for the next 11 years | In 1642, Charles tried to arrest some of Parliament's MPs and put them in prison. This caused riots and demonstrations in London. Charles left the city to raise an army to fight Parliament | Charles spent a lot of money on paintings, his family and the expenses of the royal court |
| In 1626, Parliament refused to raise money for the king | There were long-term money problems in England which went back to the days of Elizabeth I. Anyone who was on the throne would have to raise more money in taxes | In 1640, Charles fought a war against the Scots. He had to pay them money to maintain their armies while they occupied two counties in Northern England |
| In 1634 Charles extended the use of an unpopular tax called 'Ship Money' | In 1628, a military operation against France was a failure | In 1625, England fought an unsuccessful military expedition against Spain |

**Figure 5.2** Using processing to understand causation (NCET, BECTa and HA, 1998a)
*Source*: BECTa Improving Students' Writing in History using History and Word Processing (1998a)

step 2, and that the real active learning begins when they begin to explore the interrelationship between different causes.

## Layers of inference and evidence sandwiches

Another active strategy which helps students to develop their understanding of evidence is commonly referred to as the layers of inference model. The idea was originally developed to help analysis of visual sources but in reality it can be applied to any kind of evidence. The technique is designed to help students dig deep into a source. The idea was originally suggested by Hilary Cooper as a way of helping primary pupils engage with historical evidence. It is nowadays one of the standard teaching techniques in the history classroom.

The variant described by Claire Riley (1999) in *Teaching History* consists of a series of concentric circles which begin with simple observations. The outer circles require deeper thinking.

- What does the source tell me?
- What guesses or inferences can I make?
- What does the source not tell me?
- What other questions do I need to ask?

The activity can become part of the routines of history teaching and help pupils to work with evidence in a systematic and challenging way.

While the layers of inference model can be a useful strategy to be used within any lesson, the next active strategy is one which is more suited to developing and structuring more detailed student work. From reading the previous chapter you should not only be aware of the National Strategy, but you should also be developing your awareness that history teaching involves far more than just teaching students about the past. History also makes a significant contribution to the development of students' general skills. The very nature of history means that it is ideally placed to contribute to developing literacy in particular. Every history teacher has, at some point, to confront the literacy paradox. History is a literate subject and students' poor literacy skills can be a significant barrier to understanding. By developing their literacy skills, history teachers are helping students to become more effective learners of history. In the National Curriculum the key processes are concerned with constructing historical understanding. The National Curriculum expects students to apply their literary skills – speaking, reading and writing – to understand and to communicate their understanding of the past. Helping students to develop their ability to communicate in what is sometimes termed 'extended writing' is a key skill which not only helps them to develop a deeper understanding of history, but also helps them to develop logical and orderly ways of thinking. Christine Counsell (1997) uses the term 'analytical and discursive writing' alongside extended writing and this is a useful term which reflects both the nature of historical communication and our expectations of what and how the students write.

The key process: 'communication about the past' outlines a series of expectations. First, that there are disciplinary conventions:

- History imposes a variety of structures which may be chronological or conceptual.
- Communicating an understanding of history is not just about re-creating a narrative, but developing historical argument.
- Historical argument itself imposes particular conventions in terms of structure and coherence.
- Historical argument also involves the use of evidence to substantiate an argument.

Margaret Mulholland first suggested the idea of the Evidence Sandwich in 1998. The technique described by Mulholland develops a particular approach to constructing paragraphs by using the analogy of a deep-filled sandwich, or a hamburger. It is a memorable analogy and does help students to remember how to develop an argument within a paragraph. Counsell made the all too familiar observation that often A-level students found it difficult to structure an essay and the results more resembled a passage from James Joyce than a structured analysis of Bismarck's foreign policy. The concept is simple and memorable – a paragraph begins with an opening argument – the first slice of bread; this acts as a signal for the content of the paragraph – the meat and salad. The meat and salad filling is the evidence which can be used to prove or demonstrate an argument. The final slice of bread is the concluding remark of the paragraph which can provide both a conclusion and a summation of the evidence. It can also act as a link to the next paragraph which might examine counter-arguments. The hamburger approach helps students to develop an understanding of structure but it is only a beginning. Commenting on two Year 7 essays, Counsell notes that 'Essays like those … do not happen by magic. Nor do they happen as a result of spending a lot of time writing essays' (Counsell, 1997: 7). To understand what Counsell means it is worth looking at a sequence of lessons described by Dale Banham (1998). This provides a valuable demonstration of the ways that an active approach can be sustained over a lengthy teaching sequence and how the idea of the evidence sandwich can be used to provide real depth and structure. Banham develops a sequence of lessons which have the focus question: 'King John was the worst monarch ever to sit on the English throne': do you agree with this statement? Banham's article demonstrates that if teaching and learning are going to be effective and active there has to be a point in the sequence of lessons where students have the ability to engage with the subject in real depth. The value of approaching a topic in more depth was referred to in the previous chapter when reviewing the work of Gardner and MI theory, and it is a point that Banham himself makes. The King John activity provides an 'opportunity for Year 7 pupils to deepen and extend their understanding ... a chance to develop evidence evaluation skills in a rich and motivating context' (Banham, 1998: 6).

The techniques described have become part of the repertoire of active teaching and learning approaches; during your early observations it would be worthwhile looking out for these ideas and variations of them. For example in Peter Duffy's classroom there are wall displays which demonstrate a similar approach to the evidence sandwich but which has its origins in English teaching, POINT–EVIDENCE–EXPLAIN, which uses the memorable acronym PEE. However, for the Jamie Oliver generation perhaps the hamburger analogy is equally memorable.

### Points for reflection

- The references to Hamburger paragraphs might sound like clever gimmicks yet both Banham and Counsell write about the importance of approaches which are 'systematic' and 'holistic'. Do you think that Hamburger paragraphs are just clever tricks or can they provide students with the tools to become analytical and discursive?



## THINKING SKILLS: LEARNING HOW TO LEARN

The illustrations earlier in the chapter demonstrate how many history teachers have developed a series of active strategies and incorporated them into their teaching repertoires. They might be thought of as tricks of the trade but it is also possible to understand them as a significant element of the history teacher's pedagogical knowledge. There is an awareness that these strategies engage learners and help them to work with the history; as teaching strategies they are flexible and adaptable. For beginning teachers they are also valuable models and it is important to see them in this context. Think of these strategies not so much as off-the-peg lessons but as patterns or templates which are adaptable and flexible, and can be applied in a number of different contexts. A variant on active history involves a more considered approach to learning, and is sometimes referred to as thinking skills. Guy Claxton writes about developing the capacity to learn and has coined the phrase 'building learning power'. If you refer back to the discussions about the direction of whole-school curriculum reform, in Chapter 2, you should be able to appreciate how this idea fits into the 'successful learners' area of the curriculum.

Claxton's ideas are applicable in a wider curriculum than just learning history. The philosophy behind these related approaches to teaching and learning is concerned with helping students understand how they learn: in effect engaging students with their metacognition.

Thinking skills have been lurking in the curriculum for a number of years. In Curriculum 2000 (DfEE / QCA, 2000: 9) there was a specific reference to history promoting thinking skills: 'through work on processing and evaluating information, describing and explaining events and actions and carrying out investigations of past events'. There is also a reference to the key skills which might be closer to understanding what thinking skills might involve: *communication* – which probably also includes *working with others* to *solve problems*.

In the latest version of the curriculum the thinking skills are more explicit from 'making and testing hypotheses', one of the key processes, to the more general but more obvious personal learning and thinking skills:

(PLTS), together with functional English, mathematics, and ICT, cover the areas of competence that are most often demanded by employers. Integrating these skills into the curriculum and qualifications will provide learners with a platform for employability and further learning. PLTS are:

- team working
- independent enquiry
- self-management
- reflective learning
- effective participation
- creative thinking. (www.qca.org.uk/qca_10327.aspx)

Thinking skills might be viewed as another element of the drive to improve teaching and learning in schools. The rhetoric suggests that there is more to this and a guide to the PLTS framework provides a useful insight. Thinking skills is an attempt to make every aspect of the curriculum relevant to the world outside school. Claxton again provides a more developed and a more persuasive series of arguments. Building learning power involves:

- helping young people become better learners
- developing their portable learning power
- preparing young people for a lifetime of learning.

These ideas can be explored more fully at the Building Learning Power website, a link to which can be found on the companion website.

The problem for the new teacher is trying to understand what distinguishes active history from thinking skills in history. Hopefully, you are developing an eye for subtleties. Investing an idea with a grand title like 'thinking skills' implies that it is somehow important and serious. To give thinking skills an official seal of approval might endorse the initial view. On the other hand, it might encourage an element of scepticism. As for the relationship, it might best be summed up in the following terms: thinking skills will inevitably engage learners in active history. Employing active history techniques does not necessarily imply that you have adopted a thinking skills approach to teaching.

This distinction is highlighted in the comment below by an NQT describing his first impressions of working in a department and school where the philosophy of learning to learn pervades the whole curriculum. What is also clear is that it is just as important to involve students and parents in these approaches to learning if the approach is going to be effective.

> One of (the school's) main aims for this year is to increase challenge in pupil learning (especially in boys). The Head of Faculty uses mind maps extensively, in fact since working with him I have stopped writing lists and started to naturally draw concept maps to make notes. My first impression of the history department is that it is tuned into the idea of pupil learning. The schools where I worked on placement did similar activities but here there is a more connected approach. Many of the activities are based on learning theories. This affects the children who are well versed in learning theory and understand their own learning styles/profile. As a result of Year 7 'Unlocking learning day' the children are taught how to do these things correctly. (For example) when I ask students to draw a concept map they can without having to be shown how. Unlocking learning is done for parents as well as the students.
>
> As for my personal challenges, it's not been difficult to adapt the way that I teach, the different methods are not harder, they are just different; as such I am finding that I am having a lot more variety in my teaching. It's also good to look at my own learning style profile, because I didn't realize that if I learn in a particular was then it is most likely that I will teach that way. It's probably a bit too soon to say what the children's reactions are but I don't get the impression that the kids are getting bored because I am doing different things every lesson. (Gary)

## THINKING SKILLS APPROACHES

### Organizing and recording thinking

The NQT above referred to the extensive use made by his department of concept maps. Thinking skills and concept-mapping are related. Concept-mapping is simply one technique for developing or reinforcing thinking skills. It is a way of recording understanding of a topic. There are advantages over more traditional ways of recording ideas and understanding. It is a process which is dynamic and might therefore demonstrate a developing understanding of a topic over a period of time. Essentially, concept-mapping is a diagrammatic representation of an individual's understanding; it demonstrates an awareness of links between related concepts or a series of facts. What distinguishes a concept map from a spider diagram is the way it is used. It is more complex and more studied than a random list of ideas which could appear in a spider diagram. It helps to connect ideas and explain such concepts as causal links. A concept map therefore could be considered to be a dynamic record of learning and understanding. For example, the school referred to above asks pupils to develop a concept map about the Holocaust; it is added to week by week. In assessing students' learning they are asked to talk their teachers through the concept map and issues such as causation or significance can be explored in depth.

An understanding of some of the principles of concept-mapping can help you develop a range of strategies which can make teaching more effective and consequently make pupil learning more effective. The benefits of mind-mapping techniques for history teaching might therefore be summarized as follows:

- helps to develop pupils' subject knowledge
- to construct sustained narratives
- to develop conceptual understanding of issues such as cause and consequence and significance
- to develop pupils' analytical skills.

Another school which has approached the idea of learning to learn is St George's Church of England High School in Blackpool, the head of history, Jason Brierley, explains how living education attempts to engage and develop students' metacognitive abilities. This approach is part of the National Strategy Leading in Learning strand but the learning to learn philosophy underpins all aspects of the department's teaching and learning strategies. St George's is also involved in a wider LA initiative developing thinking skills resources in association with the Ireland in Schools project. The link to Fighting for whom – 1916?, the Easter Rising, and the Battle of the Somme is a thinking skills resource based around a relational diagram (opposite).

## THINKING OUT LOUD: METACOGNITION FOR YOUNG THINKERS

In the previous chapter one discussion focused on the role of the plenary. It began to explore the difference between simply consolidating the learning that had taken place in a lesson and the 'debriefing' and 'bridging' activities that are an important feature of a thinking skills lesson. There is a tendency to view a thinking skills lesson as a series of neat tricks, clever ways of working with students, rather than a coherent approach to teaching and learning in the history classroom. If you have an opportunity to observe a thinking skills lesson, you will naturally be drawn to the activities that the students are engaged with. Instead, try to focus on the way that the teacher manages the debriefing. The focus is less on the students providing a solution and more on their ability to articulate how they reached their conclusions. Even more skilful is the teacher who can develop the debriefing and move to the bridging phase where students are encouraged to see how their thinking might be applied outside the confines of the subject. Managing this element of learning in an open forum is difficult and challenging. Peter Fisher's *Thinking Through History* (2002) is therefore a valuable resource which not only provides a number of worked examples; it also gives you an opportunity to read the teachers' evaluations of the lessons. *Thinking Through History* also makes clear this link between active history and thinking history in a very practical way. The book suggests that there are different levels at which the activities outlined in the text can be used: either as ready-made resources or as a series of models or exemplars which you might want to adapt for different topics, groups or abilities. As you gain confidence you can move up a level and focus on the thinking aspects and developing students' metacognitive abilities.

**Use of Thinking Skills at St George's C of E Business and Enterprise College, Blackpool**

**Background**

The work arose out of discussions at the Blackpool History Teacher Network. We had been considering ways of implementing Thinking Skills during 2004–2005. At the same time Blackpool LEA was approached to take part in the Ireland Project as a way of raising awareness of the Irish conflict and bringing about reconciliation.

I had been interested in developing lessons around the First World War, particularly the experiences of different soldiers; therefore it seemed logical to work on the experiences of Irish soldiers fighting in the Somme. This was then tied into the Easter Rising, which had occurred just months prior, with Catholic nationalist soldiers in particular, potentially having divided loyalties.

The project itself was able to take on a life of its own. I was unwilling to embark on this work for it to merely stand alone and was therefore able to tie it into a new assessment task on Michael Collins. As a consequence the Irish Unit that was inserted into the scheme of work, whilst self contained also linked in with the First World War and the rise of nationalist politics after the war.

**Rationale**

I had agreed to look at relational diagrams as a way of assessing responses to a given situation. This fits snugly with Key Skill 3: Interpretations of History. The rationale of the unit was to assess the interpretations of Michael Collins. This required an understanding (at a basic level) of Republican, Nationalist, and Unionist responses to Collins. These were the same interpretations required to respond to the events of 1916. Therefore, after background lessons on the Irish conflict and Collins himself, we considered the Irish responses to recruitment for the war from the three perspectives before reinforcing this through the relational diagram.

**Concept**

The principle of the relational diagram is that having considered two pictures, 'The birth of the Irish Republic' by Walter Paget and the picture of the Ulster Division advancing at the Somme

*(Continued)*

*(Continued)*

(whose name and artist I don't have at hand), the group considers the similarities and differences of the Republican and British Unionist combatants, they then consider written sources about combatants from 1916. The sources are based upon primary accounts, secondary interpretations and generic statements and are deliberately ambiguous. For example:

'these very men of the Norfolks (a British regiment) had quitted Belfast … owing to the menace in their midst of the very men who were doing them (the guard of) honour now.'

The obvious response is that these were a nationalist regiment offering a guard of honour, but a closer reading identifies Belfast and is a reference to the Ulster Division made up of UVF volunteers who had been fighting to maintain the Protestant supremacy up until 1914. Similarly the following quote is ambiguous:

'At times they were jeered at and spat upon by the (Dublin) crowds.'

This in fact refers to the response to Republican combatants during the Easter Uprising, and not to nationalists in British regiments as is usually suggested.

However, the ambiguity is to allow students to place these cards into interlocking circles and recognize that for example both republican and nationalist in British regiments could be spat upon, or that mainland British soldiers fought alongside men who, whether nationalist or Unionist, may have fought against them prior to the war.

**Impact**

Initially the response of the pupils has been that the Irish conflict is 'too difficult' and [they] are confused by the use of Unionist, nationalist and republican, particularly when people such as Patrick Pearce are introduced, who was both Republican and Protestant. However, as this unit is driven by the same key skill and repeatedly reinforced through the use of a variety of exercises such as tables, questioning, both oral and written before the relational diagram their confidence has been developed.

When presented with the diagram, which they recognize as a Venn diagram, they understand the concept but may need support to associate Unionist with the Ulster Division, nationalists with the Connaught Rangers and the Republicans with the Irish Volunteers. Having made this connection they are then challenged by the ambiguity of the statements. But having completed the exercise and discussed their responses they are more confident when revisiting the interpretations of Michael Collins.

The initial trial, and subsequent evidence has backed this up, demonstrated that compared to the previous assessment pupils made significant progress. The prior assessment had seen grades on average a level below their target grade at 0.9 for the class. After completing this assessment the average was 0.06 below the target level. Two pupils recorded a level two grades above their target level and nine pupils exceeded their target grade by one grade.

Pupil responses have indicated that this was a popular unit and assessment due to their familiarity with the material and variety of tasks.

**Metacognition**

As part of the discussions pupils have been asked to consider how they have reached their conclusions, to justify their responses and identify examples of how this activity could be applied to both other lessons and other contemporary events, e.g. the war on terror, support for different sports teams, etc.

Lesley Ann Buxton is an experienced head of department working in the North East of England who is an enthusiastic advocate for the use of thinking skills in history lessons. Again, her approach is important; it is the element of connectedness which distinguishes a thinking skills philosophy from active history. For her the key element of the lesson involves connecting the learning: managing the debriefing process.

**Preparing and Managing the Debriefing**

A few years ago I was part of the Leading in Learning Strategy and I worked with colleagues across the school coaching thinking skills lessons. One of the elements we looked at was managing the debrief/plenary. Sometimes when you ask a student what they have learned in the lesson, they can easily recall facts they have acquired in the lesson, if you ask them how they have learnt, they draw a blank, and fall down: 'oh! We read!', 'erm! We talked about!' ... Students do not fully understand the processes of how they have learned or how they acquired this new knowledge. We as teachers need to familiarize students with this terminology. The thinking chart allows students to focus and use the correct thinking skills vocabulary. I ask the students to select 3 skills they have used in the lesson.

1. How did I learn today? (choose 3 skills)
2. What will I do next time?
3. Where could I use this skill again?

On the companion website you will find a thinking sheet to focus the debrief/ plenary. It is based on the Standards.

For an inexperienced trainee the debrief can be the most challenging part of a thinking skills lesson. It is far more than simply asking for a report from each group. They are doing more than providing answers or writing their own version of history.

- Be prepared – be proactive; as the pupils are working in groups listen to their discussions and make a note of the good points they make.
- Ask them to be prepared to raise that particular issue at the debrief.
- Try not to intervene or dominate their discussions.
- Intervene if they appear to be getting stuck.
- Don't provide answers but ask them to review or summarise their ideas so far and then try to get them to rethink their ideas.
- Give plenty of advance warning: 10/5 minutes to debrief, etc.
- Remind them about organizing their contribution to the debrief.
- Make the pupils aware of the particular questions they will be asked. This gives them time to consider their ideas.
- The questions should be open ended.

*(Continued)*

*(Continued)*

This plenary technique will help a teacher focus on how much learning took place during the lesson, something Ofsted inspectors look for when grading lessons. It will help a teacher improve lesson plans in the future, when looking at how and what you want a student to learn.

I used the Thinking Chart with Year 7 today. I have a huge mounted display outside my room on 'what have the Romans done for us?' and the students picture from memory exercise ... make a mind map of information after only 30 secs per person in their groups of 4. I then ran through a debrief: see PPT on website. (Lesley Ann Buxton)

Just as it is possible to model good active teaching and learning strategies so it is important with thinking skills tasks to recognize that they can be used in a number of different ways. The advantage of making thinking skills activities explicit is the focus on metacognition. The closing comments of the bridging activities based on the Motte and Bailey task asked 'when could you use this strategy again?' Lesley Ann Buxton below describes how these learning strategies can be very practical.

I used this approach recently with Year 10 using the Source 'The Gap in the Bridge' – a British cartoon of 1920 – showing America refusing to join the League. The pupils had not been previously exposed to this particular source and I was interested to see what they made of this activity. After using this activity I found an added benefit, the pupils' source skills became much more effective ... they discussed what could be inferred, the provenance, the reliability, the purpose. The cartoon from memory activity was much more enjoyable than looking at the source from an OHP or textbook and the teacher dominating, asking questions to the whole class. This activity involved all the pupils thinking!

It is possible to see the positive impact this strategy had on student learning, although cartoons can be a very difficult sources to use, particularly at GCSE level. Students have first to develop an understanding of the historical context and subject knowledge. From this they have to understand the perspective of the cartoonist and what light this then sheds on the attitudes, values and beliefs of the time. By developing a thinking skills approach, students become more conscious of different learning techniques. They not only know how an activity works but they know why it works. The activity becomes more memorable, the students develop a deep understanding of the content of the cartoon and are able to construct a more considered interpretation of the evidence.

## THE NATIONAL STRATEGY AND THINKING SKILLS: A DISCONNECTED APPROACH?

It is worth comparing thinking skills as a coherent approach to teaching and learning with the National Strategy approach in the Leading to Learn strand. Subject-specific guidance is available and this opening statement highlights the different philosophical approach: 'This is the perspective that teachers are asked to adopt when, for an occasional lesson, they subordinate subject concerns for a common focus on a selected National Curriculum thinking skill' (Key Stage 3 National Strategy Leading in Learning Exemplification in history 2005).

The whole purpose of active history and a thinking skills approach to history is that the learning styles and the learning approach are integral elements of learning history. There is a real weakness in the approach outlined in the National Strategy given that the focus is on developing critical thinking or on learning to learn there is a distinctive lack of connected thinking when the Leading to Learn guide suggests that just for once teachers subordinate subject content and focus on a National Curriculum thinking skill. By separating, or suggesting that it is possible or even desirable to separate, history and thinking it reduces the Leading to Learn approach to a series of disconnected tricks. So far the discussion has tried to develop an understanding of active history and how and why these strategies can be effective. The important point, however, is to understand how these different strategies can contribute to a particular approach to teaching and learning which is summed up in the idea of thinking skills. As a teacher it is important to be able to develop an informed and critical perspective. The standards might demand that you are open to new ideas and innovations but they do not demand unqualified acceptance. There might be significant weaknesses in the approach outlined in the Leading to Learn exemplification. They begin with the attempt to match 'history skills' with thinking skills. Causation is seen as little more than reasons why something happened. The exploration of reasoning skills below provides some idea of the limited nature of historical understanding on the part of the authors of this document.

**Reasoning skills**

*These enable pupils to give reasons for opinions and actions, to draw inferences and make deductions, to use precise language to explain what they think and to make judgements and decisions informed by reason or evidence.*

In history, teachers should plan for pupils to:

- *Give reasons for opinions and actions* - for example, when they substantiate their answers with relevant knowledge and understanding or they assess the opinions of others according to factors such as bias, completeness, accuracy or whether the author wishes to inform, persuade or popularise history, they are able to provide reasons for their judgements.

- *Draw inferences and make deductions* - for example, when they use a range of sources to answer questions about the past which go beyond simple observations or when they use prior knowledge and understanding of a historical character to explain what motivated them during certain key events.
- *Make judgements and decisions informed by reason or evidence* - for example, when they reach a conclusion by selecting appropriate evidence from a broad range of sources and articulate the reasons for choices made. (DfES, 2005: 7, emphasis in original).

The guide then devotes most of the time to describing a range of thinking skills devices. In themselves they describe valuable strategies or teaching and learning models. Unfortunately, the examples they use are shallow and trite.

The guidance suggests that advance organizers could help Year 7 students handle copious amounts of text:

> Advance organisers can be used to great effect in history because it is a subject which requires pupils to sift through extensive information and evidence, to undertake research, and to analyse complex relationships. Pupils benefit from having an appropriate mental representation on which to hang their developing historical knowledge and understanding. For example, in order to assess '*how successful Anglo-Norman monarchs were at extending their boundaries*', pupils are required to process and evaluate copious text. To avoid pupils feeling overwhelmed, a **KWL grid** is introduced to activate prior understanding and 'scaffold' reading.

| What do I **know?** | What do I **Want** to know? | What have I **Learned?** |
|---|---|---|

> Pupils note down what they already know about a given topic, categorizing information through pair talk. Pupils then decide what they want to find out. Key questions are agreed. Information cards describing episodes in the story of the relationship between England and its neighbours are read and answers to the pupils' key questions recorded and shared. (DfES, 2005: 8, emphasis in original)

It would be useful to compare this idea or approach with Dale Banham's (1998) King John Grand Prix, remembering that the techniques Banham develops and the ideas suggested above both focus on similar thinking activities:

- sifting through extensive information and evidence
- analysing complex relationships.

Both techniques also use devices, or mental representations:

- Banham makes extensive use of the evidence sandwich.
- Leading to learn uses a grid.

## Points for reflection

Developing a critical perspective

- The leading in learning exemplification material makes quite a pointed reference to history which requires students to process and evaluate copious amounts of text. You might like to refer back to earlier discussions which focused on ways in which pupils of all abilities might be helped to work with text and 'information' and alternative active strategies which can help them read for meaning, sort, categorize and then evaluate text.
- There are a number of other examples of thinking skills tactics in the guide. It might be useful to evaluate two or three of these approaches. In developing a critical perspective you might like to consider why two of these ideas might be particularly suited to the history classroom. The third tactic might be one which you felt might not be effective.
- You should have developed an understanding of active and thinking approaches to the extent that you can suggest quite specific criteria. It might be useful to use these criteria in your evaluations above.



### What does the research say?

The ideas of active learning and thinking skills approaches to learning are playing a significant part in changing the way history is taught. It is also one aspect of teaching which has been significantly influenced by cognitive research. The logical premise is that if it is possible to understand how people learn, then it is possible for teachers to create more effective teaching and learning activities. There is also an added benefit in that this approach depends on the learners themselves developing self-awareness. Under these circumstances learning becomes much more of a conscious activity and is a useful 'life skill'. Some of the work of cognitive psychologists is not necessarily new but has enjoyed a renaissance with the advent of the National Strategy. Researchers such as Guy Claxton have synthesized some of these older traditions with more recent knowledge provided by neural scientists. This understanding about the ways that the brain works have added a new dimension to ideas about effective learning.

This research is far more accessible and you might want to follow up three quite generic leads, all of which can be found on the companion website, www.sagepub.co.uk/secondary:

- Carol McGuinness, from the School of Psychology, Queen's University, Belfast produced an evaluation of thinking skills in 1999 for the DfES: *From Thinking Skills*

*(Continued)*

(Continued)

to *Thinking Classrooms: A Review and Evaluation of Approaches for Developing Pupils' Thinking*.

- Similarly Pete Griffin's 'Encouraging children to explain or verbalise their thinking and their activity' considers ways of raising students' levels of consciousness in the way that they think about thinking.
- Guy Claxton's home page also contains useful links to ideas about learning to learn and building learning power.
- As you develop your understanding of thinking skills and active learning strategies you might like to relate this back to learning in history and why learning history is difficult. See Chapter 2 'Putting Principles into Practice: understanding History', P. Lee in M. S. Donovan and J. D. Bransford (eds) 2005. Committee on How People Learn: A Targeted Report for Teachers, National Research Council.
- Finally, Dale Banham: 'Getting ready for the Grand Prix: learning how to build a substantiated argument in Year 7', *Teaching History*, 92: 6–15. As you develop an understanding of active history it would be valuable to read this article and try to identify what makes the Grand Prix an effective learning experience.

## Further reading

Banham, D. (1998) 'Getting ready for the Grand Prix: Learning how to build a substantiated argument in Year 7', *Teaching History*, 92:6–15.

Counsell, C. (1997) Analytical and Discursive Writing at Key Stage 3. Shaftesbury: Historical Association.

Fisher, P. (2002) *Thinking Through History*. Cambridge: Chris Kington.

Mulholland, M. (1998) 'Frameworks for linking pupils' evidential understanding with growing skill in structured written argument: the evidence sandwich', *Teaching History*, 107: 17–19.

## Useful websites

Live links to these websites can be found on the companion website.

www.dfes.gov.uk/research/programmeofresearch/projectinformation.cfm?projecid=12823&resultspage=1.

www.devon.gov.uk/dcs/maths/nletter/verbalise.htm.

www.guyclaxton.com/resources.htm.

# 6 ASSESSING FOR LEARNING HISTORY

This chapter considers the following issues:

- measuring and managing students' learning.
- the purposes of assessment
- the connection between assessment and learning and the importance of formative assessment
- the role of the history Attainment Target in measuring student progress and the range of opinions on their real value.

The focus of this chapter is on assessment – measuring and managing students' learning – and begins by asking you to consider your own experiences of having work assessed – particularly at University. Having some awareness of what you wanted to get out of having work assessed and how you hoped it might help you should help you to understand what students might feel about assessment. This is one of the key Standards areas and one which Ofsted has real concerns about – not the assessment practices of beginning teachers but the difficulties all teachers experience trying to manage assessment. The opening discussion focuses on the 'burden' of assessment and then begins to look at the purposes of assessment in the hope that this might help you to undertake more purposeful assessment. The most significant aspect of your practice is in making the connection between assessment and learning, and the importance of formative assessment. Hopefully, you will develop a more critical understanding of this and come to realize that much assessment is an integral part of your everyday teaching.

In the good old grammar school days you did history as opposed to learnt history. The routines of GCE history were described in a previous chapter and it was recognized that you had to know a lot of facts. The drills and routines worked, banging facts into heads. Success, the measure of learning, was to get high marks in an essay and good grades in an examination. To get a good mark for an essay on Bismarck's foreign policy you had to remember a number of facts, in sequence. Using these criteria I was a successful history learner. Getting better at history simply meant being able to remember more facts. At university for some reason I was also a successful learner – I could write essays that resulted in marks such as 'alpha/beta/plus/plus/question mark/plus' with the comment from the professor, 'very good: a cogent survey'. Understanding how or why you were eventually awarded a 2.1 or a 2.2 was down to the mysteries of the guild. History undergraduates today are in a very different situation. The modularization of degree programmes, end of year assessments and assignments that count towards final marks (rather than being completed simply for fun) often mean that undergraduates have a good idea of where they are and how they need to improve, or the marks they need to get to achieve the desired result.

Biography can be a useful 'way in' to help you develop an understanding of assessment. Consider these questions:

- Did you know how to write a good essay?
- Did you know how to improve your essay-writing skills?
- Did you know how to write at a higher level?
- Did written or oral feedback from a tutor help you to raise the level of your work?
- How did you feel if the essay you had spent days crafting, was ticked in a few places, had the occasional 'good' and a few cryptic comments in the body of the text, was topped off with a grade or percentage and a vague comment such as: 'analysis needs to be more sustained'?

If you have been on the receiving end of a history education within the past few years, you will either think that the quality of your assessment was impressive or maybe you feel let down. Hopefully the bullet points enable you to see the purpose of assessment from the perspective of a learner. It would be interesting for you to work out your PGCE perspective on assessment. As a prospective history teacher it is worth considering the impact assessment will have on your professional life. You might have noticed that history departments are smaller than English or science departments. You should also have worked out that students have fewer history lessons than English lessons. A useful observation to make when you first get into your placement school is to compare the number of different groups a history teacher and an English teacher might teach in Year 7 or Year 8. If you are teaching four Year 7 groups you could be teaching somewhere between 100 and 120 students per week. This might mean:

- 120 sets of parents or carers to talk to at parents' evening
- 120 reports to write and the end of the year
- 120 examination papers to mark
- 120 end of module tests to assess at the end of a module – with the students completing perhaps six modules in a school year
- 120 exercise books to mark each week.

This little sequence was prefaced by the comment, 'the impact assessment will have on your professional life'. Reading through these figures you might be thinking is there anything outside a professional life? You then need to balance the expectations which you had as a learner. Assessment presents a significant logistical problem and, therefore, managing assessment is a significant issue, one that the discussion will return to.

## ASSESSMENT OF LEARNING V. ASSESSMENT FOR LEARNING

Nationally there are some hefty expectations on you as beginning teachers, particularly with regard to assessment. There are four big QTT Standards (numbers 10, 11, 12 and 13) which have a focus on all aspects of assessment and there is a real and significant connection to Ofsted reports. Successive comments point to improvements in the quality of teaching and link this to the effects of National Strategies. There is always at least one 'however' and this inevitably relates to assessment. In 2005 the HMI Annual Report for secondary schools commented: 'assessment remains a general weakness, the more so at Key Stage 3. In the majority of schools, pupils do not have a good understanding of how they can improve their work'.

These comments are important because they enable you to understand the following expectations:

- You are expected to assess students at the end of Key Stage 3 and report on their level of attainment based on the level descriptions in the history National Curriculum Attainment Target.
- You are also expected to prepare students for national examinations at the end of Key Stage 4 GCSE and in Key Stage 5 for GCE A/S and A level examinations.
- It is also highly likely that you will be expected to assess students at the end of a module of work or at the end of the year.

This type of assessment is referred to as *summative assessment*. Students' performance is measured against criteria and their level of achievement recorded as a GCSE or GCE grade or as a National Curriculum level. Other summative assessments will be used to monitor progress either through Key Stage 3 or GCSE courses. These assessments are part of the process of accountability, enabling schools to report individual student progress to parents and carers. They also help schools and individual departments to set, meet and review targets – a measure both of accountability and teacher effectiveness.

A head of a history department is more accountable than ever before: to the head teacher and for target-setting and results. Part of this function also involves monitoring the effectiveness of other history teachers in the department.

To a beginning teacher this element of the profession might appear to be intimidating, and from the way summative assessment has been described it might feel that history teachers are subject to a series of shocks during the year as test results pile up. However, another kind of assessment helps the teacher keep in touch with what is happening in the classroom lesson by lesson. *Formative assessment* is the day-to-day evaluation of student progress, it is a process which is part of teaching and learning, and integral to the lesson. Formative assessment is that continuous dialogue between the teacher, the individual student and the whole class. It is recognizing in a question and answer session that there are problems with a particular idea or being aware that the class has grasped that idea and is ready to move on.

Formative assessment is one of the important aspects of professional craft knowledge that you will develop as a teacher, and to be effective at using formative assessment you need to, yet again, develop that metacognitive, reflective approach. If you refer back to the Kolb cycle in the previous chapter:

- Effective learning is cyclical so is effective teaching.
- Formative assessment is your professional reflection on students' progress but you need to complete the cycle.
- Formative assessment informs the next stage of your planning.
- Your formative assessment helps you plan the next stage of your students' learning.

If you look at the Ofsted comments in Figure 6.1 you can see that the major area of concern is the way formative assessment is used to inform planning and student learning and to help teachers be more systematic in directing future learning. This is a whole-school issue, and some subjects are managing assessment less well that others. History was not named and shamed but the history subject reports highlight these concerns.

Figure 6.1 clearly indicates that there are some difficulties that will not go away. This is not because history teachers or history departments are 'disobedient' or not 'good at doing assessment'. It suggests that assessment in history is fraught with problems. The final cell in Figure 6.1 outlines the issues which Ofsted feels are significant. Some of the difficulties relate to what might be considered principles of assessment. In the terminology of Sellars and Yeatman (*1066 and All That*) these are the 'good things' about assessment that Ofsted has identified:

- sharing criteria with students
- using criteria that students can understand
- enabling students to set their own targets for improvement
- providing constructive and useful feedback.

These four points also illustrate how good assessment involves the students themselves and requires a degree of reflection on their part. Other aspects of

| 2005 | 2007 |
|---|---|
| • The quality of marking and assessment is improving.<br>• In too many schools, pupils are not given clear enough indications of how well they are doing. This occurs mainly in Key Stage 3 and has two contrasting characteristics.<br>• The first is that in some schools, marking is not linked tightly enough to clear objectives. Part of the problem is the ambiguity in National Curriculum-level descriptors which many teachers and others find difficult to interpret and turn into workable criteria.<br>• In the absence of local or national moderation facilities, the ambiguity also undermines the accuracy of some overall teacher assessments and annual reporting of levels to the QCA.<br>• The second feature is that some schools have gone the other way and produced assessment systems which are overly bureaucratic and which confuse pupils.<br>• To address both these problems, a review of the history attainment target and level descriptors is necessary. | • Pupils are not given clear enough indications of how well they are doing.<br>• Increasingly, pupils tell inspectors which level they have reached; sometimes this is meaningless because they are not sure what this represents and what they need to do to improve.<br>• Part of the problem is the National Curriculum level descriptors which many teachers and others find difficult to interpret and turn into workable criteria against which to assess.<br>• This is made worse by the absence of effective monitoring to ensure consistent and accurate assessment.<br>• In 2004/05, Ofsted reported that these problems also undermine the accuracy of overall teacher assessments and annual reporting of levels to the QCA.<br>• Ofsted's report went on to recommend a review of the history attainment target and level descriptors to make them more functional and so improve the feedback to pupils.<br>• The QCA is now undertaking a review and we await the final outcome. |

| Ofsted and Assessment: Issues |
|---|
| • Some teachers and others argue that National Curriculum levels should not be used for within-key-stage assessment as they were not designed for this purpose.<br>• Experience has shown that they can be made to work and have benefits, particularly when they use language with which pupils are familiar in all subjects.<br>• Another advantage is that, when used in all subjects, they can help schools monitor overall progress closely.<br>• To reach this stage, the levels need to be translated into learning objectives that pupils can understand.<br>• The assessments themselves need to be informed by teachers' shared understanding of the standards implied.<br>• Schools that are far advanced in this respect have compiled portfolios of exemplar work, moderated against National Curriculum levels, which can be used for discussion and benchmarking. |

**Figure 6.1** Ofsted, history and assessment

the report imply that there is an element of disagreement about what is assessed and how this might inform students' understanding. Time for some critical engagement (QTT Standard 7). At the heart of the problem is the

status of the National Curriculum history Attainment Target and the level descriptors.

## HOW MIGHT THE LEVEL DESCRIPTORS BE USED TO INFORM ASSESSMENT?

The Office for Standards in Education believes that there is a lack of consistency and lack of agreement in the way that achievement is measured and reported. Their default position appears to be that the history Attainment Target is the lowest common denominator, therefore it is better than nothing and might deliver an element of consistency and uniformity. They also point out that some schools are using the level descriptors in a systematic way and this is helping to motivate students and raise standards.

At this point it would be worthwhile taking a look at what assessment in the classroom looks like. If you examine the closing sequences of the Thomas Beckett lesson, the students have completed their freeze frames. They have also watched a short audio visual presentation on the whiteboard and they are beginning to write the concluding piece explaining who they think is responsible for the murder of Beckett. The relevant sequence begins at 27 minutes. Peter Duffy provides some advice about the way to construct an answer which is effectively a historical argument. You might care to refer back to Chapter 5 and the discussion on the 'evidence sandwich'. You should also be aware that this links to the key process, 'communicating about the past', where students 'present arguments that are coherent, structured and substantiated'. This is important and by focusing on the PEE formula the students are developing an understanding of how they write their response. If you listen carefully, Peter Duffy also relates the type of answer on the whiteboard to level 5a: 'the level 5 success criteria, but to get a higher level you need to back that up with historical sources. If you do that in your answer you are reaching the top end of a level 5 answer'.

Following this, the students get on with their work. From this point on, Peter Duffy is monitoring their progress and developing an idea of their levels of understanding. At times he will discuss quietly with individuals their ideas, and occasionally he offers advice such as, 'you may need another sentence in there'. At other times he commends pupils for the way that they have constructed their answers and feeds back ideas to the whole class. At first glance this might appear to be the teacher simply doing his job but it is more subtle than that; monitoring progress also means forming an idea about students' progress – either individually or as a whole class. This is more obvious in the Home Guard lesson where the students were from a less able group. They needed more support and structure. In Chapter 5 you focused on some of these interactions as a practical demonstration of scaffolding learning, but it also represents a point in the lesson when the teacher is forming an idea about students' levels of assessment. The process of measuring learning in the classroom during the course of the lesson used the term 'forming an idea'. This might be a crude demonstration of the notion of formative assessment but, hopefully, it helps you to understand that assessment can be a continuous process in the classroom, and teachers create opportunities at frequent intervals in a lesson to get some idea of how students are learning. It might also give you an idea of how assessment can be made more manageable.

- Formative assessment can provide almost instant feedback.
- It helps you to understand if pupils are learning.
- You can intervene immediately to help move students' understanding on.

More significantly, it might give you an idea that there is a common problem which you might not have foreseen when you were planning the lesson.

- Formative assessment enables you to discover the problem.
- It raises the issue with the whole class and provides additional help.
- This could involve further explanation.
- It could involve you in a more structured question and answer session.

As you become a more competent practitioner in the classroom, this should enable you to understand your next move: how you take on their learning.

The assessment that what was taking place in the Thomas Beckett lesson would make Ofsted happy.

- Assessment was linked explicitly to learning objectives.
- Assessment criteria are shared with the students.
- They have an understanding of what they need to do to achieve a particular level.
- They are beginning to develop an understanding of levels and how performance can be matched with levels.
- The language used to describe the levels is student-friendly.
- As a consequence students would be able to set targets for improvement.

This lesson sequence demonstrates both how good formative assessment can work and how a system of levels can help students improve their performance. It would be appropriate at this stage to have a look at the levels in more detail. You should have made the connection between learning objectives and assessment: put simply your learning objectives also provide a framework for assessment. The Attainment Target therefore acts as the missing link connecting planning and assessment. It outlines a series of national expectations – what we can expect students to understand, to know, or be able to do in history. The history Attainment Target describes a series of levels which link closely with the key concepts and the key processes. This sounds too good to be true and it probably is. The Attainment Target was described as a missing link and in some respects this is probably an appropriate analogy. The levels in the Attainment Target are not fully formed, their status and precise relationship with the statutory requirements of the National Curriculum are subject to disagreement and they might be described as intellectually challenged. As a device for measuring or describing levels of understanding in history – well, it is a bit like using a hand axe to perform keyhole surgery. The next point for reflection illustrates some of these difficulties

## Points for reflection

The extract below is taken from the history National Curriculum Attainment Target. It describes the typical achievement of a student at level 7. The descriptors go from level 4 to level 8 in Key Stage 3. They also include a paragraph which describes 'exceptional performance':

**Level 7**

Pupils show their knowledge and understanding of local, national and international history by analysing historical change and continuity, diversity and causation. They explain how and why different interpretations of the past have arisen or been constructed. They begin to explain how the significance of events, people and changes has varied according to different perspectives. They investigate historical problems and issues, asking and refining their own questions and beginning to reflect on the process undertaken. When establishing the evidence for a particular enquiry, pupils consider critically issues surrounding the origin, nature and purpose of sources. They select, organise and use relevant information and make appropriate use of historical terminology to produce well-structured work.

- Link phrases from the Attainment Target to the key concepts and key processes.
- Ofsted believe that the level descriptors (above) provide a valuable benchmark for measuring attainment. From what you have read do you think that these statements help you to understand the type of work that students might be expected to achieve? (DfES, 2000: 39)



## NATIONAL CURRICULUM LEVELS: A CRITICAL EVALUATION

The level descriptors have been described as a blunt instrument. If you felt that you were unable to come to any significant conclusions about what a student might be expected to achieve or demonstrate at level 7 perhaps the full range of achievement presented in Figure 6.2 will help you to understand the problems. There are five grades that are designed to describe student progression within Key Stage 3. Level 4 describes the average expectations for a student beginning their secondary education in Year 7. Naturally some students will not be achieving at this level and some may be able to work at a higher level. An accountant's view would suggest that students should move from one level to the next in exactly 1.8 terms (or 7.8 weeks or 39 school days). This assumes, of course, that every student is going to move to level 8. You should begin to appreciate the blunt instrument analogy; in reality a student might reasonably be expected to move from one level to another over the course of a year. This tends to imply that students will be plugging away at the same type of task week after week.

The second difficulty with National Curriculum levels is the actual descriptors themselves. If you look at Figure 6.2 it highlights 'progression' through the levels in terms of understanding key concepts and the key process, 'communicating understanding'. This is a combination of blunt instrument with imprecise science – a little like early gunners trying to estimate how much gunpowder to put in the cannon to get the cannon ball to crash into the walls of a castle – you just keep adding more and hope you do not blow the thing up. Working from level 5 to level 6 you can see that students have to move from

- 'suggesting relationships between causes', to
- 'explaining relationships between causes'.

In terms of being able to communicate their historical understanding:

- At level 5 they are aware of causal relationships so the expectation is that their work would be structured and they would be able to use the correct terminology.
- At level 6 their work would be 'better' because they had organized, as well as structured their work but they were still using the correct terminology.

As you begin to analyse the level descriptors you might begin to appreciate other difficulties (probably a level 6 activity). Figure 6.2 has highlighted the progression in understanding as it relates to similarity and difference and causation, and in terms of the ability to communicate an understanding of history. From reading the key concepts you must be aware that some are more difficult than others and it is inevitable that students will make better progress in one area than in another. This might also reflect the nature of teaching. It is probable that students will spend more time on developing their chronological understanding and describing the key features of a particular society or sequence of events. It is also likely that they will spend

| Key concepts: change/causation | Key process: communicating understanding |
|---|---|
| Level 4<br>They describe characteristic features of past societies and periods to identify change and continuity within and across different periods and to identify some causes and consequences of the main events and changes. | They begin to produce structured work, making appropriate use of dates and terms. |
| Level 5<br>They begin to recognise and describe the nature and extent of diversity, change and continuity, and to suggest relationships between causes. | They select and deploy information and make appropriate use of historical terminology to support and structure their work. |
| Level 6<br>Beginning to analyse the nature and extent of diversity, change and continuity within and across different periods. They begin to explain relationships between causes. | They select, organise and deploy relevant information and make appropriate use of historical terminology to produce structured work. |
| Level 7<br>Analysing historical change and continuity, diversity and causation. | They select, organise and use relevant information and make appropriate use of historical terminology to produce well-structured work. |
| Level 8<br>Constructing substantiated analyses about historical change and continuity, diversity and causation. | They use historical terminology confidently, reflecting on the way in which terms can change meaning according to context. They produce precise and coherent work. |
| Exceptional performance<br>Pupils show a confident and extensive knowledge and understanding of local, national and international history. They use this to frame and pursue enquiries about historical change and continuity, diversity and causation, constructing well-substantiated, analytic arguments within a wide frame of historical reference. They analyse links between events and developments that took place in different countries and in different periods. | They evaluate critically a wide range of sources, reaching substantiated conclusions independently. They use historical terminology confidently, reflectively and critically. They consistently produce precise and coherent narratives, descriptions and explanations. |

**Figure 6.2** Progression in historical understanding: the National Curriculum perspective

relatively less time developing an understanding of the idea of interpretations of history. Plotting a student's progress through the different elements of the Attainment Target could well resemble the temperature chart of a malaria patient.

The final problem with Attainment Targets and level descriptors relates to their 'official status' in the National Curriculum. The Attainment Target provides criteria which enable teachers to report on the standards 'that pupils of different abilities and maturities are expected to have by the end of each key stage'. This is statute law, the Education Act 1996, section 353a. What this means is that there is no requirement by law to use the level descriptors or the Attainment Target to report progress except at the end of Key Stage 3 for students in secondary schools. The notion of different abilities and maturities is also a tacit recognition that progress or attainment across the Attainment Target might not be uniform. As well as a blunt instrument used to measure an imprecise science, the level a student achieves in the history Attainment Target might best be described as 'best fit'.

Part of the problem lies in the nature of history itself, the Attainment Target attempts to gauge historical understanding rather than knowing a number of facts about medieval monarchs or the ins and outs of twentieth-century history. If you look at this sequence taken from the science Attainment Target you might be able to understand why progression in historical understanding can be problematic:

- Level 5: They use line graphs to present data, interpret numerical data and draw conclusions from them.
- Level 6: They record data and features effectively, choosing scales for graphs and diagrams.
- Level 7: They record data in graphs, using lines of best fit.

You may or may not understand the process but you should be able to work out that these describe a series of very precise achievements which are demonstrable and quantifiable. The science levels are also absolute – the ability to draw a line graph is going to be the same in a school in Cornwall or Cumbria. Ideally the history Attainment Target is describing national standards but it is possible to see that there could well be differences in the way that the guidelines are interpreted. It is worthwhile comparing the descriptor for 'exceptional performance' with the QAA History Benchmark descriptors which describe criteria for a 2.1 examination response. Depending on your interpretation, it might appear easier to write a 2.1 answer in a final examination than reach the level of 'exceptional performance'.

This discussion has considered some of the difficulties the history Attainment Target presents. It is important to be aware of these issues because they will impact on your practice. The Office for Standards in Education tacitly acknowledges some of the difficulties in their report (Figure 6.1), the main issues being:

- problems interpreting the levels
- no effective monitoring, that is, no national end of key stage tests for history
- legitimate disagreement about the nature and status of the level descriptors.

A careful reading of Fig 6.2 should enable you to appreciate some of the problems faced by history teachers – particularly if you compare the science examples on page 129. In the Standards there is an expectation that you will 'critically engage' with them. This might be an appropriate time and place.

## Points for reflection

Points for reflection

There is a recognition that the history Attainment Targets are less than perfect. The Ofsted rationale for continuing to rely on them boils down to that favourite Thatcherite concept of 'TINA' – There Is No Alternative. TINA was a signal to end discussion. It might be time for you to critically engage with the levels outlined in Fig 6.2. As a 'commonsense' graduate historian why might you (or why should you) find it difficult to blindly accept the levels?

Don't worry about providing answers at the moment, hopefully the next discussion might help to point the way.

## MAKING YOUR ASSESSMENTS USEFUL

If there is an element of disagreement between the advocates of level descriptors and the critics who view them as un-historical or a-historical this clearly places a beginning teacher in a difficult situation. When you begin teaching it is inevitable that the assessment policies and practices in the history department where you are on placement or where you are an NQT will reflect whole-school policies. It is highly likely that they will also reflect the ideas which have become central to the National Strategy: Assessment for Learning.

There are some very accessible materials produced by the Assessment Reform Group which outline the principles of effective assessment. Inside the Black Box is a valuable summary. There is also a useful guide which outlines the main principles of *Assessment for Learning*. One of the first points the report makes is the importance of distinguishing between assessment of learning and assessment for learning. The authors are convinced that good assessment is one of the most significant factors in raising achievement.

In trying to understand how the history teacher might try to square the circle, it is worth trying to learn from good practice. There was a recognition that the levels approach to assessment was causing difficulties and the editorial board of *Teaching History* asked for examples of good practice. The result was in 'Assessment without levels?' *Teaching History* (2004), vol.115. Christine Counsell's editorial comment neatly sums up the dilemma facing history teachers:

> Most intriguingly of all, the principles of 'assessment for learning' have sometimes worked in curious ways. For some, they have pointed to the need for more careful reflection on what historical learning is, what progression might be and how we might assess it in a way that supports pupils' thinking and learning about history. But in other settings, the 'assessment for learning' principles have actually harnessed the idea of teaching to Levels and assessing with Levels and talking about Levels in every lesson, all in the name of a well-intentioned desire to make things transparent or explicit to pupils. Other factors, too, such as the drive for measurement and accountability have also been behind this curious distortion of 'assessment for learning' into (as far as history is concerned) a puzzling closing down of thinking about progression in history, and, instead a pressing of the Level Descriptions into inappropriate service. (Counsell, 2004: 2)

There is a tendency to describe important bits of paper as 'Key documents' but the idea can be overused. Suffice to say that 'Assessment without level descriptions' by Sally Burnham and Geraint Brown makes a very strong case for not using level descriptions to assess students' work. The system they describe fits the principles of Assessment for Learning; it is helpful for teachers and understandable for students. On page 8 of Burnham and Brown's article there is a reflective observation which focuses on students developing an understanding of imperialism as a cause of the First World War. What is described is good formative assessment within a lesson which enabled some students' thinking and learning to be moved on, it also enabled the teacher to identify students whose first language was not English: their conceptual understanding of imperialism proved more problematic and the teacher knew that she would have to revisit these ideas. However the formative assessment can inform a wider aspect of practice: imperialism is a concept that recurs in the history curriculum. Burnham made a note to look at where the idea of Imperialism crops up in Years 7 and 8 and consider how students' understanding might be strengthened. You have looked at the idea of formative assessment earlier in Peter Duffy's lesson; the account by Burnham and Brown is valuable as it provides that first-hand reflection on student understanding.

The significant aspect of assessment which Burnham and Brown feel is more relevant to the needs of teacher and student focuses on the mark scheme.

- A mark scheme is not an 'answer book'.
- It is closely linked to planning and the learning objectives either for a lesson or for a series of lessons.

- A mark scheme is very specific to the task which students are undertaking and measures their learning, or understanding, in the lesson or over a series of lessons.
- When learning objectives are shared with students, students should also have an understanding of the mark scheme.
- A mark scheme reflects a series of expectations – or different levels which students might be expected to achieve.

There is a very detailed mark scheme on page 11 of Burnham and Brown's article which focuses on the issue of causation. What is worth remembering here is that the KS3 Scheme of Work revisits the issue of causation across the key stage. The Year 9 mark scheme is therefore progressive; it helps to demonstrate how students have become 'better' at causation between Years 7 and 9. This is far more valuable than stating that the students have reached level 6 or 7 in causation. The mark scheme takes into account the 'nature' of causation and how students' understanding might have become more sophisticated. It is worth exploring this mark scheme in more detail because it is a technique which is used at a number of different levels in history teaching.

The mark scheme has two components

- response type/mark
- characteristic features of pupils' responses.

The responses range, Lowest–Low–Medium–High–Highest, and marks are allocated to each level. The most significant element of the mark scheme is the responses themselves. The teachers have been able to suggest a typical answer along with examples to illustrate each level. Do not confuse this with National Curriculum levels, though. The qualitative difference between these levels outlined in the mark scheme is that they are exclusive and informed:

- exclusive to the piece of work
- exclusive to the particular learning objectives
- informed by students' previous work.

In other respects this mark scheme demonstrates good practice. It is possible to understand what a student needs to do to move from one grade to another, which enables targets to be set. It is also possible to share these criteria with students so that they understand why they have achieved their grade and what they need to do to improve.

This is yet another 'must read' article for the way that it demonstrates how assessment in history can be managed at a departmental level. What is important for you to appreciate is how this approach can be useful at the level of an individual lesson.

For this it would be useful to watch the following Teachers' TV programme, *Assessment in History* a link to which can be found on the companion website, www.sagepub.co.uk/secondary. In the film you have an opportunity to hear Sally Burnham describing her ideas about assessment. However, the most relevant aspect of the film for the purposes of this discussion is where Reuben Moore describes the levels in his mark scheme for the Black Death Story (7 min 40 secs). What he describes is a range of attainment. He expects student responses to range through:

- understanding the progress of what happened in the village during the Black Death
- understanding something about the short- and long-term results
- using ideas and understandings from previous lessons about the nature of the medieval village
- understanding the importance of underlying consequences of the Black Death.

This mark scheme relates to the series of lessons based around the Black Death. The advantages of this way of assessing and recording achievement is valuable because of the benefits for both teachers and students:

- These overall expectations are presented in terms which students understand.
- The more specific assessment criteria are again presented in ways which the students understand.
- The levels in the Attainment Target are not referred to but there the work does make incremental demands on the students. This enables teachers to identify achievement and progress.
- It is possible to identify the key concepts and key processes in the history National Curriculum in the mark scheme.
- The mark scheme also takes account of previous learning, in this case how students' knowledge/understanding of the medieval village has helped them to appreciate the effects of the Black Death on the social structure of the village.

This list demonstrates the immediate benefits of using a mark scheme in this way. There are obvious longer-term benefits:

- The mark scheme enables teachers to revisit specific skills and areas of understanding – the Black Death story was building on an earlier piece of extended writing which focused on the Battle of Hastings.
- Teachers are able to both increase the demands of the most recent activity and help the students improve by referring back to previous work.
- Developing understanding in history does not involve learning 10 more facts or 20 new words. Developing conceptual understanding involves practice. By using and applying their understanding of ideas like cause and consequence in new or different contexts helps students to learn more effectively.
- Teachers have concrete evidence which demonstrates areas of competence and levels of achievement and these can be expressed in terms which are both historical and relate to real achievement.

- This can be seen in the discussion on the film where Reuben Moore links the possible reaction of villagers to the death of the reeve. The students have to relate this to previous lessons on the medieval village and need to understand something about the significant role of the reeve.
- Evidence of achievement and progress can be related to parents in a meaningful way. The filmed extract from the parents' evening demonstrates how this way of reporting progress is valuable. The effectiveness of this way of reporting can be judged by the involvement of the students themselves reporting their progress to their parents.
- The system also provides meaningful feedback for teachers which helps them to plan future learning – both of individual pupils and of whole classes.

## Points for reflection

Points for reflection

The mark scheme for the Black Death sequence of lessons in the film you have watched, expected students to demonstrate their understanding a number of different areas. Taking just two of these areas, flesh out the mark scheme by identifying a range of possible responses or different levels of knowledge or understanding which you might expect students to demonstrate:

- understanding the progress of what happened in the village during the Black Death
- understanding the importance of underlying consequences of the Black Death.

## WHAT DO YOU MARK AND HOW DO YOU MARK IT?

Earlier in this chapter reference was made to the assessment burden, the sum total of books, homework and examinations which history teachers – along with all other teachers have to mark. The next discussion focuses on the nature of the assessments themselves. A colleague, a head of history in a local school, described the school's assessment policy: everything had to be marked on a weekly basis. Such an approach resembled the British Army in the days of National Service: if it walked, salute it; if it did not, paint it white. This colleague described his assessment load as a one-bag or two-bag night – referring to the number of carrier bags of pupils' work he had to take home. All beginning teachers recognize that assessment is part of the job and you may well find that you have a sense of anticipation marking that first set of books. You will want to assess the work carefully and thoroughly and provide each pupil with valuable feedback. Before you know it, that class set of extended writing about the Battle of Hastings has taken you about 90 minutes to mark. The logistics soon become terrifying: three sets of books to mark, followed by four lessons to prepare, each lesson, with resources, taking perhaps two hours to put together.

Hopefully we have moved away from the Everest approach to assessment – we do it because it is there. Before we really begin to focus on managing assessment it might be useful to consider the following issues in relation to day-to-day assessment practices:

- What do you assess? Should you mark everything that students produce: notes? class exercises? homework? anything else?
- Why do you assess? Do you or your students need to know week by week how they are performing? What kind of feedback would be useful?
- How do you assess? Do you need to grade everything that students produce? Can students self-assess? Can students assess each other.

Some schools and departments will have a rational and considered assessment policy which outlines expectations for teachers, students and parents. An assessment policy is likely to indicate expectations with regard to measuring attainment, monitoring progress and setting targets, and these are often displayed prominently in history classrooms.

**Features of assessment policies**

*Notes and class work*

Is it necessary to provide marks for routine class notes? You may need to ensure these are completed and up to date. You might however like to question the validity of class notes: what purpose do they serve? Are they an effective way of building subject knowledge and understanding? Are there more effective ways of building understanding such as mind maps? If your department or school feels notes are important do you simply acknowledge that they are complete? Do you offer advice about compiling effective notes as part of study skills?

*The nature and frequency of homework*

The Office for Standards in Education believes that homework should be an integrated part of learning. Finishing off class work might not therefore be a good use of homework time. It penalizes the slow and encourages the less conscientious to rush. Managing homework is key to managing your assessment load. Research work preparing for the next lesson can be effective – but it needs to be structured *and* you need to ensure that it does feature significantly in the next lesson.

*(Continued)*

*(Continued)*

Homework can be used effectively to consolidate learning. Managing homework routines is important, students need to know when and where work is handed in and they also need to know that there is no hiding place.

*Providing feedback*

Students need feedback which is constructive, sets clear targets and is useful. Commenting on work is time-consuming. You need to be focused and you need criteria which students are aware of and understand. How does feedback relate to learning objectives? Feedback is an important element of teaching and learning: do you build time into your lesson to review feedback with students as individuals or as small groups or as a whole class? Are students encouraged to review and comment on their own progress and to set their own targets?

*Grades and grading criteria*

Are grades and criteria clearly understood by students? How do you award grades – are students rewarded for effort as well as attainment? How do students use grades; do they just look at grades at the start of the lesson and move on? Do they understand how they are awarded grades – are they generic across the department or school or are the criteria different for each piece of work? Are the grades and the system for awarding grades the same across all classes? Are less able groups only able to score 'lower' marks or are criteria appropriate and particular for each group? If you are teaching mixed-ability groups should each student have individual targets?

*Correcting spelling, punctuation and grammar (SPG)*

Is there a school policy on SPG – do you correct everything, is the policy to correct 'subject specific' words? Are the expectations of SPG the same for different groups of students, for example, you take a more rigorous approach with more able groups or students, or a more focused approach with less able groups of students? Do you simply highlight errors or is there a policy of correcting mistakes, for example, 'write out spelling mistakes five times'? In some schools there is a policy of close marking the first paragraph or half page. Is it important to set good habits for future work and learning and thereby encourage students to produce work which communicates effectively?

*Monitoring student progress and 'compliance'*

This involves checking that homework has been handed in at the correct time and completed. It either requires ruthless efficiency or a methodical and consistent approach. Students soon work out which teachers are less effective at tracking down missing homework. If there are department or school policies, stick to them and use procedures and sanctions where appropriate. Monitoring progress also involves recording grades, completion of tasks and targets; you have to be able to provide accurate records of your own teaching, and for your department as well as for parents and carers. It is important that you use this evidence to identify levels of achievement, pleasing or worrying trends in student performance or application.

*Lead by example*

School policies will also require students' work to be marked and handed back within a reasonable period of time. Ensure that student work which needs to be marked is assessed and returned. Returning assessed work can be a useful personal point of contact between you and the student. It is an opportunity to praise or encourage and occasionally cajole. Verbal feedback can be immediate and valuable. One department uses written targets as an occasional starting point for a lesson. Students are asked to read targets or comments in the opening phase of the lesson and to then use the information to set their own personal learning goals for that lesson. With more challenging groups these targets can sometimes focus on management. For example, one of Tommy's personal learning goals was to put his hand up if he wanted to answer a question rather than shout out. The teacher asked Tommy what his goal was and reinforced this with the rest of the group, asking them if they could help Tommy to achieve his target.

## HOW AND WHAT TO ASSESS

The first time you sit down with an exercise book or a piece of a student's work must be like trying to write that important first page of your novel. What to write, where to write it, how to write it. Using examples of students' previously assessed work might well give you some idea and it is important to work closely with your mentor to develop an insight into the process of assessment.

If you return to Sam's essay about the Princes in the Tower you might like to consider:

- how the work was marked: *two ticks per page*
- any comments which were made: one on the final paragraph '*cop out!*'
- the final grade: and comment '*B– good account, awful conclusion*'.

There are other examples of work which you might want to refer to on the QCA National Curriculum in Action website, a link to which can be found on the companion website. These provide real examples of students' work but the examples are to some extent dated – they were compiled in 2001. You might also question some of the key concepts that they were supposed to illustrate; for example, would you agree that the Cromwell essay really is an example of 'Interpretations of History'?

### Points for reflection

You have already looked at Sam's essay in Chapter 4 in relation to the National Literacy Strategy. It would be useful to look at the Features of Assessment Policies; focus on Feedback and Grading Criteria (see pp 135–8) and retrospectively try to work out learning objectives for the activity – these could be based on key concepts and key processes.

- What formative comments might you make on Sam's work?
- What targets would you set for Sam's future work

## MAKING YOUR COMMENTS EFFECTIVE

Commenting on students' work is probably one of the most effective and practical ways of assessing understanding. The examples you have looked at are not very helpful and some positive reinforcement might be in order. The Burnahm and Brow article has a particularly useful example of students' work which has been commented upon (see 2004: 7). This feedback is particularly valuable for the following reasons.

- The style – it is conversational; the teacher's written comments could just as easily have been made in a face-to-face discussion; they are positive and encouraging.
- References to criteria – the students have to focus on how a piece of work like this is structured (communicating understanding). There are key comments on 'signpost' sentences for example.
- Aid to improvement – again this refers back to criteria and to structure. Developing historical argument depends on using examples to support a point.
- The summary comments are encouraging and offer appropriate praise but also set focused and specific targets to help build on and improve the student's work, first the reference to the hamburger and then to the previous card sort. This would help the student to improve the structure of their work and also to develop their reasoning. Both student and teacher are aware of targets for future work like this.
- No grade was awarded but the student was given a merit, rewarding her individual achievement.

*Teaching History* (2004), volume 115, provides a valuable insight into a range of assessment practices and as such is exceptionally valuable.

A useful seminar activity which works equally well as a face-to-face task or as an on line activity. Working as a reading group the different articles are shared amongst individuals or groups and the report back under the by line Assessment is ... The intention is to demonstrate the range of views and ideas about what makes for effective assessment.

What is worth noting is that each article has a shared dislike for using the history Attainment Target levels as a basis for everyday assessment. Equally, it is possible to identify a shared enthusiasm for the ideas of the Assessment for Learning Group where the focus shifts to helping students to become better learners. There might be two reasons to explain this enthusiasm. The obvious answer is that Assessment for Learning is clearly a 'good idea'. The less obvious answer lies in the belief that learning in history, and therefore measuring learning and understanding, is complex. If history involved nothing more than learning names and dates assessment would be straightforward. At one level learning history involves different levels of understanding; look again at the key concepts and the key processes. At another level learning history involves children making sense, or making their own sense, of the past. This is developmental, it is messy and can be very uneven. Project Chata (concepts of history and teaching approaches) focused on students' understanding of causal structure and rational explanation, and some of its broad conclusions demonstrate the problematic nature of trying to understand student progress in historical understanding.

**Project Chata: some broad conclusions**

- At any given age students' ideas about historical explanation differ widely.
- Some 8-year-olds have more sophisticated ideas than most 12- or even 14-years-olds.
- A student might show progression in ideas of causal structure but not in rational understanding, or vice versa.
- It is possible that developments in different conceptual areas may occur at different times.
- In some concepts, especially (understanding) evidence, there were often changes in skills (for example, cross-referencing a pair of sources) with no accompanying conceptual development. (Lee and Ashby, 2000: 213)

Assessment for Learning therefore supports good history teaching and good assessment practice in so far as it is far more attuned or aligned to the way students learn history. Becoming a good history learner involves revisiting different concepts and different processes – in short becoming better at working with or understanding the nature of evidence, or developing a more complex understanding of causation. Good assessment enables teachers to identify how students are becoming better learners, better at doing history. They can share these ideas with students so that they begin to recognize how they are learning and how they can become better at learning history.

**What the research says**

There is a great deal of accessible research-based evidence about the nature of assessment and effective assessment. One obvious starting point is the website of the Assessment Reform Group and their publications, *Inside the Black Box* and *Assessment for Learning: Beyond the Black Box,* which provide a useful overview of the ideas and the principles which underpin what is now recognized as good practice.

The views of Ofsted with regard to National Curriculum levels have been referred to and it would be worthwhile revisiting their ideas. There is a sense that they are half-hearted about Attainment Target levels and decide to opt in favour of them on the grounds that 'they are all we have'. In some areas Ofsted appears to be willing to be guided by the History Community of Practice but not on this occasion. You are then faced with the problem of squaring the circle.

Evidence of good assessment practice and evidence which demonstrates why the Attainment Target levels are not a good idea can be found in the Assessment edition of *Teaching History* (2004, vol. 115) and in Lee and Shemilt's (2003) 'A scaffold not a cage' in *Teaching History*. Lee and Ashby's, (2000) Progression in historical understanding' provides a concise introduction to the Chata Project and demonstrates why measuring learning and understanding in history is difficult.

## Further reading

Burnham, S. and Brown, G. (2004) 'Assessment without level descriptions', *Teaching History*, 115: 5–15.

## Useful websites

Live Links to these websites can be found on the companion website.

Web Site Link to QAA Benchmark Statement Document – http://www.qaa.ac.uk/academicinfrastructure/benchmark/statements/history07.pdf

Inside the black Box and Principles of Assessment for Learning http://arg.educ.cam.ac.uk/index.html

Web Link to Teacher's TV Assessment in History http://www.teachers.tv/video/3323 Km to check Teachers TV permission

Web site link to http://www.ncaction.org.uk/search/comment.htm?id=1278

http://arg.edu.cam.ac.uk/index.html

http://www.teachers.tv/

# 7 TEACHING ACROSS THE AGES: GCSE AND A LEVEL

This chapter considers the following issues:

- teaching GCSE and A level history and the different demands facing students and teachers
- how the examination frameworks, assessment objectives and syllabuses can influence teaching approaches
- strategies to enable teachers to address the elements of syllabus demands
- how you can use your recent and relevant experience of learning history at university when teaching at A level
- developing and understanding of good practice at GCSE and A level.

## TEACHING ACROSS THE AGES: HISTORY 14–19

The QTT Standards make references to correcting students' misconceptions; and it could be that trainee teachers have a few misconceptions about the nature of GCSE history and A level history. As a beginning history teacher you are probably rightfully concerned about the subject knowledge demands that GCSE, and particularly A level, will impose on you. You might also be worried that the students you are going to teach after KS3 are bright and articulate and looking for an opportunity to trip you up. By way of consolation, however, they are keen, budding historians and they will be very willing workers. Students post-16 are a matter of months away from becoming history undergraduates and you will be more like an intellectual equal rather than the fount of all wisdom. These may be misconceptions, they are certainly gross generalizations. Some of the students you teach at GCSE and A level will be keen, bright and articulate, while others may have opted for history because it was the least worst alternative; in Year 12 history could well be their fourth or fifth A/S subject. Once you have spent some time in school you will also come to realize that the summer holidays between

Years 9 and 10 and between Years 11 and 12 are not marked by some remarkable Damascene conversion. Year 10 boys can be just as problematic as Year 9 boys. Outwardly confident Year 11 students can also be awkward and sullen Year 12 students. If this sounds worrying, you might be pleased to know that some of the active and fun strategies which you have perfected with KS3 can be just as effective with Year 10 or Year 13.

## WHERE DID GCSE COME FROM?

The first GCSE examinations were sat in the summer of 1988, and replaced the two tier GCE O level and CSE (Certificate of Secondary Education) examinations. The difference between the two examinations was a problem: a GCE pass was a pass, a CSE grade 2 was just a CSE grade 2. Unless you achieved a grade 1 at CSE which was the equivalent of an O level, a CSE carried far less weight and there was undoubtedly a perception that even a CSE grade 1 was not quite up to the mark. A single examination at 16+ was seen as being more efficient administratively and more equitable; students would have the opportunity to enter a single examination and know that his or her performance would be nationally recognized.

From the late 1970s there had been a number of attempts to unify these qualifications and history departments in some parts of the country were able to enter students for a single 16+ examination. Significantly history teachers themselves played a part in developing these unified courses. Coursework, for example, was a valuable feature of both CSE and 16+ which carried over into GCSEs and again ensured the active involvement of history teachers. The introduction of GCSEs also witnessed the drafting of national criteria, examinations in every subject and across the, then, six examination boards would work to the same subject-specific criteria. At the time they represented good practice and were welcomed by history teachers who felt that an emphasis on the use of evidence as well as knowledge, reflected good history teaching. The introduction of the GCSE also saw the reduction of 14–16 history courses to the three which are still on offer today: Schools History Project, Modern World, and British Social and Economic History. There have been some minor, but regular, modifications to content since 1995 which have focused on the addition of an identifiable element of British history in all courses, but the universally disliked KS4 National Curriculum proposed in 1991 died when the Dearing Review made history an optional subject after KS3.

## UNDERSTANDING THE CRITERIA AND THE SYLLABUS

When you begin to teach GCSE history there is a natural tendency just to get stuck in. Your school is following the Modern World syllabus of a particular examination board and you have been asked to take responsibility for the section on the USA 1918–45. Quite a nice topic – largely social and economic history – looking at the years of 'boom and bust' followed by Roosevelt's New Deal – could not be simpler. In some respects this might be right but it still may be necessary to look at some of the less comprehensible elements of the syllabus. Hopefully with the KS3 programme of study you have come to realize the importance of the key processes and the key concepts – in many respects the *syllabus aims* and *assessment objectives* are just as important – possibly more so if you want your students to do well in the final examination. You have possibly heard or read accounts of hapless English teachers who neglected to read the fine detail of the syllabus; students spend a term 'learning' the *Merchant of Venice* only to find that the set play was *King Lear*. You might think that Roosevelt's New Deal is the New Deal but unless you are aware of the different emphases that each paper has, your students might not achieve their full potential. Understanding the structure of the GCSE process is just as important as knowing the historical detail.

## GCSE Assessment Criteria

The criteria are generic, they are 'defined' by the QCA and apply equally to every history syllabus. You should therefore be able to read the criteria and understand how they might apply to a Modern World course or to the rapidly withering British Social and Economic History GCSE or the Schools History Project GCSE. You should also be able to make links between the GCSE criteria and the key concepts and key processes of the KS3 curriculum. One of the purposes of the GCSE review which was under way as this chapter was being written was to investigate ways in which KS3 history and GCSE courses would be able to become more coherent and progressive.

If you look carefully at Table 7.1 you should be able to make those connections with the KS3 concepts and processes. Table 7.1 also enables you to consider the changes which the current review is proposing. The first impression is that the QCA is piling on the criteria: there appear to be more of them! If, however, you consider them more carefully you can see that the QCA is also trying to provide a 'useful' rationale for the study of history. The usefulness of history is expressed in personal terms of history being a valuable leisure pursuit, in terms of its intellectual worth helping to develop critical thinking and, finally, in terms of its civic value – history as a preparation for an active citizenship. There is, however, one big change in the draft criteria, and that is in the area of interpretations. It might not appear to be different; interpretations is there in the current criteria. But this is one area where perhaps the GCSE practice becomes more aligned with the KS3 view of interpretations.

**Table 7.1** Comparison of current (2007) criteria and draft criteria

| AQA Syllabus B aims | QCA draft criteria aims |
|---|---|
| • Acquire knowledge and understanding of selected periods and/or aspects of history, exploring the significance of historical events, people, changes and issues | 1. Develop a personal interest in why history matters and be inspired, moved and changed by studying a broad, coherent, satisfying and worthwhile course of study |
| • Use historical sources critically in their context, recording significant information and reaching conclusions | 2. Develop their knowledge and coherent understanding of selected periods, societies and aspects of history |
| • Develop understanding of how the past has been represented and interpreted | 3. Develop an awareness of how the past has been represented, interpreted and accorded significance for different reasons and purposes |
| • Organize and communicate their knowledge and understanding of history | |
| • Draw conclusions and appreciate that historical judgements are liable to reassessment in the light of new or reinterpreted evidence | 4. Develop the ability to ask relevant questions about the past and to investigate them critically using a range of sources in their historical context |
| | 5. Actively engage in the process of historical enquiry to develop as effective and independent learners and as critical and reflective thinkers with enquiring minds |
| | 6. Organize and communicate their historical knowledge and understanding in creative and different ways and reach substantiated judgements |
| | 7. Recognize that their historical knowledge, understanding and skills help them understand the present and also provide them with a basis for their future role as active citizens in employment and society in general, as well as for the possible further study of history |

## Assessment objectives

The assessment objectives (Table 7.2) help you to understand how the broad criteria are translated into outcomes. The ultimate outcome is the examination itself and each syllabus demonstrate how the different examination papers will address each assessment objective. Again there is a close link between the key concepts and key processes and again you should be able to make direct links between KS3 and GCSE. The assessment objectives, however, have been aggregated or combined together to make them more

**Table 7.2** GCSE assessment objectives

| | Assessment objectives | % weighting |
|---|---|---|
| AO1 | Recall, select, use and communicate their knowledge and understanding of history in an effective manner | 30–35 |
| AO2 | Demonstrate their understanding of the past through explanation and analysis of:<br>• key concepts such as causation, consequence, continuity, change and significance within an historical context<br>• key features and characteristics of the periods studied and the relationships between them | 30–35 |
| AO3 | a) As part of an historical enquiry, understand, analyse and evaluate a range of appropriate source material<br>b) Understand, analyse and evaluate, in relation to the historical context, how aspects of the past have been interpreted and represented in different ways | 30–40 |

manageable. The assessment criteria have to be linked to an examination paper and if the objectives were as numerous as the key concepts and key processes this could be unwieldy. Each assessment objective does 'cover' a number of the criteria but there is an element of 'unity' in the way that this is achieved.

## Points for reflection

It is important to develop a really clear understanding of the way that the criteria and the assessment objectives work together. Using the assessment objectives in Table 7.2 you should first attempt to match them with the criteria numbered 1 to 7 in Table 7.1. It is inevitable that each assessment objective will cover more than one criterion.

Once you have done this it would be valuable to decide what aspects of an examination paper, or the type of questions, which would be appropriate for the assessment objectives. Remember the examination also includes a coursework element.

Once you feel confident that you have developed this understanding, it would be useful to relate this to the GCSE syllabus and examination board that your partner school follows. You need to match up the syllabus options and the examination papers and understand how this will affect the way you approach each topic.

Before you begin teaching GCSE you need to be able to say (convincingly):

- I am teaching Syllabus X.
- Paper A or B or coursework.
- The assessment objectives for this paper are ...
- This means I have to ensure that students know and understand how to ...

## GIVING YOUR TEACHING STRUCTURE: DEVELOPING CRAFT KNOWLEDGE AGAIN

To some extent this focus on criteria and assessment objectives suggests an approach to teaching GCSE which appears to be quite mechanical. There is an element of truth in this and certainly some of the criticisms that are made of GCSE highlight the mechanical and repetitive tasks that students sometimes undertake.

**Teaching GCSE: what does it feel like (part 1)?**

*This extract, and parts 2 and 3, may give you an idea of what teaching GCSE involves. To some extent the comments do reflect some of the points made in the body of the chapter. Hopefully part 3 will restore your confidence.*

In my experience so far, teaching GCSE History is a lot like 'teaching by numbers' – you look at the overall picture from the syllabus and then teach pupils facts and arguments for both sides of the 'key question'. You must ensure that you cover the specified content. There is little time to cover anything in depth, and all the interest is sucked out of the content because of the need to ensure that the pupils understand 'the point' of every topic covered and where exactly it will be assessed in the examinations. This Gradgrindian emphasis on 'getting the facts into their heads for the exam' limits both the student's enthusiasm for the subject, and the teacher's ability to deliver engaging lessons. I have a jaded collection of Year 11 pupils this year, and it is exceptionally difficult to motivate them because of the demands made by the syllabus. When studying 1920s America, I longed to be able to take them on an intellectual journey through the seedy side of the Roaring Twenties which I knew would inspire them. They showed great excitement at the prospect of studying 'gangsters'. However, at the back of my mind I knew that we could only spare one lesson on this topic as we had 'mocks' coming up, and we still had Russia to get through before the summer.

The structures of a GCSE course are, however, important and are more difficult for a beginning teacher to get their head around than the actual subject knowledge. Most trainees have a good understanding of Modern World history and feel comfortable teaching twentieth-century topics. This confidence is less evident when trainees find that their partner school follows the Schools History Project (SHP) syllabus and they are going to have to teach the History of Medicine, or Crime and Punishment. The common problem is that they have not 'done Medicine' before and are equally concerned that it is too scientific. The science is not a problem and the syllabus makes it clear that detailed scientific knowledge is not required – but a basic understanding of human anatomy can always come in useful. In previous chapters, comments have been made about the eclectic and at times magpie-like ways that history teachers develop and acquire resources, it would seem that an essential contact for the History of Medicine is your friendly science department and the range of anatomy models and occasionally specimens that they have casually lying about the biology laboratories. Being able to name parts might not be essential but it can help to build confidence. The key to understanding the History of Medicine, though, is an awareness of the conceptual purpose of the course: to give students the opportunity to understand how change has taken place over a significant period of time and to understand something about the nature of change. The syllabus identifies agents of medical and scientific change and it might be valuable to try and understand change over time from the viewpoint of a student. Shemilt (2000) suggested that some students view change 'differently'. They might be able to understand '*when*' change takes place and '*how*' change takes place but their overview or their holistic view of change more resembles someone signalling with a torch. Progress – or events – are seen as the brilliant flashes of light; if there is no light nothing is happening. There are gaps in the syllabus, for example in 'the Dark Ages' nothing happens, change and progress only occur at particular moments in time.

The pace of PGCE teaching is not always conducive to reflection, perhaps where 'subject knowledge' is concerned and a reductive view of subject knowledge as content might just encourage that 'roll up your sleeves and immerse yourself in facts' attitude. Perhaps what you need to develop with GCSE teaching is a wider view of subject knowledge. Again this goes back to improving and developing your professional craft knowledge which encompasses 'facts' and also a developing pedagogical knowledge – this time an understanding of the structures and nature of an examination syllabus.

To understand why you need to be consciously developing your professional craft knowledge you need to know why students might find GCSE, and other examination, courses difficult. If you appreciate the student perspective you might be able to understand the emphasis on examination structures.

### Why is GCSE difficult?

- Not understanding the assessment objectives
  Students fail to see or to understand the purposes of their work. They do not understand the bigger picture or how the different 'bits' of the course fit together. This macro view is compounded by a micro problem where they do not understand how to tackle questions or how to approach using sources.
- Deployment of knowledge
  There is a great deal of content to cover, students need to develop strategies to help them remember, manage and organize syllabus content. Are pages of notes always the answer to building knowledge?
- Use of sources and interpretations
  Students can find some of the sources difficult; they can be used in different ways: as stimulus materials where they need to relate the source to their 'knowledge'. In other parts of the exam they will be asked to comment on the source as historical evidence.
- Quality of written communication
  Assessment Objective 1 not only requires them to use knowledge and understanding, but to communicate their understanding. The key words are: logical, structured, coherent.
- Poor examination technique
  This combines a number of features already described. This is about avoiding exam room panic but it involves ensuring that students are comfortable and familiar with the exam process and are able to recognize what different papers and questions require.
- Challenges of revision
  Effective revision plays an important part in developing confidence and improving exam technique. Good revision not only revisits previous topics but considers thinking and learning activities rather than the mechanical going over of old notes.
- Boredom
  Training for the exam does require students to recognize and remember how to tackle particular kinds of questions. Managing the syllabus content might also encourage repetitive tasks: answering exam question after exam question, making pages of notes. There was a view that passing exams is hard work and the students just have to get used to it, however, memorable and enjoyable teaching usually results in effective learning.

(*Source*: J. Main, Key Stage 3 teaching and learning consultant, St Helens LA)

You might feel that you want to add to this list and you should feel free to do so but it might be useful to turn the list into a card sort activity and put all the issues relating to 'knowing facts' on one side and those relating to teaching and learning on the other side. This might be a clever Marxist ploy as all the factors have been pre-selected to prove the point; hopefully the discussion helps to demonstrate that effective teaching and learning strategies are not just suitable for KS3 but are key to good performance at GCSE – and beyond. It would be useful to return to the GCSE lesson that focused on the Vietnam War. Peter Duffy was revising work that the students had previously covered which focused on the involvement of the Superpowers in Vietnam. There is a discussion of the techniques used by Peter Duffy in this lesson and it would be useful to read through this section again. This is what would be described as an active lesson but it would be useful to refer back to problems which students face at GCSE and try to consider how he addresses some of these problems. The significant issues for beginning teachers when faced with a GCSE group (and always a concern for mentors) are related to confidence.

- Are you and your mentor confident that your students have understood the content?
- Are you and your mentor confident that your students will be able to apply their understanding in an examination setting?

At one level the answer to these questions might appear ludicrously simple: give the class an examination question to answer – under examination conditions – and keep re-testing them until they get it right. As always this is not so simple. Content is a significant issue and it is signalled clearly to students in the examination questions along the lines of 'Using Source 1, and your own knowledge ... '. This lead in is then followed by 'describe or explain how or why or what were ... '. Issues relating to recalling and deploying content will be explored later in this chapter.

To understand how teaching to the examination can be difficult it would be useful to examine the lesson plan and resources on the companion website and look at how a beginning teacher, towards the end of their first full-time placement planned to teach a GCSE lesson. The topic was Britain and the First World War and focused on the Home Front and the threat posed by German air raids. The specified content was based on the focus or key question: *How did the war change life in Britain*? It required the students to know about:

- changing attitudes at home
- censorship and propaganda
- the changing role of women
- recruitment
- rationing and effects of submarine warfare.

The trainee combined content with developing the specific skills which would enable students to understand how to tackle a particular kind of question associated with the 'document' paper. Both the planning and the lesson were good, there were clear learning objectives which were shared with the students, and the trainee managed the series of tasks in a very confident and competent way. At regular intervals in the lesson the trainee referred the task back to the examination.

- This is the kind of question ... .
- This is how you can approach this kind of question.
- This is how you build a better answer.

In terms of positive and effective learning the group had reinforced their understanding of the threats posed to British civilians during the Great War. They had also reinforced their understanding of the techniques associated with answering examination questions and at the end of the lesson the students were able to explain how to write a good answer to a document question and why some answers were better than others. Their discussions were quite animated and they knew that they had achieved something by the end of the lesson.

To emphasize the importance of understanding what different types of questions required, the students marked each other's answers from grading criteria. They then had to explain how and why the answer they had assessed was worth three or five or eight marks. Of the 60 minutes in the lesson, approximately half were devoted to understanding the question, understanding the examination. The technique is effective and the history department's results in this particular partner school have steadily risen and are among the best in the school.

Looking closely at the lesson plan and at the resources you do get the impression that there is something mechanical about the process of teaching GCSE and this is not down to the experience of the trainee or particular practices in the department. If you look at the key resource – the photograph of the Zeppelin – you can see the kind of question which all too often is asked in examinations: 'How useful is Source B to a historian?' Well the answer is probably, 'not very', but then a student would not be likely to pick up the eight marks that were available for that question. Instead they are forced into a series of artificial responses which might consider the fact that the photograph was contemporary, it was published in a British newspaper, it proved that Zeppelins did raid British towns and the photograph probably had propaganda value, but the British press during wartime was subject to censorship and it was also going to be biased.

If this type of response appears to be stereotypical and in some respect 'unhistorical' it would be useful to understand how teachers might have been pushed in this direction. Examination board mark schemes are available online and *'these documents are quite useful for a beginning teacher who is trying to understand why GCSE history might not be too reliable'* (author's emphasis). The irony is intentional. The example is from the same examination board and demonstrates how students need to answer a source-based question which focuses on the 'Evaluation of a source for utility (AO6.2) in context (AO6.1)'. The mark scheme makes comments about 'generalised or learned responses' and makes it clear that these answers will only be awarded low marks. What the mark scheme fails to acknowledge is that it is just as likely that higher level responses might also be formulaic. To complicate matters, enterprising examination boards now endorse syllabus-specific texts written by examiners. The synopsis on Amazon claims that the book, targeted at a particular examination board syllabus, will:

> provide all the information students will need for paper one and paper two, with exam-style questions to help them prepare for the exam proper. This revision guide concentrates on improving the students' grades by summarizing key issues and highlighting practical issues concerning exam performance.

The format of these books replicates the key questions of the syllabus and 'Exam-Style' assessments occur at the end of each section and these tend to replicate the dull mechanical style of answers which appear in the syllabus mark schemes.

**Teaching GCSE: what does it feel like (part 2)?**

While getting through the content superficially is one key problem with the GCSE syllabus, another problem lies within the content of the examination itself. Here is another example of 'teaching by numbers'. Every history teacher knows the magic formula for answering examination questions. The exam board even tells us exactly how they want pupils to answer the questions at the annual 'Examiner's Report' meetings. There are even documents available that provide writing frames for all the different types of questions (reliability, utility, penny points) in the examination. With all this help available, what surprises me most about the GCSE is that more pupils do not achieve 100% in the examination. It is clear that the GCSE History exam does not test a pupil's knowledge or understanding of the past – or even a pupil's understanding of what a source can tell us about the past. It is simply a means of testing a pupil's ability to use the magic formula for a particular question.

## WHY IS THE GCSE UNDER ATTACK?

For an examination which had the overwhelming confidence of history teachers at the start of its life, the current format of the GCSE is facing problems. Part of the problem lies in the fact that the examinations do not appear to have changed much since 1988. There have been periodic reviews, examination boards have merged to the Big Three – four if you include the Welsh Board (somewhat like the Big Three at the Paris Peace Conferences, four if you include Italy) – and there have been modifications and amendments, but they are

essentially the same. After the 2003 review the examination boards had to indicate how and where key skills and citizenship are addressed and where there might be opportunities for candidates to develop their ICT skills. This does not reflect the state of the KS3 curriculum where there has been a significant change in the way that teachers view, understand and teach history. Christine Counsell referred to KS3 history as the engine room of change, while GCSE has effectively stagnated. This could well reflect the reality of history teaching – the community of practice has ownership of the KS3 curriculum; the increasingly large, and market-driven examination boards are less responsive to change. Sean Lang makes a very telling comment about the tension which exists between innovative teaching and the inflexibility of examination boards:

> If there is one moment which convinced me that a new curriculum project is needed it came in the coffee break at the Historical Assocation's 'Past Forward' Conference held at the Cherwell School, Oxford, when the history subject officer of an A level Awarding Body drily noted that the examples of excellent classroom practice which Christine Counsell had just delineated in her opening address were all very well, but that they did not fit the assessment criteria. (Lang, 2004)

In 2005 the Historical Association produced a response to the *14–19 Curriculum* proposals. It was a comprehensive critique of the current provision of public examination courses. Section 7 focuses its attention on GCSE examination questions and highlights what many feel is wrong with GCSE history. Examination boards are named and shamed and their 'un-historical' practices roundly condemned. Using historical sources which are not sources but 'extracts' from the same syllabus-specific text was referred to earlier. In examining a question which focuses on the action of Captain Neville of the East Surrey Regiment on the first day of the Battle of the Somme, the report makes the following stinging comment: 'the question here is about how far examiners necessarily understand their own sources' (HA, 2005: 37, para. 7.2.12). The point is being made that the examination boards are, in reality, distorting the history to serve the ends of a particular style of examination question. In a *Teaching History* article in 2002 the Director of the SHP Chris Culpin summarized the problems with GCSE history and suggested ways of making the examination work. The structural problems which have been highlighted above were having an impact on students, and his opening paragraph neatly illustrates that the difficulties might be structural but the effects are personal:

> Jake doesn't like history any more. When he was in Years 7, 8 and 9 he loved it; he loved getting involved with real issues, which took account of his own developing points of view, he loved the mix of different activities; he thought it was hard sometimes but he could see himself getting better at it. Now, in Year 11, he wishes he had taken art instead. Every week he writes practice essays to old examination questions; he finds going over revision factsheets boring. His teacher is nervy, anxious, bad-tempered. (Culpin, 2002: 109)

## Points for reflection

Go to the companion website, www.sagepub.co.uk/secondary, and follow the link to the Culpin report (issue log of *Teaching History*).

The HA report and Chris Culpin's *Teaching History* article are highly critical of the GCSE examination system. It would be valuable to match this criticisms with practice in the classroom. You are probably just beginning to develop an understanding of the GCSE system, but does your mentor feel that the situation in your partner school is different?

Culpin has some distinctive ideas for the way GCSE could be changed. Do you think that any of these changes are possible – or desirable?



## CAN GCSE HISTORY REALLY BE SO BAD?

Chris Culpin made a key observation in his *Teaching History* article: 'Let's get one thing straight about any examined course: The course should come first, then the assessment' (Culpin, 2002). Are students following a course in World History from 1914 to 1990 or are they doing GCSE history, Assessment of Learning v. Assessment for Learning? History teachers might be confident about what they are doing at KS3 but at GCSE there are other pressures. Results count, they might reflect the healthy state of a department; they can affect the reputation of a school. The truth, or a version of the truth, should be beginning to dawn. The emphasis in previous chapters about good teaching and effective learning, the focus on learning to think hopefully proves that good history teaching promotes good learning and if students become reflective and aware thinkers they will prosper at GCSE. The focus of this discussion tries to make a link between some of the perceived problems that students face and effective approaches that might help them to get over these problems.

There is a great deal to be said about continuity between KS3 and GCSE. Earlier in this chapter the emphasis was on the differences that are apparent between the challenge of history in Years 7 to 9 and the weary drudge of GCSE. A key issue for any department is planning for continuity and progression between KS3 and GCSE.

## HOW DOES A DEPARTMENT CONSCIOUSLY BUILD ON SKILLS AND CONCEPTS ACROSS THE KEY STAGES?

Organization and communication are GCSE assessment objectives and are KS3 key processes. The hamburger paragraph and all the other literary structures and devices should be developed and extended. There could well be content overlap between Years 9 and GCSE. The overlap is not a problem. Again conscious planning might 'revisit' Nazi Germany: this could mean throwing more content at Years 10 or 11; on the other hand, you could consciously consider how concepts and skills make increasing demands. All the work on how students learn history emphasizes that it is not a matter of learning more facts but coming back to ideas like causation or evidence. How is causation made more challenging between Years 7 and 9. How do you use this model of progression to make GCSE teaching more challenging?

## PLANNING AND PLANTING A GCSE ALLOTMENT

Michael Riley's ideas about planning for the new KS3 curriculum in 2000 might be equally useful for planning how to deliver a GCSE syllabus. There is an element of logic to the way that examination boards set out the content but this does not mean that you have to follow this dogmatically. While each section in the examination has a focus or key question, you might feel that these are too prosaic and you might want to change or break up the way that these questions are framed. This need not just be a matter of trying to be smarter than the examination board – more intriguing questions could give the work more purpose or a different direction. In the Modern World syllabus there is a significant block of work which focuses on a single country. The most popular choices are the USA 1919–41 (or thereabouts) and Germany 1919–39, some schools substitute Russia for Germany. These area studies are often taught in isolation. It would be possible to prepare a more thematic overview and consider the histories of the USA and Germany (or Russia) as linked. Both countries were involved in the First World War but their histories post-1918 are very different. It is a history of winners and losers, but imagine how much more intriguing the history can be if this is somehow related to the psychologies of winners and losers rather than a narrow examination of one nation. Making deliberate links enables students to see a bigger and different picture. We are used to the idea of overviews in Key Stage 3, providing the bigger picture but also enabling students to make more sense of the depth. The balance between overview and depth is supposedly addressed in the GCSE syllabus but this is often limited to the claim that students can see an overview in a specific section of the syllabus. An overview in a Modern World history syllabus could quite easily be plotted on a living graph with a three-way focus on the changing fortunes of Europe, the USA and Russia. Such an approach to understanding the history of a period is important. Again 'The caliph's coin' illustrates this problem of partial understanding. The structure of a Modern World syllabus does not preclude an examination of the impact of Mussolini or the Spanish Civil War, but it does not include it either, and can you really teach the history of the interwar period without really considering the history of the Soviet Union? Filling in the gaps might be good history, but it might also be important to help students construct a coherent view of a period.

## BUILDING KNOWLEDGE AND APPLYING UNDERSTANDING

Being successful at GCSE does involve mastering a significant amount of content and students have not only to be able to recall content but apply it in appropriate places and in coherent ways. Knowledge-building is a skill which begins in Year 7. Again the emphasis is on the conscious linking of teaching and learning approaches across the key stages, students do not suddenly have to learn more once they are in Year 10. For you as a GCSE teacher this means trying to find more effective and efficient ways of managing content. For example, you might consider that mind maps are an appropriate way of helping students to manage and organize information, but you might need to supplement the mind map with other resources. Under these circumstances the mind maps would work as pointers to further information.

Building and applying knowledge also links to developing skills. Extended writing if progressively built in to schemes of work will help students to organize and communicate their understanding but they also need to understand how to use or deploy knowledge. This cumulative developmental work is highlighted by Kate Hammond (2001) in 'Getting Year 10 to understand the value of precise factual knowledge'. This links progressive planning across the key stages and developmental strategies to improve the quality of students' written work. The strategies, like the hamburger paragraph or the King John Grand Prix, are memorable and demonstrate how engaging students with their own thinking helps them to write better answers. This is not about helping them to remember facts better, but helping them to realize why an answer might not be 'good' and how they can use factual detail or examples to strengthen an argument.

**Teaching GCSE: what does it feel like (part 3)?**

The chief difficulty with GCSE History is creating lessons which deliver the necessary facts (not to mention in a format that can be referred to again when students revise) in a manner which motivates and excites the pupils. One method I have employed successfully is through the use of music. At the start of a lesson about 'Women in 1920s America', I played my class the opening sequence to the film 'Thoroughly Modern Millie' and gave them a copy of the lyrics. From this source, pupils were able to identify the key attributes of a flapper, as well as gaining an insight into the moral outrage such women provoked through analysing the lyrics to the song. For another

*(Continued)*

*(Continued)*

lesson, I turned out the lights, got the pupils to close their eyes and I played Fats Waller's 'This Joint is Jumpin'' in an attempt to encourage pupils to empathize with the historical period. Before the song had ended, they were barely able to sit still and were filled with the energy of a 1920s nightclub. Whilst both these methods were noticeably different from referring to the ever-reliable textbook, I still found it necessary to encourage the pupils to make notes of important facts to ensure success in the examination as I was worried that they would not necessarily remember the lessons when faced with the mountain of other GCSE History syllabus content.

## Points for reflection

Points for reflection

The teacher's experiences detailed in parts 1–3 of 'Teaching GCSE: what does it feel like?' provide a useful insight into the demands of GCSE. After reading the three extracts, is GCSE history all bad?

Earlier discussion in this chapter focused on understanding the structures of GCSE courses. This would be a suitable opportunity for you to reflect on:

- the rationale
- the assessment structure.

## TEACHING HISTORY POST-16

The challenge of teaching A/S or A2 history can be even more daunting for a beginning history teacher. The issue of subject knowledge looms larger; a perception that the stakes are higher for students and teachers added to a natural concern that A level students' intellectual abilities might present a challenge, and post-16 history becomes intimidating. The subject knowledge difficulty might be illustrated by this recently observed university session. History PGCE trainees were faced with an active history task which focused on the changes in Henry VIII's foreign policy. Some who had not covered this topic before were outside their comfort zone. Analysing their experience, the vague notion of 'no subject knowledge' became more considered and it was a combination of confusing detail and a fragmentary or partial understanding. The session was based upon an activity on Ian Dawson's 'Thinking history' website which is designed as an introduction to the topic and is meant to develop students' abilities to read for deeper understanding. A link to this activity can be found on the companion website, www.sagepub.co.uk/secondary. In other words as 16- and 17-year-old students begin to read for themselves the confusing details of princes, emperors, popes and principalities will have a chronological and geographical context.

I am not an expert on this topic and I found the material difficult to get my teeth into – despite having done some reading, I felt that anything I had learned deserted me (and anything that was left only confused me during discussion – hence my fixation with Mary Tudor – and yes, I was talking about Henry's youngest sister, not Margaret his other one or Mary his daughter). In many ways, I think a little knowledge is a dangerous thing – it warps and distorts your judgement. If this exercise is meant to be an introductory lesson, then the pupils wouldn't have *any* knowledge – which may or may not be in their favour. They would probably be able to respond appropriately to the leading questions the teacher asked. (Gemma)

Gemma's analysis of her thinking is useful and provides an insight, not into the difficulties of Year 12 students trying to understand Henry VIII's foreign policy, but from the perspective of a history trainee grappling with new subject knowledge. In the earlier discussion which focused on preparing to teach GCSE, similar observations were made about effective ways to approach new subject knowledge. The immediate and automatic response is to reach for a book, but as Gemma's comment points out reading might not always be effective and understanding can always become confused and fragmentary – not good for your confidence. This may be symptomatic of trying to assimilate knowledge without a context: reading in a non-specific, way hoping it can be transformed into something useful. To make reading or learning effective it needs to have a context, a purpose. For a trainee trying to turn reading into useful new subject knowledge the examination syllabus and the wealth of support materials is an essential first step.

When you begin to plan teaching your first A/S or A2 lessons it is more than probable that you will have observed the group being taught. It would be useful to develop a deper understanding of teaching at this level by making a series of comparative observations (see Fig 7.1).

The emphasis in this observation framework is based on the liable historical concept of similarity and difference:

- Are teaching strategies which you have observed or used in KS3 or GCSE lessons also used in Years 12 and 13?
- How are these strategies used in the more academically challenging atmosphere of Year 12 and Year 13?

| Teaching and learning strategies |
|---|
| • Expectations of students in terms of their preparation and contribution to lessons<br>• Effectiveness of student preparations and their contributions to lessons<br>• Strategies for building and developing subject knowledge and understanding, e.g. notes, organizational diagrams handouts, study skills advice<br>• Developing syllabus/examination techniques – essay writing, document skills, exam questions<br>• Discussion of and questioning techniques |
| KS3 and GCSE teaching approaches |
| • Scaffolding and structuring strategies to develop extended and analytical writing<br>• Layers of inference/relevance diagrams in evidence/source-based activities<br>• Use of ISMs and plenaries<br>• Thinking skills activities such as living graphs<br>• Student presentations<br>• Group and pair work tasks |
| Similarities and differences |
| In many cases teaching strategies might be similar but there are going to be qualitative differences.<br>Are tasks made more challenging?<br>Are they more appropriate for older learners?<br>Are students expected to be more independent learners? |

**Figure 7.1** Key Stage 3 and GCSE teaching and learning strategies

As you develop your awareness of the different demands of A level teaching it will be valuable to begin to understand the demands of the syllabus. While teaching strictly to the syllabus can result in a tiresome and lacklustre approach, it can possibly be excused as a first attempt to understand the different demands of A/S and A2 teaching and help to build your confidence as you attempt to prepare those first lessons.

When trying to put your first A level lesson together you might want to try comparing the syllabus with an examination question. The example referred to in Figure 7.2 is based around Henry VIII's foreign policy. This is often an unfamiliar aspect of English history. Most of the material referred to in Figure 7.2 is available online at one of the examination boards' websites and these sites often prove a useful first point of reference. It would be useful to try and construct your own planning document based on Figure 7.2. This outlines a way of developing a structured approach to A level lesson preparation and, while this might appear mechanical, it is only intended as a beginner's guide to help you pull together the

<table>
<tr><th>Syllabus</th><th>Examination paper</th></tr>
<tr><td>Focus question: Who controlled English foreign affairs 1515–29: Henry or Wolsey?<br><br>Content:The relationship between Wolsey and Henry in the conduct of foreign affairs 1515–29, Wolsey's and Henry's aims, an assessment of success in foreign affairs by 1529.</td><td>Who was more important in directing foreign policy from 1515 to 1529: Henry VIII or Wolsey?<br>Explain your answer.<br>(OCR June 2006)<br>Questions set up argument – On the one hand Henry … /However Wolsey ...</td></tr>
<tr><td colspan="2">Understanding the question<br><br>Developing exam technique, recognizing continuity with KS3 GCSE teaching strategies:<br>• Communicating ideas in logical/coherent/structured way: constructing paragraphs – making point, using evidence to provide example – explain importance<br>• Developing skill of historical argument: relate to nature of question – Oh yes he was – Oh no he wasn't. Recognizing how structure of question promotes rhetorical approach</td></tr>
<tr><td colspan="2">More help?<br><br>Syllabus assessment objectives:<br><br>AO1a recall, select and deploy historical knowledge accurately, and communicate knowledge and understanding of history in a clear and effective manner;<br>AO1b present historical explanations showing understanding of appropriate concepts and arrive at substantiated judgements;<br>Focus: Comparative assessment of a king and minister in directing foreign policy.<br>• A valid case might be made for either Henry VIII or Wolsey.<br>• The explanations should be supported by appropriate knowledge drawn from the period from 1515 to 1529.<br>• As always, the quality of the argument will be most important in the assessment.<br>• High marks can be achieved by answers that are well-argued and contain succinct factual references.<br>For example, answers can focus on particular developments to substantiate their claims</td></tr>
<tr><td colspan="2">Selecting and deploying the historical knowledge with a little help from the mark scheme</td></tr>
<tr><td>Wolsey<br><br>• One of Wolsey's major concerns in foreign policy was to meet the wishes of Henry<br>• Wolsey was charged with the execution of policy and had considerable leeway, for example in dealing with diplomatic dispatches<br>• The later years showed the decline of Wolsey's influence.</td><td>Henry VIII<br><br>• Henry VIII was a strong king who was not a cipher to be controlled by any minister.</td></tr>
</table>

**Figure 7.2** Constructing an A level Lesson *(Continued)*

**Planning framework**

- Combination of resources from syllabus, assessment objectives, examination paper and mark scheme provides a beginner's framework.
- The framework could provide the bare bones of a lesson or short sequence of lessons.
- The framework provides a focus for your further reading and as you read concepts/structures will begin to fall into place.
- Developing teaching and learning strategies:
  1. Building on KS3 or GCSE approaches to structuring extended/analytical writing: linked to development of study skills
  2. Students demonstrating understanding: notes/mind maps/structured paragraphs/presentations: paired–group.
- Working with assessment criteria: understanding banding/levels – how to write to a higher level/self- and peer evaluation.

**Figure 7.2** (*Continued*)

different threads which are important components of successful teaching at A level.

The framework also provides a useful structure to support your subject knowledge development. If you are having to teach a completely new topic you should be able to read with more 'intent'. It is also worthwhile using this structure with an A level topic with which you are familiar. Again graduate ideas about subject knowledge can be different and approaching a topic in this structured manner might help you to avoid presenting your A/S or A2 students with diluted undergraduate notes.

## COHERENCE AND STRUCTURE

Developing your understanding of what an A level lesson might look like and your ability to construct that important first lesson demonstrates the significance of coherence and structure. As you begin to teach more A/S or A2 lessons you also need to develop your understanding of the larger structures. From the personal perspective of your own sequence of lessons, effectively constructing your own slimmed-down scheme of work, you might begin to appreciate how complex Year 12 and Year 13 history can be. Your mentor has, through experience and over time constructed a programme of study for Year 12 and Year 13 which meets a range of criteria. In schools or colleges with large numbers of students opting for history there may well be a range of courses on offer. Students might, for example, be able to select a course which has its main focus on the history of the USA or opt for British and European sixteenth-century history or modern European history which has, as its main focus, Nazi Germany and the Soviet Union.

Unlike GCSE where there are only three choices of syllabus – along with variations within an individual syllabus – the choices on offer at A/S and A2 can be confusing. If you followed the A/S and A2 route into studying history at university it would be worthwhile trying to remember the different courses you studied and trying to work out how your A level course provided you with a coherent course of study. More difficult is recalling the nature of the different types of questions or question papers which you had to sit. As an A level student you either had little or no choice or you were able to sign up for a course you liked the sound of. As a member of a history department you will have (eventually) the responsibility for teaching a particular module or option. Your head of department will also want to involve you in decisions about the overall structure of A/S and A2 courses. The current A/S and A2 'pathway' of a partner school is largely twentieth-century and consists of a number of geographical studies:

- the USA, the USSR and British History in Year 12
- in Year 13 the 100-year synoptic study focuses on a comparative study of British and American foreign policies from the 1860s to the Cold War and an in-depth examination of Fascist Italy and Nazi Germany.

You might feel that this is an interesting look at topics which are likely to appeal to A level students – and you would probably be correct. There is, however, a more considered coherence to this programme of study.

- Over the course of Year 12 and Year 13, students develop an overview of the USA, the USSR, Britain, Germany and Italy in the interwar years.
- All modules have a strong focus on the social and economic history.
- In Year 13 the issue of Anglo-American relations is explored in the context of the period 1860 to 1960.
- The pre-1914 background helps to provide a contextual understanding of issues such as imperialism and the great power rivalry.

This level of coherence is not only deliberate but ensures that students have an idea of how the different histories fit together.

## Points for reflection

Knowing how Schemes of Work for Years 12 and 13 are constructed is important if you are going to understand this concept of coherence. This reflection develops earlier ideas about the nature of historical content in

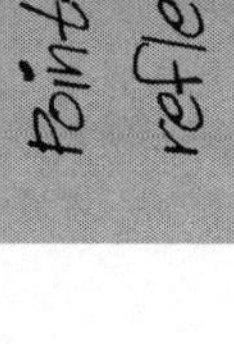


the Key Stage 3 curriculum. It would be useful to consider the KS5 programme of study in your partner school. Look at the specific optional topics across the key stage and try to assess the extent to which it offers a coherent history course.

Coherence does not simply imply that all modules cover roughly the same historical periods.

You could also take into consideration other factors such as:

- geographical coherence
- themes
- the balance of depth and overview
- the contrasting requirements of assessment patterns
- the 'terms and conditions' of GCE examination boards.

If you are not working with a department with A level classes you could construct your own A level scheme of work using one of the examination boards' websites.

## THE NEW A/S AND A2 SPECIFICATIONS

From September 2008 the GCE A level programme is changing. The number of study units is being reduced to four allowing schools and colleges to develop a more measured approach. In October 2007 the *Observer* asked the question: 'What links the British empire, witch-hunts and the Wild West?' The subsequent report on the proposed A levels claimed that: 'History lessons that focus on traditional periods such as the Tudors, the Victorians and post-war Britain will be dropped as part of plans for a new A-level that will instead concentrate on historical "concepts"' (Asthana, 2007).

As always the reality is different from the news. The impression has been created that students will be presented with an incoherent pick-and-mix selection of 'interesting' topics making it impossible to develop a deep understanding of period or place. The *Observer* was highlighting OCR Specification B but then that would not make a good story. On the other side of the coin, Ian Dawson observed that:

> At A level one of the criticisms of SHP GCSE has been that it doesn't fit very well with traditional A level courses. I would dispute that but if you are looking for a course which definitely leads students on from where they left off in the GCSE course, look hard at OCR Specification B. (*SHP Newsletter*, October 2007)

Specification B is different – there is no getting away from it, even OCR is marketing it as new and innovative. Trying to explain how the syllabus is different in ways that the average *Observer* reader will understand is straightforward. First, students will have to follow two modules of British history, second, the 100-year synoptic period remains. In terms of period study it remains possible to follow courses in medieval, early modern nineteenth- and twentieth-century history. The changes are in the way the history is presented. Yes the history is different – a sixteenth-century module will not require students to answer questions on Henry VIII, Wolsey and foreign policy. Instead Specification B takes a more conceptual approach. In Year 12 students focus on the 'theory and critical use of evidence' or examine the 'construction, revision and validity of historical explanations and interpretations'. In Year 13 there is a focus on historical controversies and a personal study which focuses on historical significance. This thematic approach is challenging but it is possible to see important conceptual links being developed across the secondary history curriculum. It is also worth considering the nature of some undergraduate courses. Tristram Hunt, the *Observer*'s in-house historian said that:

> ... bringing in lessons about 'historiography', which involves looking at methods used by historians, would be too advanced for A-level. 'I teach second and third-year undergraduates and for them that is hard enough. That would be a lot of running before they could walk'. (Hunt, quoted in Asthana, 2007)

One is tempted to ask if historiography is difficult for second- and third-year undergraduates simply because it is new. It may be that Specification B requires students to think differently about history but is this a 'bad thing'?

## Points for reflection

The publication of the OCR Specification B provides a suitable opportunity for you to consider the nature and purpose of historical study at a higher level. You need to download Specification B from the link on the companion website and first work out the structure of module combinations in terms of period and place. You then need to understand the conceptual nature of the different modules in Years 12 and 13. The language of the syllabus detail can be intimidating but if you reference this to the sample examination questions, the nature and purpose of the modules becomes clearer.

It would be useful to consider Specification B from a number of perspectives.

1. The 'old' idea of historical entitlement: are A level students (or should A level students) be entitled or required to study more conventional periods?
2. If you consider some of the modules that you may have studied as part of your undergraduate course, is Specification B a good preparation for degree-level history?
3. We use concepts such as change and continuity, similarity and difference to help us understand the nature of change. Do you think Specification B provides somewhere for SHP GCSE students to go?

## PREPARING YOUR STUDENTS FOR A LEVEL HISTORY

So far the discussion has focused on helping you to understand what teaching A level history involves. This has ranged from developing your awareness of subject-knowledge issues to trying to gain a coherent overview of the nature of A level courses. This is important because you need to be able to approach teaching A level history with confidence.

Sometimes it is difficult for you to realize just how valuable your recent experience of learning history is. We are thinking about the development of your professional craft knowledge again: experience is an important element of a history teacher's craft knowledge, but experience is not just about years served in the history classroom. Consciously, but judiciously draw on your university experience:

- Did you study similar topics?
- Were there aspects about a period or topic which you found difficult – how did you make that breakthrough, what enabled you to clarify your ideas or your understanding of the topic?
- In your teaching it would be more than appropriate to refer to 'my lecturer at university believed ... '

The average or typical A/S student beginning their course will find the history different. The most obvious difference is that the content will be new. Consider what it must be like moving from Modern World history to the reign of Henry VII. Yes there is new subject knowledge to master but if students are to develop a deeper understanding they need to begin to get a feel for the period as well. The attitudes and outlooks, values and beliefs of late fifteenth-century Europe are markedly different from those of the mid-twentieth-century. On the other hand, students might be going over old ground – revisiting the Nazis or the New Deal. The challenge is to help students to realize how they can move up a gear, and the realization that an A level course requires different thinking, not simply more detail.

Schools and colleges realize that GCSE is not necessarily a good preparation for A level courses, and time and much thought goes into the creation of extensive induction programmes. These might be generic study skills sessions as well as subject-specific induction activities, and students and A level teachers might devote quite some time to settling-in activities. This can be particularly important in a tertiary setting where students might come from a large number of 11–16 schools. A sensible approach to teaching in the early weeks of Year 12 could involve raising students' awareness of the thinking that went on at GCSE and how the thinking at A level is different. Once again it is developing students' awareness of metacognition, but this bridging phase between GCSE and A/S could be quite explicit:

- How did you develop an answer at GCSE?
- What level of thinking does a GCSE answer require?
- What do you have to do differently at A/S level?
- How should you think differently at A/S level?

This is not as difficult as it might seem. Angela Leonard's (2000) article in *Teaching History* pointed out some ways in which progression from GCSE to A/S can be managed. Students therefore need to:

- manage new and unfamiliar content
- manage the demands of more independent study, even down to basics like reading effectively and building subject knowledge through notes or mind maps
- get a feel for the period – this is important if they are going to be able to answer document questions at an appropriate level
- be introduced to different views/perspectives including those of other historians. This is a qualitative difference between GCSE and A level.

In Leonard's view the most effective way to appreciate the different demands is to analyse an A/S document paper. The example she uses is the Edexcel British seventeenth-century paper entitled: 'The World Turned Upside Down', a link to which can be found on the companion website. Effectively this

involves 16-year-olds getting to grips with the Levellers. To know what the Levellers stood for you have to have a reasonable understanding of their mental outlook. A GCSE question on Nazi Germany might simply require a series of linked ideas:

- Herr von W said this because he was a Prussian aristocrat.
- Hitler wanted to overturn the Treaty of Versailles.
- Therefore Herr von W would support the Nazis because they wanted to restore Germany as a great power.

The ideas of the Levellers might be 'visible' in what they wrote and what they said, but it is also important to understand that what they said and wrote was a reflection of their mental outlook, which in turn was shaped by their radical religious and political ideas, altered and shaped by the Civil War. This is what we mean by a sense of period; this is the qualitative difference between GCSE and A level. As a history teacher it is important that you know the subject, but it is equally important that you are aware of the nature of the demands that teaching history to different age groups imposes on you and requires of you. Teaching A level therefore is doubly demanding, not just in terms of the 'subject knowledge' but in understanding the barriers that are likely to stand in the way of your students' understanding. This is yet another element of your developing professional craft knowledge.

## Points for Reflection

Points for reflection

Students expect A level to be more demanding. They may not realize it but the very layout of the examination paper signals these raised expectations. In terms of the document paper, this might be apparent in the following ways:

- increase in the time allowed to answer questions
- a decrease in the amount of structuring of the questions
- less adaptation of the language of sources.

If you were to compare GCSE and A/S 'document papers' what would you perceive to be the significant qualitative differences between the two?

How then might you change or develop your teaching approaches to help A/S students understand the demands of studying history at a higher level?

**What the research says**

Ideas about effective history teaching at GCSE or A level are mostly practitioner based and largely pragmatic:

- teachers analysing their own practice
- aimed at improving the nature of students' learning and the quality of students' learning experiences.

Over a period of 10 years, articles in *Teaching History* which focused on GCSE and A level have grown significantly. There are some important trends which demonstrate first the growing influence of the community of practice. More importantly, they demonstrate practically the idea of reflective practice. Using *Teaching History* articles chronologically and thematically is to develop another understanding of the idea of depth lurking within an overview. The point was made in this chapter, both with regard to GCSE teaching and A level teaching, that there is a great deal of cross-fertilization across all key stages. Ideas for engaging and developing students' understanding in KS3 are adapted and applied in Year 11 or Year 13. Similarly the understanding that being a good learner in the history classroom requires students to think historically and to pose questions is now a common feature of history teaching. The final piece of the jigsaw is communicating understanding, which brings together engagement, questioning and thinking. Consider how the evolution of the hamburger paragraph has become an effective teaching tool across the history curriculum and has been developed to help students develop substantiated arguments at GCSE and at A level. More significantly the progress is not all one way from Year 7 to Year 11 and beyond. Ideas for developing students' abilities to develop a deeper understanding of causation include – Arthur Chapman's (2003b) unfortunate broken-backed camel which is used as a device to help Year 7 students develop a more sophisticated understanding of causation. It is important, then, when reading articles in *Teaching History*, to consider the following issues:

- How do the articles relate to the following themes:
  - engagement
  - historical thinking and questioning
  - communicating understanding and developing argument?
- How does the article I am reading relate to earlier articles?
- How is the practice or the thinking in this article progressive, that is, takes ideas from an earlier article and moves thinking forward?

The articles listed below in Further reading are simply representative of the work available via the *Teaching History* Archive which can be accessed by members of the Historical Association. It is worthwhile undertaking some detective work of your own by following up references to other articles referred to in the end notes at the end of each article.

*(Continued)*

## Further reading

### GCSE


- D. Banham and C. Culpin (2002) 'Ensuring progression continues into GCSE: let's not do for our pupils with our plan of attack', *Teaching History*, 109: 16–22.
- P. Benaiges (2005) 'The spice of life? Ensuring variety when teaching about the Treaty of Versailles', *Teaching History*, 119: 30–5.
- K. Hammond (2002) 'Getting Year 10 to understand the value of precise factual knowledge', *Teaching History*, 109: 10–15.
- I. Luff (2003) 'Stretching the straitjacket of assessment', *Teaching History*, 113: 26–35.
- P. Smith (2002) 'International relations at GCSE – they just can't get enough of it', *Teaching History*, 108: 19–22.


### A Level

- The A level articles referred to below have been selected because they demonstrate many of the ideas referred to earlier in the Chapter.


- A. Chapman (2003b) 'Camels, diamonds and counterfactuals: a model for teaching causal reasoning', *Teaching History*, 112: 46–53.
- R. Harris (2001) 'Why essay-writing remains central to learning history at AS level', *Teaching History*, 103: 13–16.
- D. Hellier and H. Richards (2005) 'Do we have to read all of this?' Encouraging students to read for understanding', *Teaching History*, 118: 44–8.
- G. Howells (2002) 'Ranking and classifying: teaching political concepts to post 16 students', *Teaching History*, 106: 33–6.
- A. Leonard (2000) 'Achieving progression from the GCSE to AS', *Teaching History*, 98: 30–5.
- R. Ward (2006) 'Duffy's devices: teaching Year 13 to read and write', *Teaching History*, 124: 9–16.

## Useful websites

A Live link to this website can be found on the companion website.

http://www.OCR.org.uk/qualifications/subject/history

# 8 INCLUSIVE HISTORY TEACHING

**This chapter considers the following issues:**

- inclusion: how can you meet the learning needs of all the students in your classroom?
- making the curriculum accessible for students with SEN
- how to meet the needs of the most able young historians
- working with students who have English as an additional language.

A line in a Victoria Wood play, delivered by Thora Hird, sums up the real nature of generational change in British education. Referring to her 'slow' son she claimed 'they didn't have dyslexia in them days, they just sat them at the back with raffia work'. From a personal perspective, when I began teaching, some of the most challenging classes I faced were those Years 10 and 11 groups in the 'bottom set' who often went by a variety of names: combined studies, non-specialists, foundation studies. Apart from mathematics and English it was unlikely that they would be entered for CSE examinations in any other subjects, except perhaps woodwork or metalwork for the boys and home science for the girls. The humanities faculty was responsible for teaching approximately 25 per cent of their timetable and had to construct purposeful and valid non-examination courses which could deliver a mix of history, religious education (RE), social studies and community service. The teaching was challenging, as were the students at times. This scenario might appear to represent a dim and distant past but this was in the post-Warnock 1980s and operated almost until the introduction of the National Curriculum. Effectively it had been decided that, at the age of 14, up to 20 per cent of the school population had been identified as low achievers and offered a restricted curriculum and fewer opportunities to leave school with recognized qualifications.

At one level these anecdotes simply appear to confirm a view that the school system was, until relatively recently, willing to accept failure in that a significant proportion of the school population might not reach its potential. These views demonstrate a lack of understanding of the nature of underachievement; these children were often just thought of as 'slow' or as 'remedials'. By the 1980s teachers began to develop a deeper understanding of the learning difficulties which students might face. Dyslexia was possibly one of the first recognized explanations for a particular kind of underachievement. Teachers began to be more aware of students who had real difficulty with reading and writing but were noticeably articulate and were often skilled in other ways. As teachers began to understand why some children were having problems, so measures began to be put in place to address the difficulties facing children with special educational needs.

Planning for pupils with special educational needs during the early years of the National Curriculum was not necessarily a priority. The extensive planning guidance focused on how to teach a particular Attainment Target and how to assess the same Attainment Target. The assumption was that less able students might just 'not achieve' a level or might be approaching the level, and the remarkable term 'visiting' the level was invented, used to describe students whose answers were weak. Levels of response mark schemes suggested that students would be able to produce an 'irrelevant answer' and therefore could not be awarded a level. If students with special education needs appeared to be overlooked at the planning and implementation phase of the history National Curriculum, there was a realization that practice in schools would be more accountable. The National Curriculum and Ofsted were often different sides of the same coin. Local Authority Advisory Services – who in many instances also became subcontracted inspectors – made it clear that schools and subject departments in schools would need to demonstrate how students with special educational needs were catered for. Differentiation was born.

The position of students with special educational needs in the first version of the National Curriculum was uncertain; they were entitled to a rewarding and challenging curriculum, but it was also possible to apply for some students with SEN statements to have the curriculum regulations 'disapplied'. In reality this happened infrequently in mainstream schools, hence differentiation. This was a term which was much used but little understood; again LA advice suggested that history departments needed a 'policy statement' of SEN in departmental handbooks which outlined how differentiation might work. Again a standardized generic statement about differentiation might read as follows:

> Provision for pupils with Special Needs may be made in the following ways:
>
> Differentiated tasks which enable slower pupils to achieve at a lower level whilst the most able have the opportunity to work at an additional, appropriate level. (Lancashire County Council Guidelines for the construction of a Departmental Policy Document, Styles and Willoughby, 1992)

While this document was focused on preparing for Ofsted, history teachers had to begin to give some thought to what differentiation meant in practice. There was a neat semi-official definition of differentiation as a '*planned process of intervention in the classroom to maximise potential based on individual needs*' (author's emphasis). This was interpreted in a number of very different ways and led to a hierarchy of differentiation:

- *Differentiation by task.* Typically this could mean having different worksheets for less able students or a range of resources to meet the needs of a range of abilities.
- *Differentiation by resource.* This could range from having distinct texts for the less able students, or individualized departmental resources.
- *Differentiation by outcome.* Here allowances could be made for SEN students in terms of expectations. They might attempt the same task as other students but their work could be assessed against targets which were specifically geared for their abilities.
- *Differentiation by intervention.* Here the teacher is able to provide focused help and support for special needs pupils within a lesson.

These descriptions are somewhat old now, but they are useful indicators into ways in which teachers might be able to build access and challenge into their work. Differentiation was seen as a real challenge to all teachers in the mid-1990s, the explanation that students were placed in teaching groups according to ability was not acceptable, the range of ability within a set also had to be catered for. For history teachers, trying to second guess what Ofsted Inspectors were looking for, differentiation might mean two, three or four different lesson plans and an equal number of resources. It might also mean assessing to four different sets of criteria. What was apparent with the differentiation and the provision of a suitable curriculum for students with SEN was that it was not led by the needs of the students. It became a system driven by regulation; it was a process largely designed to cope with the hurdle of inspection and the solutions to these perceived problems were equally mechanical. This is best exemplified by some of the first 'Foundation Level' texts, which appeared in 1994 and ran alongside the 'core' text. It could be possible that some of these are still lying around in departments, hopefully gathering dust. As a head of department you were responsible for meeting the needs of students with learning difficulties so the ability to buy texts which matched, page for page, illustration by illustration, the main text was an advantage. Mixed-ability groups would all be working from a text which looked the same. The significant differences: the font was larger, the sentences shorter and the questions easier. One has to ask about the value of missing word exercises and comprehension questions, and how exactly they contribute to student learning. In 1994 these resources appeared to meet the needs of history departments and therefore enabled them to satisfy Ofsted.

In reality, teaching tended to be aimed largely at the middle. The more able were not sufficiently stretched, the less able were often left behind. Under these circumstances it is hardly surprising that special needs groups or bottom sets were often thought of as being difficult, challenging and poorly behaved. In

October 2007 a series of programmes entitled *Lost for Words* was broadcast on Channel 4. Over the course of four nights, filmmakers followed the progress of a school in East London as it implemented a whole-school literacy programme. One key issue was the problem of pupils who failed to become functional readers by the end of Year 3. They were effectively excluded from learning – unable to take part in lessons. They became bored and disaffected, and often were disruptive. This pattern of poor achievement and poor behaviour in time becomes a problem for secondary schools. The focus of the series was on literacy not on SEN, but the programme highlighted the consequences of excluding a significant proportion of a school's population from active participation in the curriculum.

## WHAT YOU NEED TO UNDERSTAND ABOUT SPECIAL EDUCATIONAL NEEDS

It is important to have an awareness of how approaches to teaching students with SEN has developed. The process can still appear to be daunting, particularly when you are trying to make sense of the system in operation in your placement school. In some ways you are in a similar situation to a history teacher in the mid-1990s trying to understand how to manage a system when the real issue is trying to understand how you can meet the learning needs of your students. This is the key – there might be a special needs department in your placement school; there will be a special needs co-ordinator (SENCO) in your school. Some pupils will be working with classroom support; but in the end these students are in your class, they are your responsibility. It is also highly likely that part of your professional studies course will include an introduction to SEN. Your induction programme in your placement school will also provide you with a more contextualized introduction to SEN. Before you begin planning and teaching you need to understand how recent reforms affect the way you teach history in the classroom. These should include:

- history National Curriculum 2000 and the emphasis on Inclusion: providing effective learning opportunities for all pupils
- the SEN Code of Practice
- your personal responsibilities under the SEN and Disability Act of 2001
- how your department works within the pattern of stages designed to support students with learning difficulties which might precede a statement of special educational needs: for example, following the responsibilities of individual teachers through to subject departments to the whole school
- the process of drawing up statements of special educational needs.
- how Individual Educational Plans (IEPs) are used to plan students' work
- working with other adults supporting SEN learners.

You also need to become familiar with the way that your partner history department meets the needs of the SEN students it teaches. Most importantly you need to develop a deeper understanding of SEN students and awareness of their needs and their abilities and capabilities. Your earliest contacts with students in the history classroom might involve working alongside or supporting SEN students. This is a useful confidence-building activity, but it is also an opportunity to develop your understanding of SEN students.

- Who are the SEN students in any teaching group?
- What is the nature of their learning difficulty?
- What suggested strategies are in place to support their learning needs?
- How should this information help you to work with an individual student?
- How is this information going to help you plan lessons for this group?
- How might you make most effective use of any learning support or learning assistants who are assigned to a group or an individual student?
- If it is possible to look at a student's IEP, this should give you an indication of his or her problems and the range of strategies are thought to be appropriate.

Understanding this information about students on the SEN register or whose progress is being monitored by learning support is important. You might feel that gathering intelligence could simply confirm preconceptions you might have about SEN students. In reality it raises your awareness of their difficulties and enables you to support their learning more effectively. Working with SEN students in a support role is not just a case of sitting next to them and helping them to read or write. The bullet points in the previous list focus on the students themselves. To understand how you might begin to resolve some of the 'questions' it would be valuable to consider how the history teacher and learning support might work together to enhance the teaching and learning for students with SEN.

- What are the learning objectives for the lesson?
- What are the learning outcomes?
- What aspects of the lesson is the student going to find difficult?
- Are there any new words or subject specific terms which s/he might find difficult?
- Are there any conceptual issues which might be difficult, for example, developing or articulating thinking following a card sort activity?

If you have not had the opportunity to support students in this way it would be valuable to revisit the Home Guard lesson with Peter Duffy and Year 8 at North Liverpool Academy.

You will have to meet the learning needs of the SEN students you teach. You will also need to be aware of the extensive range of special needs that you are likely to encounter. A very useful text produced as a staff development resource has been written by Richard Harris and Ian Luff (2004). The opening three chapters are a highly valuable introduction not only to the nature and the processes involved in meeting the needs of these students, but also because there is a comprehensive description of the range and the nature of special needs which you are likely to encounter, together with suggestions of effective and appropriate teaching strategies.

## Points for reflection

Points for reflection

Based on any support teaching you may have undertaken with SEN students or on your observations of some of the Year 8 students at North Liverpool Academy:

- What would you think are going to be the most significant teaching challenges you are going to face, working with SEN students?
- What do you think are going to be the most significant barriers to learning that these students are going to face?
- Some of the teaching and learning problems will be generic, that is, will apply to most subjects. Do you think that there are any difficulties which might be particular to history?

## EFFECTIVE TEACHING AND LEARNING WITH SEN STUDENTS

Many of the difficulties facing SEN students will be based on their poor literacy skills; they are likely to have reading ages significantly below their chronological ages. This obviously makes understanding text difficult, which then has an impact on their ability to express themselves in written work. If you consider the nature of history you will be able to appreciate that it is a highly literate subject where much of the evidence is text based. The traditional way to demonstrate historical understanding is through essays and other forms of written work. Even for students whose literacy skills are more developed history is a challenging subject: there is a lot to read, a lot to write and a lot to remember. However, within this 'difficulty' lies, if not a solution, then an approach. Special needs is about inclusion – enabling students to access the history. You need to consider ways of making the text and the sources more accessible. You also need to consider alternative or different ways of enabling students to demonstrate their understanding. The difficulty with some of the earlier foundation textbook approaches was their replication of the problems with the early National Curriculum – trying to cover too much too quickly. The tyranny of the double-page spread is not conducive to good history teaching, and even more so with SEN. Watering down resources and tasks is not a suitable or effective strategy; you need to consider how you are going to approach teaching SEN students and provide a curriculum which is challenging and enjoyable, and where students can develop a sense of achievement.

**Observing an SEN lesson**

The Home Guard lesson has been used to demonstrate issues relating to planning. It would be equally useful to observe how the teacher works with this lower-ability group. You will already have noticed how the written abilities of these students does not always reflect their abilities to communicate their understanding orally.

The PowerPoint presentation on the website outlines some significant issues and suggests some broad strategies for developing lessons with SEN students.

- Using Slides 5–8 as a checklist, try to review the Home Guard lesson as an effective SEN activity.
- You might also like to consider to what extent the 'good elements' of an SEN lesson should also be the 'good elements' of a history lesson

You might be aware of patterns emerging as you have read previous chapters:

- Learning history is dependant upon conceptual understanding.
- Demonstrating conceptual understanding involves an ability to communicate.
- Historical understanding develops by revisiting concepts.
- Historical understanding is demonstrated by the ability to communicate in increasingly sophisticated ways.

You might also be aware that certain teaching strategies and learning activities reappear. Teaching students with SEN does not necessarily involve learning new techniques or developing radically different approaches. It is often a matter of understanding how strategies and techniques, which you might have used with other groups, can provide the basis for challenging history with lower-ability students. If thinking skills activities have an impact on the cognitive abilities of more able students, it would seem sensible to assume that similar strategies are going to make a difference with SEN students.

A previous discussion in this chapter noted the inadequacy of earlier ideas about differentiation: resources which were oversimplified, tasks which lacked challenge, resulting in dull, dreary lessons. Richard Harris's exploration of differentiation (2005) makes this link. His article takes the key features of a good history lesson and demonstrates how lessons for SEN students should:

- *Engage the learners.* Consider the important role of initial stimulus materials. How much more important is it to capture the imagination and motivate students with learning difficulties. Visual sources or short pieces of film might be even more important.
- *Build challenging activities.* Consider how card sorting activities or layers of inference tasks for example, could involve students' thinking and learning and the opportunities for developing discussions.
- *Enable them to access interesting resources.* Harris points out the dangers of simplifying texts to the point that they lose all sense of time or period. Presenting students with the real thing is challenging but if carefully selected and thoughtfully 'taught' students can develop a deeper understanding of the past.
- *Provide opportunities to achieve.* Students have to be able to communicate their understanding but consider how this might be achieved. Are there opportunities for oral reports, for group presentations. Harris mentions role-play and freeze-frame activities. You might want to look at how Peter Duffy used this technique with his Year 7 group. Look at using writing frames to structure and support student learning.

- *Make time, take time.* At first you might be surprised at the slow pace of student work but do you really need to push them through the scheme of work? Be prepared to accept that students with SEN will work at a slower pace. If this improves the nature and the quality of their learning experience, is this an acceptable outcome?
- *Recycle.* The old way of recycling probably looked at ways of watering down materials for SEN students. You do have to make resources accessible but, rather than beginning with the textbook or the worksheet, think about how you might recycle active or thinking skills strategies. A living graph activity has the potential for developing thinking, reasoning and talking. The adapting comes from making the activity accessible.

As you read Harris's article it would be useful to try to identify teaching and learning activities that you have already come across, either in earlier chapters or in the course of your observations. A practical example of this idea of recycling can be seen in the following example. In Chapter 1 you were able to read a commentary, 'Portrait of a Lesson', which focused on the Motte and Bailey castle. The trainee also delivered this lesson to a lower-ability group with very positive results. Reading the account below, it is clear that the lesson with the lower-ability students was almost identical to the one taught to the more able mixed-ability group. It required very little work on the part of the trainee to adapt the resources or to make them accessible – it was, after all based on their observations of an image. In terms of teaching strategies the only significant changes involved allowing the students to spend a longer period of time looking at the image and then allowing all group members to visit the image a second time. Completing the task required the students to remember an image, or part of an image, and then describe their 'bit' of the image to the rest of the group – effectively communicating their understanding. What is equally interesting is the insight which the trainee developed into the way that they 'remembered'. The labels on the diagram played a significant part: 'you look at the ditch', 'you look at the tower'. They were making a link between a word – or in this case a series of quite technical and history-specific terms – and a historical feature. A final significant comment referred to their ability to remember the activity over a period of weeks.

### Lower-ability students describe a Motte and Bailey castle

This lesson had already successfully been delivered to the top set Year 7 and I felt it was worth having a go with the bottom set too, particularly as it does not contain a large amount of written work. The same format was used, but as I was working with a small number of pupils, the class was just divided up into two groups. The memory task entailed pupils going to another location (outside the classroom) to look at a drawing of a Motte and Bailey castle and coming back and, as a part of their group, re-creating this picture putting as much detail down as they could in the time they were allowed.

Using my own observations while they were on task, the assessment took the form of a teacher-led discussion. I wanted to know:

- how they had re-created what they had seen, and
- how they allocated certain tasks to each other.

It was extremely interesting to see this group attempt this lesson as they are extremely low ability, but they really enjoyed the activity and were able to think through the process of slicing up the tasks. As a result of them being of lower ability and a smaller group they were given more time and a couple of goes at looking at the picture.

It was interesting to assess the way these pupils were able to articulate to each other and to me; why they, for instance, sent one person in to only look at the moat or ditch and what benefits this had to the picture overall – they had pretty much, as two groups, both split the picture up into sections, that is, words, keep, bailey area, houses, and so on, and by the time they had been in twice they had a definite plan as to what they were looking for and what they wanted to achieve.

Assessment via class discussion is a good way of observing whether the key learning outcome has been achieved very quickly. Sometimes, however, it is necessary, for instance with the memory task lesson, to extend this to be covered again in the next lesson so some written work on some elements of the lesson can be reinforced, for instance castle design, and then can be referred to by pupils on an ongoing basis. As memory span is not very long, it is essential with any lesson that requires a large amount of time given over to either role play or 'something different', that some written work is set either at the end of the lesson for homework or follow-up in the next lesson to ensure that work is able to be referenced by pupils in future.

I was particularly pleased that they were able to participate fully in this activity. And it obviously stuck in their minds for many of the following weeks, with them constantly referring to the drawing exercise as having been fun and interesting. What is more satisfying is that they managed to remember what a Motte and Bailey was, which is pleasing given the ability levels of these particular children.

As the Motte and Bailey lesson demonstrates the underlying idea of Harris's article is that differentiation is really about inclusion and access not about the creation or provision of different resources and activities. The resource on the website which focuses on the Execution of Charles I is used to demonstrate how web technology can be used to support learning, but you might also like to consider how this technique can be used to make the image more accessible. The image itself is very busy, in some ways it overturns conventional ideas about images where the most important characters are centre stage. Charles and the scaffold party are clearly the main players, but they are only visible in the middle distance. The web version enables detail to be isolated from the potentially confusing bigger picture. The image could be projected on an interactive whiteboard, or students could work on individual computers, but the effectiveness of the activity is that it can be led by students themselves discovering the detail in the image.

Refer back to the Home Guard lesson and go to Clip 7 (48 mins 30 secs). This sequence focuses on the final activity in the lesson where the students report back on their ideas about the effectiveness of the Home Guard. This part of the lesson was to some extent hurried. If you were to apply the 'Make time, take time' advice to this aspect of the lesson you might want to consider how the activity could usefully be extended.

You would need to refer to the learning objectives and learning outcomes:

- Identify the key features of the Home Guard.
- Analyse historical sources.
- Use historical sources to evaluate how effective the Home Guard were.

The only change might be needed to alter the nature of the learning outcomes – the end product, that is, the method by which the students record their understanding.

If the lesson was being extended it might be appropriate to consider how the learning outcomes might be different, or how the end product might look different. For example, you might want to consider if a PowerPoint presentation could be an appropriate vehicle or if a piece of extended writing could be a useful activity. Once again you are revisiting ideas already covered in previous chapters:

- developing students' literacy skills
- developing students' understanding of the conventions of historical reasoning or historical argument
- developing IT capability with presentation software or word processing
- using the power of ICT to sort, organize and categorize
- using writing frames to provide structure and direction.

Again if you refer to the chapter on 'Elements of a Lesson' or the IT chapter you might find useful ideas for structuring and presenting students' work which link to the Literacy Strategy. Similarly, using word-processing software can speed up some mechanical tasks allowing students to concentrate on organizing their ideas. The end product could then be a more permanent and extensive record of individual or group achievement.

The SEN PowerPoint presentation was produced by Peter Duffy in a session he led on 'SEN for history PGCE trainees' at Edge Hill University. The slides provide a series of useful summaries of issues, but you might like to consider how some of these slides could be used as a checklist to help you meet the learning needs of the SEN students you will be teaching – slide 7 might be particularly valuable here – but in reality there is nothing that should come as a revelation, and the connection to good teaching and learning activities is emphasized again. You might also like to consider using slides 6 and 7 as evaluation templates. When you have taught a lesson with SEN students, as with all lessons, it is important to evaluate or make judgements on the effectiveness of your teaching strategies and the students' learning experience. Was your teaching effective because you created a memorable learning experience as outlined in slide 7? Were the pupils able to learn effectively because you had built in some of the opportunities outlined in slide 6?

## GNT, NAGTY, YGT

They might look like a Tibetan version of I am, you are, he is. They are, in fact the changing initials which variously describe the special educational needs of the most able students, the gifted and talented (GNT), who were until September 2007 supported by the National Academy for Gifted and Talented Youth (NAGTY), but who are now reduced to the more enigmatic young gifted and talented (YGT) and who are supported via a headache-inducing black website, fronted by a new generation *Blue Peter* presenter who is, incidentally, a very gifted and talented autocue reader.

The discussion which focused on early attempts to provide for the needs of all learners in the history classroom in the form of differentiation suggested that one difficulty was the tendency to teach to the middle, where the needs of the most able and the less able might be overlooked. It is perhaps understandable that less able students can be disaffected and this then has an impact on their behaviour. In DfES guidelines published to help schools identify able students there is an extensive bullet point list which outlines a number of unsurprising 'characteristics' but the list concludes by describing some less positive attributes of gifted students who might be 'arrogant', 'easily bored', 'not necessarily be … well-behaved' and who might even 'challenge authority'. When described in these terms it is perhaps more obvious why inclusion should also focus on the needs of the more able. The traditional approach – the counter to the differentiated worksheet for the less able – is extension activities for the more able. Again it might be necessary to consider what this idea has meant in practice. An extension task often implies something for students to undertake when they have finished the class work

before everyone else. Not only might this not pick up the genuine able student, focusing instead on the student who finishes first, but you have to ask yourself, what is the incentive? More able equates with more work, perhaps better to just progress slowly and get by without making too much of an effort. Just as meeting the needs of the less able in your history classes is your responsibility, so it is with the needs of the more able. This means you need to be able to identify the very able and provide suitably challenging work which meets their needs throughout the lesson, rather than something which is literally tagged on as an afterthought.

## Points for reflection

Who are the gifted and talented young historians?

This might appear to be a daunting question but have you ever thought of it in these terms: could it be that you were an unacknowledged gifted and talented young historian?

- If you refer to the DfES publication, available through a link on the companion website, which focuses on identifying G&T students are there any of the characteristic features which you might identify with.
- At what stage in your school career do you feel that you began to demonstrate an aptitude for history?
- How do you think your school might have encouraged or developed your gift for history?

Points for reflection

Again biographical perspectives can be valuable. My own experience of doing GCE history was not inspiring: a two-year long series of predictable routines. In what was then the lower sixth – Year 12 – the possibilities of history became more interesting with a new head of department. Notes were provided, reading around a subject encouraged and argument and discussion became the focus of the lesson. Links were developed with the history department at Leeds University and interested students were encouraged to turn up to Historical Association lectures in Leeds where we encountered some big names. In another context it might appear somewhat sad but there was a genuine interest in the subject and reading the personal, vitriolic exchanges between A.J.P Taylor and Hugh Trevor-Roper over the origins of the Second World War convinced me, at least, that this subject had something going for it. In my case there was a latent personal interest, engaging teaching methods, extending the subject outside the bounds of the school and a realization that this was a living and vibrant discipline and not just another subject.

Having a natural empathy for your subject, working with gifted young historians ought therefore not be just another layer of planning but an opportunity to engage with like-minded young people. You should be well placed to recognize these talented individuals, and you should have some ideas about how to develop their interests further.

On the QCA/National Curriculum website, a link to which can be found on the companion website, each subject area has a 'gifted and talented' series of pages which provide a starting point for any new teacher who might want to develop an idea of the characteristics of students who might be considered to be gifted young historians – not that there is anything ground-breaking here. The impression is that gifted students are just good at doing history because they are good at reading and writing (just as less able students are not good at doing history, largely for the same reasons). This does not really take us very far. If you care to look at other definitions – what it means to be a gifted young mathematician or a geographer – you will see that there are similarities in approach. This is important because if the characteristics of a good or able young historian conform to a broad generic stereotype, then the solutions to providing for their needs might equally be bland and generic.

A more considered view of the nature of gifted young historians is provided by the NAGTY History Think Tank which met in November 2005 in an attempt to identify the characteristics of high achievers in history classrooms and consider how this talent might be fostered and supported. This might be considered to be the response of the community of practice but this time there is a significant difference between the developing ideas of the think tank and the way that these ideas have been mangled by the QCA. Original thought is not conducive to a formulaic quick fix. These differences in approach and emphasis are explored in Table 8.1. The QCA ideas come directly from the website; the think tank ideas from their paper which is deliberately described as 'work in progress'. The think tank headings are not theirs but have been imposed on a large bullet-pointed list; this is simply designed to suggest that there might be different 'domains' of giftedness.

The placing of an idea in one particular domain might therefore be subject to fierce disagreement and it might be that the members of the think tank would suggest different domains. This being said the important difference is in the qualitative nature of giftedness which is firmly grounded in the subject. While the advice on the QCA National Curriculum website appears to consist of generic and bland exhortations, the ideas in the history think tank report are anything but. There is a clear link to key concepts and key processes, and an attempt to describe not only what an understanding of these might look like at an advanced level but the document also explores strategies that might be employed to develop this advanced level of understanding as Figure 8.1 demonstrates.

These ideas about teaching students who have an advanced understanding of history might appear daunting; it might be difficult to visualize what a lesson or an activity might look like that addresses. For example, how do you create a lesson which develops, or enables students to demonstrate that they

Table 8.1 Different perspectives on gifted and talented

| NAGTY History Think Tank | National Curriculum G&T Version |
| --- | --- |
| **Philosophical Awareness and Understanding**<br>• An appreciation of the intrinsic value of historical learning and an enjoyment of the process<br>• A developed awareness of the complexity of the past and of the process of seeking to understand it<br>• An understanding of presentism – of the inevitable human tendency to see the past in terms of the present – and of the problems and opportunities that it presents | **Historical knowledge**<br>• have an extensive general knowledge, including a significant amount of historical knowledge<br>• develop with ease a chronological framework within which to place existing and new knowledge<br>• demonstrate a strong sense of period as a result of study |
| **Academic Resilience**<br>• An unwillingness to be easily satisfied and a desire to be challenged by and to pose real historical problems<br>• The ability to engage in open-ended historical research and enquiry and to enjoy the process<br>• The ability to cope with the unfamiliar (contexts, periods, cultures) and the ability to use historical imagination to engage with and attempt to understand it<br>• A hunger for knowledge of the past and the ability to acquire and understand large quantities of knowledge about the past | **Historical understanding**<br>• grasp quickly the role of criteria in formulating and articulating a historical explanation or argument; understand and apply historical concepts to their study of history<br>• be able to draw generalizations and conclusions from a range of sources of evidence<br>• seek to identify patterns and processes in what they study, while being aware of the provisional nature of knowledge<br>• appreciate that answers arrived at depend largely on the questions<br>• recognize how other disciplines can contribute to the study of history and draw readily on what they learn in other subjects to enhance their historical understanding |
| **Joined-up historical thinking**<br>• The ability to see links between diverse elements and areas of historical knowledge<br>• An informed awareness of the importance of historical context, the desire and ability to contextualize elements of the past and the ability to develop a sense of period and to suggest, question and critically evaluate periodizations | **Enquiry**<br>• be able to establish and follow a line of enquiry<br>• identify and use relevant information; be good at reasoning and problem-solving |

| NAGTY History Think Tank | National Curriculum G&T Version |
| --- | --- |
| • The ability to develop and internalize an 'archive' of historical knowledge and concepts and the ability to use this to frame and develop questions<br>• The ability to grasp and understand historical concepts, to develop them rigorously and to apply them in a nuanced way when constructing historical analyses, arguments and explanations<br>• The ability to make and to break historical generalizations – to see their value and also their limits<br><br>**Advanced communication skills**<br>• A developed awareness of the nature of historical argument and of the ways in which historical claims are put together and justified<br>• The ability to critically deploy historical evidence to sustain, test and develop historical arguments and to think critically about the ways in which others have done this<br>• The ability to appreciate and to deal with logical complexity in historical writing and documentary materials and to consider and to evaluate conflicting and contradictory evidence and arguments<br>• The ability to process and develop historical knowledge and to reorganize and restructure it into new historical forms and new historical arguments<br>• A willingness to construct historical hypotheses, to test and develop historical theories and descriptions and a willingness to take risks when doing so | • think flexibly, creatively and imaginatively<br>• show discrimination when selecting facts and evaluating historical evidence<br>• They may: manipulate historical evidence and information well<br>• appreciate the nature of historical enquiry; question subject matter in a challenging way<br>• be intrigued by the similarities and differences between different people's experiences, times and places and other features of the past<br>• thrive on controversy, mystery and problems of evidence<br>• show resourcefulness and determination when pursuing a line of enquiry |

(Continued)

Table 8.1 (Continued)

| NAGTY history think tank | National Curriculum G&T Version |
|---|---|
| **Advanced historical thinking**<br>• The ability to read historical materials actively and critically – to read documents and accounts for purpose and to consider the aims of authors and documents<br>• The ability to grasp, to develop and to experiment with analytical historical vocabularies and to enjoy communicating historical ideas and theories<br>• The ability to structure and to develop extended historical narrative and analysis and the ability to construct, sustain and weave together chains of reasoning, analysis, description and explanation<br>• A secure grasp of the nature of historical interpretation and the ability to historicize representations and constructions of the past, in the light of a range of considerations (such as their purpose, the questions being asked and answered, provenance, audience, context) | |

understand their awareness of 'the close relationship between causal argument and questions of interpretation'? There are hints in the report about the kind of activities which might address some of these topics but there are more concrete ideas in a short review of the think tank report in the *BBC History Magazine:*

> Tony McConnell, a history teacher who co-ordinates gifted and talented provision in his school, encourages his pupils to think the way historians think. With fourteen year olds, for example, he not only teaches about the Second World War, he also explores the nature of causation and the concept of a 'just war', using Aquinas' thirteenth century criteria to examine notions of a 'proper authority'. The key, McConnell argues, is to ask the right questions.

Some concluding remarks in the BBC article are intriguing and provide fertile ground for conspiracy theorists. McConnell's view is that raising the bar for gifted and talented students has an impact across the history curriculum and enriches the learning experience for everyone. Nothing wrong with that sentiment; it is, after all, what inclusion is about. It is just that you get the impression that the focus of the National Academy for Gifted and Talented Youth has changed and the establishment of the Young Gifted and Talented programme is more of a franchise. It is certainly difficult to track down any convincing history materials on the website and the productive and imaginative ideas of the think tank are not so evident. Perhaps their ideas proved just too gifted, too talented and too rigorous.

In your planning you could well be asked to 'take account' of the gifted students in a particular set; your partner school may also require you to be able to plan to meet their needs. Taking into account your giftedness for history, you should realize that one solution might lie in recycling. This was suggested as an appropriate strategy for working with students with SEN and it is an equally appropriate approach for working with the most able students; it is a matter of providing the challenge. Figure 8.1 suggests what advanced understanding in two 'areas' might look like; the Think Tank Report therefore can provide you with an idea of other examples of advanced understanding. From page 12, the report also outlines ways in which historical enquiries might be constructed to meet the needs of the more able and suggests a series of approaches or strategies which serve to demonstrate how giftedness and meeting the needs of the more able involves far more than requiring the students to write more, or answer more questions. The report is work in progress and some of the ideas might be dismissed as being more suitable for undergraduates, but as starting points for creating your own activities they provide food for thought.

Some of the strategies are demonstrated in *Teaching History,* volume 124 (2006) which focused on teaching the most able. It is worth trying to make connections between the approaches to teaching suggested towards the end of the think tank report and the articles in this edition of *Teaching History*. What is equally significant is matching the nature or direction of the articles with effective teaching and learning strategies.

| **What might an advanced understanding of evidence look like?** |
|---|
| • Aware of the concept of evidence – of the fact that sources only become historical sources in the context of historical enquiry and questioning<br>• Comfortable with a variety of source materials and types and with different ways of using them in pursuit of different types of enquiry<br>• Aware that sources can be used to present, develop and support different enquiries, arguments and analyses<br>• Aware that the same source can be used differently for different purposes in different enquiries<br>• Aware that the crucial component of an enquiry is the question posed and that changing the question changes everything – the sources that become relevant and the conclusions that the sources will support<br>• Aware of the choices that historians make – choices of enquiry and question, choices of sources – and of the link between these choices and differences in interpretation |
| **What might an advanced understanding of causation look like?** |
| • Aware that talk about causes is a form of historical argument<br>• Aware that historians construct causal arguments in order to explain how and why events and states of affairs in the past have come about<br>• Aware that causal arguments depend upon models of how the world works and that these are subject to dispute and debate<br>• Aware of the close relationship between causal argument and questions of interpretation<br>• Conceptually capable of both constructing causal arguments – with the analytical distinctions and hierarchies that they entail – and analysing and evaluating them in terms of their logic and in terms of the relationships between the claims they make and the evidence that they adduce. |

**Figure 8.1** History Think Tank Report: Advanced Historical Understanding

## Points for reflection.

Points for reflection

Consider the list of articles below which apppeared on the contents page of *Teaching History* (2006) volume 124, 'Teaching the Most Able'.

Deborah Eyre Expertise in its development phase: planning for the needs of gifted adolescent historians, pp 6–8

Rachel Ward

Duffy's devices: teaching Year 13 to read and write, pp 9–16

Arthur Chapman and James Woodcock: Mussolini's missing marbles: simulating history at GCSE, pp 17–28

Guy Woolnough 'Tough on crime, tough on the causes of crime:' using external support. local history and a group project, pp 37–45

Ellie Crispin A team-taught conspiracy: Year 8 are caught up in a genuine historical debate, pp 50–54

The NAGTY Think Tank Report suggests a number of ways of working with the most able history students. These range across:

- working co-operatively across schools.
- working with experts, either in or out of school

- computer conferencing
- engaging students with advanced texts
- using IT to order and organize ideas and manage text
- developing reasoning and argument.

Can you work out how many of the 'boxes' each article ticks?
Working with the principle of recycling can you suggest how some of these ideas might be applied in different contexts?

## WORKING WITH YOUNG GIFTED AND TALENTED – THE QCA PERSPECTIVE

In previous chapters significant play has been made of the idea and influence of the community of practice, but what might be emerging from this discussion is the presence of divergent or contrasting ideas about the nature of gifted students, what it might mean to be a gifted student in a particular discipline and the nature of tasks which might be appropriate for gifted students. The new YGT website appears to support the needs of the whole gifted and talented community yet it is not yet possible to track down the NAGTY History Think Tank Report or even references to the 'Teaching the most able' edition of *Teaching History*. Examples of good practice in terms of gifted and talented on the QCA website highlights work which perhaps simply demands more in terms of output, or enables gifted and talented students to work in different ways, but it is evident that work of this nature is not necessarily as rigorous as this example demonstrates.

**Unit 22: The role of the individual: for good or ill?**

The teacher used this unit with a Year 9 mixed-ability class to examine the contribution of Richard Arkwright to developments in the textile industry. He then asked the most able pupils to make a similar study of a local entrepreneur. To give the task a particular focus, the teacher explained that he wanted year 9 pupils in subsequent years to study the local entrepreneur, so he wanted pupils to think how they might use or adapt the enquiry model of unit 22 to fit the person they were researching. They spent some time discussing the range of sources that pupils might use, including the local environment. The teacher prompted them to consider the strengths and limitations of these sources. At the end of their research, the pupils were asked to make a presentation to the class to summarize their findings and to reach a conclusion about the significance of the person studied. (www.nc.uk.net/gt/history/ examples.htm)

This example drew an appropriately cynical response from an inner-city mentor: 'I can think of at least three local drug dealers who might fit the bill.' Advice about working outside the classroom is equally thin and limited to providing weblinks to the National Trust, English Heritage and the Young Archaeologists Club.

It could be useful to consider how the YGT programme is being developed in your partner school but, to develop a wider perspective, the discussion on the History Teachers' Discussion Forum which you can reach through a link on the comapnion website provides a different perspective and demonstrates that the range of practice is quite extensive. For some practical ideas about implementing YGT strategies, John Clare's website is valuable for its straightforward advice. A link to his website can be found on the companion website for this book, www.sagepub.co.uk/secondary.

## TEACHING STUDENTS WITH EAL

The final discussion in this chapter focuses on students who are not native English speakers, or for whom English is an additional language. Until recently this was seen largely as a metropolitan 'problem' but a Standard that Ofsted were particularly interested in. It could be that teachers in parts of the country distant from London would never come into contact with students who 'had EAL'. But this has changed significantly. The enlargement of the European Union (EU) in the past five years with the accession of nations new and old from Central Europe has witnessed an unprecedented rise in migration across Europe. In post-war Europe the establishment of the Eastern Bloc was accompanied by westward migration in 1945, 1956 and 1961. In 1989 the collapse of Communism was in some respects prompted by new migration as East Germans left for the West via Hungary. In the twentieth century Britain was largely an observer as European populations moved – or were forcibly moved. At times Britain became a welcome, or at times a reluctant, haven for refugees: Hungarian in 1956, Kenyan and Ugandan Asians in the late 1960s and early 1970s. In the early 1980s the children of Vietnamese boat people became part of our school communities. More recently the fratricidal wars in the Balkans saw refugees arriving from Bosnia and Kosovo.

European Union enlargement created a different playing field and workers from the new territories moved to where the work was. Again this in some ways replicates the internal rural–urban migration of the late eighteenth and nineteenth centuries. European migration on this scale is a new phenomenon, very different from the longer-established pattern of migration from the Commonwealth where communities from South East Asia, from Africa and the Caribbean have been established for almost three generations.

This history is important – not just because it helps to illustrate changing ideas about diversity, but because it helps to demonstrate why EAL is now an issue in what would at one time have been considered unlikely areas of the UK. European migration is urban and rural; it is also as much a part of small-town Britain and is no longer only an issue for teachers working in the inner cities. These new patterns of population movement throw up issues which you as history teachers might have to consider – over and above the relatively simple matter of English as an additional language. Whether it is in the heart of

Northern Ireland, or in the flatlands of Lincolnshire, small towns and rural schools are learning to teach the children of Central European workers.

Teaching history students who have EAL is again part of the idea of inclusion. In some ways the difficulties facing these students are similar to those facing students with SEN in that they have problems understanding and communicating. They are, however, very different from SEN students as the following illustration demonstrates. A partner school in Blackpool regularly receives students whose families have come to work at the Blackpool Tower Circus for the season. One family from China arrived speaking virtually no English but by the end of the season their son in Year 9 had become one of the most able students in his year, achieving some of the highest scores in the KS3 tests – proof that an inability to speak or understand English is no measure of intelligence. In a similar way the inability of the English to speak foreign languages is not necessarily a measure of our collective intelligence. This demonstrates that the EAL 'problem' is transitory and the help and support which students require will diminish as they gain confidence. Young people can be natural communicators and it is likely that students with EAL will pick up words and phrases 'from the playground'. Participating in French exchanges over a number of years, it was always impressive to observe how quickly English and French students could become effective communicators; a mixture of (mostly) English and some French ensured that there was a good level of mutual understanding, but there are always aspects of playground French, or Polish, which may not be appropriate. Working with EAL students at the level of simple communication is easily achieved but it will require direct intervention and communication on your part. If you are working in a school with a significant population of EAL students, try to work with them for one or two lessons and try to make the communication a two-way process rather than you simply explaining things.

The difficulties EAL students face are similar to some of the problems SEN students encounter and relate to subject-specific vocabulary and to conceptual understanding. It is relatively easy to hold up a ruler and say 'ruler' or point to a picture of King Charles, but how do you explain the origins of the English Civil War in terms of conflicting ideas about the power of the monarchy? On your part this needs to be thought through carefully and highlights longer-term problems. In some respects this might well be a peculiarly English problem. Reference was made in Chapter 2 to the French National Curriculum and you might have appreciated that this tended to be a little light on concepts such as causation, interpretations or significance – at least as far as we understand them. These can be difficult to appreciate and it is worthwhile trying to demonstrate some of these issues in an analogous way.

The work of Lee and Shemilt and others demonstrates that young people construct their understanding of history in particular ways and there is often a gap between 'common sense' explanations and historical explanations. At one level these words might simply be words which have ambiguous meanings such as ruler or church where the words might refer to a physical object and an abstract concept at the same time. For EAL students this makes understanding history doubly difficult. They may have a good surface understanding but at a technical or cultural level they can be completely lost. Much of the advice which is available on teaching students with EAL will focus on the practicalities of basic language acquisition, but you also need to consider how you can help these students to develop deeper levels of understanding.

The DfES has published subject-specific guidance on teaching history to students with EAL and this does provide some useful ideas. The text is largely generic and is in reality a 'cut and paste job'. The case studies do not really explore the issues of developing a deeper conceptual understanding. The guidance appears to suggest that the main focus is to develop confidence in acquiring a working knowledge of the language and believe that deeper levels of understanding will come with time:

> Acquisition of academic language can take considerably longer to develop than social language. This advanced level of proficiency in the language for learning is crucial to the attainment of pupils for whom English is an additional language in all subjects of the curriculum. The report draws attention to the 'considerable evidence that once proficiency in English was achieved, the progress for pupils with EAL across the curriculum was rapid and their attainment on a par with or higher than that of their monolingual peers'. (p.2)

Figure 8.2 might help you to understand the double problem of working with young people who do not understand English and who do not have the same 'cultural' reference points as an adult.

Sometimes it is important to develop an empathetic understanding and this contribution from a former trainee is valuable in this respect. What does it feel like to be a learner of another language in a totally alien context?

> I have been on the receiving end of EAL, well CAL really (Chinese as an additional language). The first stage I went through was complete immersion in the language. It is easy to underestimate the importance of being surrounded by people who only speak the additional language and are speaking it to you all the time. There is a temptation in some schools to separate (almost full time) those pupils who don't speak any English for very intensive English language lessons. In actual fact children learn much of their language from other children, hence my fluency in Chinese swear words. This process is a very successful and natural way of normalising the English language (in my case Chinese) and how it is used by native speakers.

A fuller account of trainees' experiences of EAL can be found on the website.

One of the final series of views considers the value of teaching history to students from a non-English and non-English-speaking background. Most of the discussions focus on the difficulties of working with EAL students and practical considerations about how effective communication can be

| *El Pais*, 2 November 2007<br>Alonso, el piloto español, al que le quedaban dos años de contrato con la escudería británica, es libre de fichar por cualquier equipo.- Ninguna de las partes deberán pagar compensaciones económicas.- Todo ha acabado bien, señala su representante.<br>www.elpais.com/ | *Hurriyet*: 2 November 2007<br>Özellikle FIFA ve UEFA standartlarina uyumlu futbolun tamamen özerk olduğu, futbolun tamamen kendi aktörleri tarafindan yönetildiği yasayi spor mevzuatimiza kazandirmak istiyoruz.<br>www.hurriyet.com.tr |
|---|---|
| You may not be able to speak Spanish but there are enough clues to help you work out that this has something to do with Alonso, the two years of his contract and his relationship with British team McCLaren F1.Team and something about reaching an amicable agreement and financial compensation.<br><br>The process of making sense of a foreign language like this is known as gist translation. The ability to understand does not depend on a knowledge of Spanish but the ability to use what you might call familiar cultural signposts within the paragraph – these might be words which have a similar meaning in Spanish and English and also words which have similar roots in Latin or French. I cannot speak Spanish but careful consideration of various words makes it possible to work out the meaning of the paragraph | Turkish is a very different language. It may use western script but is not a European language. There are some words which are deliberate borrowings, largely from English, French or German. Apart from the obvious references to football – 'FIFA'and 'futbolun' there are few of the cultural signposts which are present in the Spanish extract. As a result it is very difficult to gain any real sense of understanding from this paragraph. Even a word by word examination of the text does not prove to be useful. |
| This activity is not designed to help you understand how or why it might be easier for you to make sense of a European language than a non-European language but to help you appreciate the perspective of a teenager who would not necessarily have your level of cultural awareness. A teenager from any non-English background is more likely to view a page of English text in the same way that you view the text from the Turkish newspaper. This might help you to understand why you have to try and explain every word and why you need to consider how you might be able to help them to understand subject-specific words and ideas. | |

**Figure 8.2** Developing understanding of EAL: a different perspective

developed. This final discussion is important, and links to some of the issues raised at the beginning of this discussion and elsewhere in this book. In Chapter 10, A Diverse and Controversial Subject, Alison Stephen, from a school in Manchester, provides an insight into her students' attitudes to the Arab–Israeli dispute and how our adult perceptions of the issue – that is, the problems caused by Jewish migration to Palestine in the 1930s – were not viewed in the same light, immigration being perceived as something positive.

If working with EAL students is perceived simply as a 'problem' which can be solved by a series of approaches and strategies, you might be missing out on opportunities to connect with and involve, or include, students in your history lessons. A Roman Catholic partner school in the North West of England has a number of Polish students on roll. In 2007 the school, along with other schools in the area, was organizing a visit to Auschwitz. The head of department was able to involve the Polish students in Year 10 in the briefings before the visit took place. This personal perspective helped the rest of the group to develop a different understanding of the events surrounding the Holocaust and the Nazi occupation of Poland. The perspectives of students from across the world can be used to make connections across a range of topics in the history curriculum, which students and teachers alike could find valuable. Teachers TV has some valuable resources which can help you to develop a wider understanding of issues which you are likely to face in the history classroom.

The concept of inclusion, embedded in Curriculum 2000, marked an important change in terms of the way that the needs of all students were catered for. At one level inclusion reflects the way schools work with students across a range of learning difficulties and a range of disabilities. In the history classroom the significant focus is now on making the curriculum accessible and not making the provision different. A common theme in the last two chapters has been on the applicability of similar methods and approaches across the 'ages' and across the spectrum of abilities. Work for students with learning difficulties has, hopefully, advanced significantly from their copying and answering a range of comprehension questions, or filling-in-the-missing-word tasks. A level students are not just left to their own devices and expected to read, make notes and answer essay questions. The changes have happened because we have a clearer understanding of what the study of history involves:

- working with evidence
- developing conceptual understanding
- seeing patterns in the past
- understanding the nature and conventions of historical communication.

At whatever level students need support and structure, dealing with difference involves understanding what appropriate support and structure might entail. The types of thinking activities and strategies which were explored in Chapter 5 are effective teaching and learning tools for students with SEN and with the more able students.

**What the research says**

Working with students who have widely different abilities is a challenge. This is one aspect of your practice where the research can be valuable and help you to teach more effectively. The work of Lee, Ashby and Shemilt in Donovan and Bransford's '*How Students Learn: History in the Classroom*' can help you to develop an insight into how children think about or perceive the past. Their chapter in Stearns, Seixas and Wineburg which reports on some of the findings of Project Chata looks at the understanding of students in primary schools (Years 3 and 6) and secondary schools (Years 7 and 9). You should already be aware that progress in historical understanding is never as neat as the Attainment Targets suggest. Their findings might also help you to understand how students with learning difficulties are making sense of the past.

You should also read the NAGTY History Think Tank Report. This is both an informative exploration of issues relating to teaching history to the most able students and, as this chapter has indicated, has succeeded in defining first the characteristics of the most able history students then taking key concepts and outlining what more advanced study might entail. The report is well footnoted and the references are worth pursuing as they not only direct you to more advanced scholarship but also refer to a number of articles in *Teaching History* which might be said to exemplify some of the ideas and approaches suggested in the report.

## *Further reading*

Harris, R. (2005) 'Does differentiation have to mean different?', *Teaching History*, 118:5–12.

## *Useful Websites*

Live links to these websites can be found on the companion website.

DfES guidelines for working with EAL pupils in history, http://www.standards.dfes.gov.uk/secondary/keystage3/downloads/fshieal065602.pdf.

History Teachers' Discussion Forum: Gifted and Talented and Differentiation: www.schoolhistory.co.uk/forum/index.php?showtopic=4603 and www.schoolhistory.co.uk/forum/index.php? showtopic=2992.

QCA on gifted and talented: www.qca.org.uk/qca 6410.aspx.

# 9 INFORMATION TECHNOLOGIES AND HISTORY TEACHING

*This chapter considers the following issues:*

- developing and understanding the ways in which ICT can be used to support effective teaching and learning
- the importance of linking progression in historical understanding and ITC capability
- data handling and how it can be used both to improve students' abilities to question and work with primary sources
- the role of Virtual Learning Environments (VLEs) and online learning.

As more and more history classrooms become equipped with data projectors and interactive whiteboards access to ICT is improving year on year. The focus of this chapter is not on what to do and how to do it, but more on what does good effective use of ICT look like. The focus for beginning teachers is on making decisions about when to use technology to improve teaching and enhance learning. There is often an uncritical acceptance of technology and PowerPoint has become the digital chalk and talk. This chapter aims to raise critical awareness about the use of new technologies as well as to provide worked examples of effective use of information technology.

## JUST BECAUSE WE WERE USING COMPUTERS WE MUST BE GOOD

In January 2005 I observed a history lesson in a partner school in the North West of England. The lesson was based in an IT suite with the trainee demonstrating how ICT could help deliver a good history lesson. The lesson was based around online resources on one of the many sites that are on the web. The Year 8 lesson had as its focus the Spanish Armada and began with an examination of the causes of the dispute between England and Spain, concluding with an analysis of the reasons for the defeat of the Spanish Armada. The first activity required students to read through a series of screens which presented information about the deteriorating relationship between England and Spain. To ensure that the students had read, and learnt, there was an interactive test which required them to match up statements with 'answers'. This might sound like computer-aided learning, based on the assumption that if the students manage to match all the statements correctly they will have learnt the topic. The reality was somewhat different. The lesson was an excellent learning experience, for the trainee, who quickly realized what was really going on. The clever students had realized that the tiresome reading task was an irrelevance, the matching activity had used 'Flash' to create a drag and drop activity which meant that it was only possible to match correct responses together. Rapid mouse-work turned the activity into a multiple guess activity and very quickly the correct parts of the sentences were linked together. They were not even reading the alternatives – simply using the power of ICT to do the work for them. Instead of the work lasting for 50 minutes the students had completed the task in under 10 minutes. In terms of learning objectives the group had been able to demonstrate their ability to undermine or circumvent their teacher's intended learning outcomes and to complete successfully the task without knowing, understanding or learning anything about the Spanish Armada. This unfortunate episode highlights some of the problems of uncritical or poor use of ICT. There is an assumption that if you are using computers then the teaching is automatically good.

There has been significant investment in schools over the past 10 years, particularly in terms of learning technology, and naturally Ofsted comments on the way that this investment has been used. Since 1999 there have been two reports which have focused specifically on the effective use of ICT in the history classroom. Both reports are useful in that they highlight fairly specific issues (see Table 9.1).

The Office for Standards in Education highlights a quite specific problem – the unsatisfactory use of ICT. Between 1999 and 2004 there was a change in attitudes towards ICT and accessing resources – the 2004 Report referred to a 'stubborn minority'(Ofsted, 2004a: 4). This was always an issue raised in Initial Teacher Training (ITT) inspections – that 'trainee teachers' did not always have access to good facilities and that the facilities and good practice evident in universities were not always replicated in secondary school classrooms. This is not the problem it once was. It would be useful to assess the facilities of your partner school when you first arrive in September or October.

The 2004 Report may represent progress; from 1999 to 2004 the number of poor schools fell from 40% to 30% but the fact remains that only 30% of schools were making effective use of ICT. There is a qualitative element to this assessment as HMI/Ofsted now look at the way ICT impacts on pupil learning and achievement and the 2004 report highlights a number of examples where the use of ICT is poor or undemanding. This change in expectations is welcome. Anecdotal evidence suggested that some Ofsted school inspections in the late

1990s were uncritical in their assessments of the way that ICT was being used. One head of history in a school near Blackburn hoped that the limited access to ICT might provide a useful bargaining counter enabling the history department to integrate ICT into the history curriculum, and making it less of a bolt-on extra. Instead, the Ofsted report felt that students writing up GCSE coursework on the school network at lunchtime provided evidence of good ICT practice!

This confusion between using computers in history lessons and the effective use of ICT to improve the teaching and learning of history is important. The following report from Trimdon Grange Primary School in Tony Blair's constituency in 1998 reveals both the high hopes and the popular misconceptions that people had about the way computers were going to transform teaching and learning. The BBC news report on the companion website shows the Prime Minister watching students working with online resources from the National Archives. Tony Blair waxed lyrical about computers: they were going to improve education and they were going to help young people get jobs. It sounded convincing, but looking back on this one gets the feeling that Mr Blair would have been equally impressed with the lesson about the Spanish Armada. You can draw a number of conclusions from these examples. To the casual observe, or a computer- phobic Prime Minister, students working with computers looks very twenty-first century. If you get the chance to take part in an open evening at your partner school, look at parents' reactions to the sight of students working on computers! As you become a more competent teacher during your PGCE year, you might need to ask yourself at regular intervals: 'Am I assuming that using ICT always equates with effective teaching and learning?'

**Table 9.1** Improvements in ICT capability in history teaching

| 1999 report | 2004 report |
|---|---|
| Two departments in five fail to make good use of ICT in history | In three schools in ten, good use is made of new technology. In approaching three schools in ten its use remains unsatisfactory |
| Lack of training and negative attitudes towards the use of ICT on the part of teachers | A stubborn minority of schools where ICT in history is very limited, either because of poor access to computers or negative attitudes towards their use |
| Regular access to ICT as a planned part of the curriculum is not physically possible | There is strong evidence of improved quality and range of resources as a consequence of the ICT initiatives |
| Departments make effective use of ICT when (it is) built into the Scheme of Work, and exploit these regularly for progressive use for research, analysis and communication | Relatively few history departments have reached a situation where teaching and learning using ICT is consistently good, with a positive impact on students' progress and achievement |

## Points for reflection

- It would be useful to think about the way that you used ICT during your degree. Did you just use ICT as a tool – to help you write assignments or to put a PowerPoint presentation together for a seminar presentation?
- Did that PowerPoint presentation do anything other than present a series of ideas/notes/visual images?
- Did your lecturers make much use of ICT: would it be useful to compare IT-rich and IT-weak 'lectures'? Which appeared to be more effective or memorable learning experiences?
- Were any of your modules or courses 'online' – how different was the learning experience using a VLE (a virtual learning environment: usually Blackboard or Web Ct)?
- Did you use any software such as Excel or Access which enabled you to undertake historical enquiries?



## EXPECTATIONS AND DEVELOPING CONFIDENCE

The aim of this chapter is to help you reflect on the issue of the effective use of ICT in the history classroom. If you consider the official requirements the Teacher Development Agency (TDA) National Standards, for example, require you, among other things, to:

- have a creative and constructively critical approach towards innovation, being prepared to adapt their practice where benefits and improvements are identified
- have a knowledge and understanding of a range of teaching, learning and behaviour management strategies and know how to use and adapt them
- know how to use skills in literacy, numeracy and ICT to support their teaching and wider professional activities
- design opportunities for learners to develop their ICT skills
- use a range of teaching strategies and resources, including e-learning
- evaluate the impact of their teaching on the progress of all learners, and modify their planning and classroom practice where necessary.

Similarly, the National Curriculum contains a number of expectations relating to ICT. Some are fairly general exhortations, others more explicit:

- Students should use existing and emergent technologies where appropriate.
- Use ICT to research information about the past, process historical data and select, categorize, organize and present their findings.

The implication is clear – you are expected to use ICT in your teaching and students are expected to use ICT when learning history. This sums up quite neatly what you need to aim for over the coming year: use ICT to support your teaching and enhance your students' learning. With the Ofsted criteria in mind, you need to be able to evaluate the effectiveness of your use of ICT so that: 'teaching and learning using ICT is consistently good, with a positive impact on students' progress and achievement' (Ofsted, 2004: 4).

When you begin your PGCE year you might have to audit or assess your IT skills: what can you do? What aspects of ICT are you less confident with? Audits of this nature can have a negative effect and sometimes only serve to emphasize what you cannot do. Most graduates these days are usually confident with some or most of the following:

- using Microsoft Word
- using software such as PowerPoint to put presentations together
- searching and using the web with due regard to the provenance and the reliability of information
- using e-mail
- being familiar with virtual learning environments such as Blackboard or Web Ct, or taking part in discussion forums
- using digital cameras/digital video
- being familiar with websites such as U Tube and file share sites.

As a history graduate you are less likely to be familiar with:

- databases and spreadsheets using software such as Microsoft Access and Excel
- constructing web pages and websites
- using interactive whiteboards and IWB software.

If this describes your IT capability, you are in good company and you should be able to handle most IT applications quite comfortably. The analogy which might be most helpful is that of driving a car. You can be a good driver without having to know how to change a cylinder head gasket. However you should be able to do some basics such as know where the jacking points are to enable you to change a tyre. You should also know how to do basic maintenance which ensures that your car is fit to go on the road: tyre pressure, battery, oil and water levels etc. In IT terms this might equate to good file management, running regular anti-virus software, backing up files, and so on. This should make you feel more comfortable. If you feel that some of these programmes or applications are unfamiliar or you are lacking in confidence, try to discover what support you can get from your university or from colleagues in your PGCE group. A common concern focuses on students and ICT. One worry is that simply because of their youth they will be more familiar and confident with IT. Related to this is the concern that you might have to teach students IT. In most schools this will not be the case and when you ask your class, for example, to report their conclusions using a short PowerPoint presentation they will know exactly what to do. Just to be certain, find out what students in Years 7 or 9 or 11 are capable of doing.

## WORKING FROM FIRST PRINCIPLES

From the previous discussion you are probably aware that one of the key issues is the way that your use of ICT impacts on students' progress and achievement. There are two ways that this can happen. First, ICT can make your teaching more effective. Second, it can enhance or make students' learning more effective. Information and communication technology will inevitably become second nature to you during your PGCE year. It will also become an indispensable element of your teaching repertoire. However, second nature might also imply that you use ICT as a matter of course without considering how it might be used or deployed most effectively. Perhaps, then, ICT should become *considered* second nature; you need to get into the habit of asking yourself why you are using ICT: is it becoming habitual? Are your lessons becoming predictable? You might not be aware of it, but you could be boring your classes with the same ICT routines. This predictability can often be based on a perception of your role in the classroom, and one of the most common symptoms is over-reliance on PowerPoint presentations. Beginning teachers initially see their role as presenting information to students and PowerPoint can be seen as a useful or modern way of doing this. It might be useful to go back to the reflection points which asked you to consider how useful PowerPoint presentations were in your own learning.

It would also be useful to look at how an experienced teacher uses an application like PowerPoint. Peter Duffy at North Liverpool Academy makes extensive use of ICT – it is integrated into his lessons but does not dominate. You could select any of the online lessons to focus on the way he uses ICT, you might come to the conclusion that the lesson is not an ICT lesson but ICT does support his teaching and in places it helps students to structure and reinforce their learning. In the Year 8 lesson PowerPoint is used to highlight the focus question: The Home Guard – Dad's Army or Real Army? In all the lessons illustrated, PowerPoint highlights learning objectives and learning outcomes, and reinforces the point of the lesson: the ICT is simple and unobtrusive but it supports or enables effective teaching. You might say that using ICT in this way is not particularly imaginative, it is not making the most of the potential of the technology. However, teaching is also about making decisions and the strategies developed in the lesson extracts focused on other issues. The key issue here is making decisions about the way ICT is used to support teaching and to organize and structure learning. Lesson objectives and learning outcomes could be written on a whiteboard but this way they are a permanent recyclable resource. As you gain more experience of devising teaching approaches and teaching strategies, you might

like to evaluate the Home Guard lesson – could more use be made of ICT? For example, the opening card sort activity requires students to make decisions about the effectiveness of the Home Guard. It would be possible to use interactive whiteboard software to do this task. Students might be asked to come up to the front and move cards to one side or the other. The 2004 Ofsted report highlighted just such an activity: 'The lesson began with students' use of an interactive whiteboard to contribute to a sorting task, matching definitions with words to do with trench warfare. The task was slower than other methods, but with good gains in acquisition of knowledge.' (Ofsted, 2004: 5) Instead, Peter Duffy asked his students to work in pairs. This task engaged all the group and enabled him to work with the students individually to develop an understanding of their reasoning. In whole-class question and answer sessions it was apparent that one group of girls was less confident volunteering answers. Organizing the activity in this way ensured that everyone was involved with their learning and enabled the teacher to directly involve more reluctant learners.

## MAKING PROGRESS IN HISTORY: MAKING PROGRESS WITH ICT

The first part of this discussion focused on the decisions that you will have to make as a teacher. If you are using ICT, does it make your teaching more effective and will it have a positive impact on the learning of the students you are teaching? What this discussion has not really considered is qualitative issues, which focus far more on the nature of the ICT tasks students themselves might be asked to undertake. Again there are clues in the 2004 Ofsted Report:

> The use of word-processing software did not always add to the history being taught, and occasionally it slowed it down, with laborious copy-typing when tasks could have been completed much more effectively by hand.
>
> Other examples were observed where achievement was low, including low-level information transfer, and answering low-level questions from worksheets or published material (including some published using ICT). (Ofsted, 2004: 6)

The use of ICT in these circumstances is low level; it contributes little to learning and progression and such tasks would hardly motivate students. There is more to this criticism, however. This account might be describing a Year 7 lesson. It could equally be describing a Year 11 lesson where students could conceivably be completing GCSE coursework. The ICT does not take account of the capabilities of the students. When planning lessons for a Year 7 group, or for an able GCSE Year 10 group, you would take into account the abilities of the group. You would expect students to have progressed in their learning and their historical understanding between the ages of 11 and 15. In exactly the same way, when planning ICT activities you need to ensure that the demands you make are incremental. Again

Ofsted provides a significant pointer to the way that ICT is 'used ... *systematic(ally) to underpin students' progress*' (Ofsted, 2004: 4, author's emphasis). It is the use of systematic which suggests that ICT use needs to be far more considered and built into departmental schemes of work. The full benefit of ICT might not be felt if its use is sporadic. In your PGCE year it might not be possible to plan, design or develop a coherent strategy across KS3 for the use of ICT in the history department, but you should begin to think beyond isolated or individual opportunities to use ICT in your teaching. Many universities require beginning teachers on PGCE programmes to maintain a log or record of their use of ICT. This might be a simple catalogue of lessons which they have taught, with examples of resources which they have created. A useful addition to this log would be a curriculum map which would demonstrate the nature and range of ICT activities being planned or delivered. This framework could then be used to demonstrate how ICT use becomes more progressive, in terms of students undertaking more complex activities. Such a structure would then be able to demonstrate how the ICT enables students to work in a historically more demanding way.

Developing such a coherent approach, or at least being aware of these issues, involves two linked factors. The first of these has already been raised, that of matching or making more progressive demands of the students' ICT capabilities. This should involve liaising with the ICT co-ordinator. They should have an overview of the capabilities of students at different stages, and at what point in a year they might be expected to revisit particular applications. The second strand of a considered or coherent approach to using ICT in history focuses on the way that you can help to ensure that the improved ICT capability is used, or is matched to the students' developing historical understanding.

The easiest way to demonstrate how IT capability and historical understanding work together is to look at the way word-processing software supports learning. In 1998 the Historical Association in conjunction with National Council for Educational Technology (NCET) produced a software package which demonstrated how this simple application could be employed to develop students' analytical writing (NCET/HA, 1998b). The package had sample activities: for Year 7, the Norman Conquest; Year 8, the Origins of the English Civil War; and Year 9, the Home Front in the Second World War. The teacher's guide outlines the objectives of these tasks and demonstrates what a powerful tool word processing can be. The Year 7 activity began by using different formatting commands in Word to highlight dates, names and events to develop an understanding of chronology. Word can also be used to help students read for meaning; another activity required students to identify factors which suggested Harold was unlucky and were highlighted in bold text, while those that suggested that William was lucky were highlighted in italic. This simple approach to text enables students to identify reasons for events occurring and develop a deeper understanding of the text they are reading.

In Year 8 the Civil War activity is more demanding; the focus is on the origins of the English Civil War and this time Word enables students to sort, organize and categorize a range of causes. The ability of Word to sort and prioritize complex ideas can help students to identify patterns in the past with greater ease and this, in turn, can allow the teacher to focus on the relationships between more complex causal factors. By now these techniques are second nature to history teachers and are a familiar part of teaching and learning strategies. The techniques are so obviously transferable and can be used in a number of different situations. However, the key issue is that the IT becomes more challenging as the students move from Year 7 to Year 8, reflecting their ability to think historically at a more complex level. This illustrates the idea of progression in IT capability matching the progression in historical thinking.

There is a danger that such activities can become too mechanical and students replicate the process that was referred to at the start of this chapter – simply spotting or identifying key words or phrases and mechanically cutting and pasting without necessarily learning. This was a concern which Prior and John (2001) address in 'From anecdote to argument: using the word processor to connect knowledge and opinion through revelatory writing' (*Teaching History*, 101: 31–4). The challenge in the activities described involved:

> enriching rather than filleting existing text. We have looked at ways in which the use of anecdotes, examples and morsels of information might be woven into text to reveal the richness and depth of the past. We have also examined ways in which opinion can be filtered into (or out of) text in order to enhance the meaning and character of historical writing. (Prior and John, 2001: 33)

Again this demonstrates the flexibility of word processing and the ability to build in challenge in terms of the historical thinking which students are required to undertake. The fact that students become more familiar with Word has advantages. The speed and the convenience of ICT mean that more time can be devoted to historical thinking so that word processing can support complex and challenging history at A level. In *Teaching History* Arthur Chapman (2003a) describes how Word is used to develop the conceptual awareness of A level students. Subtitled: 'Using ICT to get Year 13 reading', the article demonstrates how the software enables high-level thinking skills to be developed. The key to the success of this activity lies in the ability of the software to handle and manipulate large amounts of information.

## USING DATABASES TO SHARPEN UP YOUR HISTORICAL THINKING

This is traditionally an area of ICT where history teachers are generally less confident and the discussion here has a deliberate instructional element. The intention is to help you see the real potential that this kind of software has to support historical thinking. The advantage of using historical evidence which can be stored in a spreadsheet or database is that you can use the power of the computer to sort, organize and categorize information. Then you can ask questions of the evidence, see patterns in the evidence that might not have been so readily accessible. There are some, but not many, commercial packages which already have data entered and are ready for use; however, the material is often limited and might not be suitable for your own particular needs. Another disadvantage is that you should be able to follow the instructions but you will not necessarily develop your own understanding of the nature of databases or spreadsheets and, consequently, begin to develop an appreciation of the potential of data-handling software to really change the way you teach history. Developing this understanding is important because it enables you to develop an awareness of the potential – what you might be able to do with data-handling software. We might not like it, but most computers will have the Microsoft Office suite installed, in which case the spreadsheet software will be Excel; the database software will be Access. Most people seem to have a passing familiarity with Excel but have an unnatural fear of Access. If anything Access is far more suitable for historical enquiries, it is more flexible in terms of the data that can be entered, it is even possible to enter large blocks of text and use it as a tool for textual analysis. More significantly, databases are designed to answer questions or queries which the user can define with relatively little difficulty, and writing your own queries really begins to sharpen up your historical thinking.

As with all IT applications familiarity breeds 'comfortability'. As part of my other teaching responsibilities I am module leader for an undergraduate IT course on a BA history programme. For one term the focus of the work is based around databases and, from experience, students on these courses become proficient through regular and frequent practice. This is not always possible in a PGCE year and an introductory session on spreadsheets and databases will not be enough to build up your confidence. These applications have a great deal more potential and can help you to access highly original and challenging history.

Liverpool War Dead 1939–1945 is a home-made database which is still in the process of being developed. The information it contains is drawn from the Commonwealth War Graves website. Instead of searching for individual casualties it is possible to search by cemetery. If you go to the document, Understanding the Impact of the Blitz on Liverpool, on the companion website www.sagepub.co.uk/secondary you will be able to follow the process of creating your own data resource and develop your understanding of how spreadsheets and databases can sharpen historical thinking and questioning. The ability to search by cemetery as well as by individual casualty can also be useful if you are organizing or taking part in a First World War field visit.

The process of entering data into a spreadsheet or database raises an interesting dilemma: ICT is meant to speed up historical enquiry; it is meant to remove the drudgery. We are also cautioned against getting students to complete meaningless cut and paste tasks, low-level activities which do not provide much of a challenge. Unfortunately the data as it exists is difficult to access, is not in a format which is useful for a historical enquiry and requires some additional work. If you want to develop your own exercises based around wartime casualties should you involve students in the initial data collecting? It may fly in the face of accepted wisdom, but these mundane repetitive tasks can serve a valuable purpose. There are some real practical issues: first, care has to be taken to ensure that records are copied accurately; second, if it is just a cut and paste activity it probably will be of little historical value but if students read some/most/all of the records they are pasting into the spreadsheet you can ask them to make a note of any patterns that appear to be emerging. Entering data can be a useful activity: making students aware of the importance of accuracy can help to foster good habits. More importantly, the very repetitive nature of the task might actually foster curiosity, questions about the evidence might begin to take shape. If you were to ask your students about the nature of the evidence held in the Commonwealth War Graves records, they would probably be able to put together a reasonable list of possible fields:

- Who were they? Name
- Where did they live? Address
- When did they die? Date of death
- How old were they? Age

These preconceptions about the information can change significantly just by entering the data; patterns emerge which then influence and change the way the database is designed. Familiarity with patterns in the evidence can then suggest queries that might confirm a hunch. You might call it getting a feel for the evidence, the unusual, the less obvious, and with the Liverpool example disturbing patterns begin to emerge. As this happens you can begin to think about the very different questions and answers which the spreadsheet might be capable of revealing. The entries below might demonstrate this

**Casualty details from CWGC website**

ATHERTON, Thomas Ernest
A.R.P Ambulance Driver, of 38 Penton Street. Died at Mill Road Infirmary.

AUSTIN, George Henry
16 Janet Street, Edge Hill. Husband of the late Mary Austin. Injured 17 September 1940, at 16 Janet Street; died at Alder Hey Emergency Hospital.

BANKS, Margaret
32 Eastwood Street. Daughter of Margaret and of the late J. Banks. Died at Ernest Brown Junior Instructional Centre.

BOTTER, Jan
Netherlands Mercantile Marine. Son of Arend and Anna Stokman Botter, of van Oldenbarneveldstraat, 65, Amsterdam, Holland. Died at H.M. Prison, Walton. Also commemorated at City of Westminster (Paddington) Mill Hill Netherlands Field of Honour, Screen Wall.

CONDLIFF, Joyce
Aged 6 months; of 85 Goldsmith Street. Daughter of Pte. Sydney Condliff, The King's Shropshire Light Infantry, and Mrs. Condliff. Died at 85 Goldsmith Street.

This is more than just a list of names, and the examples do not of themselves reveal any significant patterns. First, the way the names are recorded is significant. The names of civilian war dead were not just randomly collected but were official records, required under a Defence of the Realm Act. Other aspects of the data suggest that the records were used in Coroner's Courts. Thomas Atherton was a member of the ARP and died at Mill Road Infirmary. George Austin died at Alder Hey hospital but was pulled out alive, just, from his bombed house. The two records are subtly different. Thomas Atherton died on duty when Mill Road Infirmary received a direct hit. George Austin, mortally injured in the ruins of his house, died at Alder Hey. Margaret Banks died in the basement shelter of the Ernest Brown Instructional Centre (formerly the location of Edge Hill College). She was not alone – there are numerous other examples of air raid shelters receiving direct hits resulting in multiple casualties where whole families were wiped out.

As the data accumulates, more and more questions can be asked and the record of Liverpool's civilian war dead provides quite a detailed picture of what total war really meant and can provide solid evidence that can support enquiries about the nature of the war on the Home Front during the Second World War. Using this data in a spreadsheet is clearly valuable; being able to transfer the evidence across to a database can make it even more useful as is outlined in 'Understanding the Impact of the Blitz on Liverpool'. Again the process requires some careful historical thinking. In a database it is possible to create fields to tag or identify particular records. A simple yes/no field therefore could identify foreign servicemen killed in Liverpool or identify the numbers of Civil Defence workers killed, or discover how many air raid shelter disasters occurred. Again there are a number of assumptions that we make about the Home Front and a database enables students to frame their own questions, or queries. One assumption we make is that most of Liverpool's children had been evacuated to the Welsh countryside to be puzzled by cows and sheep. Simple searches of an age field could throw up some interesting results. Were there proportionately more children under the age of 3 killed than in the age range 6–12? The school leaving age in 1940–41 was 14. Once children became 15, did they no longer count as evacuees?

In the space available it is not possible to do more than highlight how valuable data-handling software is and how it can be used in a very practical way to undertake challenging, original and valuable historical enquiries. Even very simple databases can be useful, sometimes the simpler the better. They are easier to construct, take far less time to compile and provide a real challenge to students' historical thinking. Significantly, they might provide an opportunity for students to work out a number of hypotheses and then use the database to test the validity of their theories. Simple burial registers, which record name, age, address and date of death, provide sufficient information to come to a series of conclusions about sanitary conditions in nineteenth-century towns. Collecting data across 10-year periods would demonstrate change – or lack of it – over time. Effectively, workhouse registers are now more accessible via online census sites such as Ancestry and they provide a useful snapshot of the inmates at a particular moment in time. One workhouse, in your local Poor Law Union, would provide some interesting data but comparative data would be even more useful.

- What differences might you expect to find between an urban and a rural Poor Law Union?
- Might there be any differences between the workhouse inmates in 1850 or 1860 compared with in 1901?
- Are there any patterns evident relating to occupations?
- Are there any patterns evident relating to where the inmates were born?

The very fact that the data is collected in a number of limited fields makes this type of enquiry manageable.

Using databases and spreadsheets is one of the areas where it is possible to demonstrate the ideas of progression – making more demands in terms of the ICT but, more significantly, greater demands in terms of historical thinking. The stages of historical questioning and enquiry that databases encourage can range from the relatively simple to the complex:

- What does the evidence tell me?
- How can I use the spreadsheet or database to find out?
- How do I ask questions of the database?
- What fields do I need to combine to give me an answer?
- How does a database help me to construct a hypothesis?
- How do I interpret the evidence?
- Can I explain the unexpected?

## USING DISCUSSION FORUMS

This is one area of IT use where there has been a significant amount of development and progress in recent years. It is also an area where universities have a great deal of expertise and an area where there is an established pedagogy of e-learning. If you are a recent history graduate there is a high degree of probability that you may have been at the receiving end as an e-learner studying an online course. There is also a high degree of probability that Blackboard or Web Ct is supporting your PGCE programme. If this is the case then you are only too familiar with the real benefits of a virtual learning environment.

- A VLE enables you to maintain contact with the rest of your group when you are on placement.
- It can be a valuable forum for sharing experiences about partner schools.
- It is an ideal medium for sharing teaching ideas and resources.
- A VLE can also put you in touch with a wider community of practice if mentors, NQTs and former PGCE trainees contribute to discussion forums and advice clinics.

## LEARNING HOW TO USE A VLE

It is highly likely that the way you use your VLE is instinctive and functional: instinctive in that you see the VLE as an extension to the university classroom and you readily adapt to the way the VLE enables you to extend you professional and personal links; functional in that the VLE serves a utilitarian purpose; it meets a particular need. If you have been an online learner or an e-learner you might also see that the way your PGCE VLE functions is very different; it is likely to be far less structured. A traditional online course will begin and end at identifiable points. There will be a formal and structured programme of readings and activities. There will also be an expectation that you will contribute to a discussion forum and it is here that the real learning can take place. You need to be clear about the distinction between online learning and computer-aided learning. If you were simply reading text on your computer screen and then composing a response and posting it to a teacher this might more properly be described as supported self-study: a very lonely way to go and replicating an old outdated view of an Open University course where everything came in a box apart from the television programmes which were usually broadcast at 1.30 in the morning by physicists wearing improbable ties. Twice a year there was a Saturday tutorial and, dependent upon the module, an annual Summer School.

E-learning could not be more different. Online learning is a social process. It is dependent upon the interaction of learners, effectively in an electronic seminar. Chapter 4 examined ideas about learning theories and that it is important that you try to understand the processes of online learning in the same way that you tried to understand the interactions between teachers and students in the more usual classroom.

## ONLINE LEARNING AS SOCIAL CONSTRUCTIVISM

If you try to consider how an undergraduate seminar was supposed to help you learn, try applying the model to online learning.

- You might have begun with a question linked to a lecture or based around reading – which everyone would have read!
- Two or three students might then have been required to present their ideas and lead the session.

- The understanding, the learning, does not come from your fellow students' fact-filled PowerPoint presentations but from the discussion which hopefully develops subsequently.
- The exchanges of ideas, the new understandings, the resolved preconceptions are the result of discussion and argument.
- As a member of the seminar group you are collectively helping to create or construct a better understanding or attempting to find an answer to a question.
- The ability to explore ideas might help you to construct your own new understanding; it may have been your fellow students who provided a scaffold or the way your lecturer managed the dialogue, but you succeeded in bridging that gap, crossing the zone of proximal development.

It is worth considering this example in some detail; even if this was not your experience of a university seminar you might be able to understand what was supposed to happen. This is also a useful counterpoint for you to refer to when you are trying to make sense of the way you are using your PGCE VLE.

The other important idea from Chapter 4 which is worth trying to understand and apply in the context of online learning is Kolb's learning cycle. Here the learning takes place, or develops, in the reflection and evaluation phase. Reflection and evaluation are perhaps more formal elements or aspects of online learning. In a face-to-face seminar where the emphasis is perhaps on an immediate exchange of ideas, almost an off-the cuff response, the online experience can be more considered. First an immediate response might not be required; you might be picking up on a discussion which is some hours, or perhaps days, old. You also have the luxury of reflecting on your original reflection. Under these circumstances learning can be a more considered process and again it is worthwhile developing an awareness of the way you function as an e-learner. You will then be more able to manage the e-learning of students.

## MODELS OF E-LEARNING

The idea of a pedagogy of e-learning was referred to earlier and it is worth considering one particular model which appears to have cornered the market. Gilly Salmon's (2000) progressive five-stage model (Figure 9.1) is useful in one respect because it recognizes that successful online learning involves belonging to an online community and a willingness to contribute and take part in online discussions. Salmon also recognizes the central role that the teacher or online moderator plays in developing an effective online community.

This model might work well within the confines of a 'traditional' online course or a blended learning course which uses a mix of face-to-face and online teaching and learning. It might be worth exploring in a little more detail what can make online learning so effective. The analogy of the university seminar is valuable if

- Stage 1 Access and motivation: role of teacher is to welcome and encourage members to feel part of online community.
- Stage 2 Online socialization: role of teacher to help users to feel comfortable working with technology and develop familiarity with online learning environment.
- Stage 3 Information exchange: teacher's role to explain/facilitate tasks and use of learning materials.
- Stage 4 Knowledge construction: teacher's role to act as facilitator, most of exchanges taking place between members of online community.
- Stage 5 Development: teacher's role to support and respond to needs of the online community.

**Figure 9.1** The role of the teacher in developing online learning (adapted from Salmon, 2000)

you consider the nature of the discussions and exchanges which take place in a traditional face-to-face seminar. The degree of success to some extent depends upon the level of preparation. If all members of the seminar group have done the preparatory reading, the discussion can be quite fruitful and there is a genuine sense of collaborative learning. You might also have been thinking that there were seminars when participants were less than prepared. Under those circumstances there was usually one of two outcomes: a series of uncomfortable silences or people talking off the top of their heads – exchanging generalities and vague opinions. The key distinguishing feature of the seminar is that it happens within a limited period of time and the exchanges are immediate and almost conversational.

Now consider the differences, and the advantages, of online seminars. Discussion need not be immediate, there is a longer time frame for members to engage with the issues. Looking at the practice of a colleague, his blended sessions work effectively together.

- A face-to-face session explores a particular aspect of eighteenth-century enclosure and raises a number of questions.
- The online seminar begins after the face-to-face session and lasts for up to a week.
- During this time the students have an opportunity to read, reflect, post a contribution and read the contributions of others.
- There is then time for further reflection which results in a second, perhaps more considered post.
- The space and opportunity for reflection and consideration results in much deeper learning.

You might be wondering how this applies to your PGCE programme and to the way that you might want to implement e-learning in your own practice. If you turn back to Salmon's five-stage model and try to relate this to your PGCE practice, there are immediate differences. Salmon's approach is almost leisurely – developing an online community, the socializing, the confidence-building phase, allowing participants time to develop their confidence with the technology – might take weeks. The online module might represent the totality of the e-learner's workload. You should be able to appreciate that a PGCE trainee does not and cannot work at such a leisurely pace. It is highly likely that you will have a one- or two-hour face-to-face session in an IT laboratory introducing you to Web Ct or Blackboard, and by the end of the session not only are you expected to be familiar with the technology but you are contributing to online discussions. You might even find that you have a number of online tasks to complete week by week. The PGCE is noted for its steep learning curve. By week four you are often expected to be developing good e-learning habits; however, taking time to stand back and reflect on your e-learning practice might be valuable.

Try to contrast the model of effective classroom learning which you are beginning to understand with the way in which you are using you own VLE. There is often a tendency to view e-learning activities as another series of tasks to complete. The list below describes some of the most common online tasks to which PGCE trainees are asked to contribute:

- Reflect on or evaluate taught sessions.
- Read journal articles and post views on the articles.
- Post reflections on classroom observations or impressions of school practice.
- Evaluate teaching resources.

There is a tendency to think that the important element of the task is posting the review or the evaluation. The result can be a collection of individual contributions, all valuable but the element of interaction is limited. In a face-to-face seminar it would be the equivalent of each member making a statement until everyone had contributed – and then going home. Remember the real learning comes from the discussion. There are a number of possible solutions:

- A two-stage reflection, whereby everyone reads the initial posts and then reflects on the reflections.
- Journal reviews: one person reviews per week and becomes the 'expert' and is asked for views/opinions by the rest of the group.
- Instead of posting observations, reflect on the focus of the observation, for example, instead of posting a narrative describing questioning, try to reflect on the effectiveness of different styles of questioning.
- Evaluating resources or websites: this could be a paired activity where one person posts a review and the second person then reflects on his/her expectations and how these were or were not met.

Of course, the simplest thing would be to read each other's postings and react to them. This is where the Pilgrims PGCE Progress might militate against effective online learning. Consider the idea of developing a discussion focused on classroom observations: it is early November and you are beginning to plan and/or prepare teaching resources. You have a number of other tasks to prepare including focused observations. You have managed to distil your views which you post on your VLE. The next day you are back at university and things move on. There is little time to reflect on your own posting, let alone the postings of others. You might just think that like 'bad things' your VLEs just happen, but as a historian you should have some suspicion that nothing ever happens accidentally. The ever-growing pedagogy of e-learning has informed the design of VLEs used to support PGCE programmes. Equally, a number of history PGCE tutors have given a considerable degree of thought to the way VLEs can be used effectively within the quirky parameters of a PGCE course.

## VLEs IN THE HISTORY CLASSROOM

Schools are beginning to make more use of VLEs and are seen as playing an important part in 'personalizing' learning for students. In some ways the ideas about, and the claims made on behalf of, VLEs are similar to the more general claims made about computers by Tony Blair in the late 1990s. In some respects they are seen as the new 'must have' and the way they are being used in some schools replicates some of the blind alleys that universities were pursuing some time ago. There is a tendency to see the VLEs as a place where course content can be dumped on a school network – a technique imaginatively described as 'shovelware'. Students can access school networks from home and there is an assumption that this both personalizes learning and enables homework to be managed more effectively. As a history teacher you need to develop a more objective viewpoint and consider the use of VLEs in schools from a number of perspectives. These might range from increased expectations of teachers and students alike, to ideas about effective e-learning. From your perspective as a history teacher you would need to decide if uploading course content onto the school network was going to improve the quality and effectiveness of learning.

### Points for reflection

You have probably come across some history department websites that are 'advertised' as links on a site like the History Teachers' Discussion Forum. It might be a useful activity to examine and compare two or three of the departmental websites. You would need to decide or formulate quite rigorous criteria and ask yourself some difficult questions:

- Is the site mainly intended to raise the profile of the history department?
- Is the site promoting the history department in a positive manner?

- Is the material simply illustrative?
- Is there evidence that students are actively involved as online learners?
- Is the site mainly used as a resource bank?

## USING VLEs TO DEVELOP HISTORICAL ARGUMENT

Over recent years the Historical Association has attempted to develop a number of online debates with varying degrees of success. The HA are able to call on the services of well-known academics. Barry Coward contributed to an online discussion on the role of Cromwell. This was aimed at A level students and the level of argument was impressive, but levels of participation were limited. These were debates rather than online discussions and the students were producing a series of staged posts. Online learning is more reactive or interactive and could, amongst other things, support the development of historical argument. In theory the use of discussion forums should promote effective teaching and learning, but the reality presents more of a challenge to teachers. Perhaps the challenge and the solution lies in a clearer understanding of the pedagogy of online teaching and learning.

Using discussion forums in the classroom is a relatively recent development. In 2006 and 2007 Dan Moorhouse and Dave Martin made readers of *Teaching History* aware of ways in which VLEs could support pupil learning in history but it is likely that this way of teaching and learning is still in its infancy in the secondary history classroom. As a beginning teacher, perhaps with experience as an e-learning undergraduate, you have a level of expertise and a degree of insight which could prove valuable. Developing good e-learning habits takes time and like all IT applications this approach to learning needs to be revisited and developed through KS3 into GCSE and beyond.

The pressure of time has to be a factor in the successful development of e-learning approaches and it is clear that the project which Martin describes required hard work. As with all e-learning activities you have to ask if it is the most effective strategy. Is e-learning more suitable for more mature learners – do 13-or 15-year-old students need more direction and more face-to-face contact with a teacher? Again this emphasizes the difference between mediated e-learning and computer-aided learning where students simply answer questions on screen. Martin's short experiment demonstrated that pupils could develop the ability to construct historical arguments online and his evidence suggests that the level of argument improved over the period of the activity. Again it is important to draw on your own experience, either as an undergraduate e-learner or as a VLE user on your PGCE programme. Do you need different skills or aptitudes as an e-learner? As an e-teacher (or e-moderator) do you need to develop different types of skills?

### Points for reflection

The comment is often made that young people are natural communicators on social networking sites. If you reflect on your contributions or discussions that take place on these sites are there any similarities with historical argument?

If you are aware of the level and the nature of these discussions how might they prepare you to moderate an e-learning activity in the history classroom?



It will be important in future to consider more carefully the pedagogy of e-learning, particularly in a school setting, if only to understand how it might align with well-established ideas about learning in history. Dave Martin's caveat about the role of teachers in online learning is important. The three-week enquiry provided useful evidence about the ways students developed their historical understanding but it would take longer to develop an effective and a viable blended or online learning environment. This will inevitably be an issue in the immediate future; schools are going down the learning platform route. Experience suggests that school VLEs could simply be used as repositories for course content and that an understanding of effective e-learning might not be a priority. If VLEs are part of your PGCE programme, or were part of your undergraduate programme, it is likely that you will have some significant experience. Again this goes back to metacognition and reflecting on your learning. Salmon has a model of e-moderator competencies (Salmon, 2000: 54) and one of the foundations for becoming a successful e-moderator is the personal experience of online learning. In particular she highlights 'empathy with the challenges of becoming an on line learner'. It would seem that the PGCE trainee who has this experience of being an online learner and can reflect on this experience has a great deal to offer.

It has been suggested that the Salmon five-stage model might not be appropriate for the development of a PGCE VLE, but the gradual development of an online community might be exactly the way to develop their effective use in schools. Our understanding of the process of online learning and online moderating has largely come from work with adult learners. Some of this work has focused on developing the capabilities of reluctant learners who might not be familiar with the technology, or who are wary about committing their ideas to an online environment. There might equally be an assumption that young people are completely at home in an online environment, but again there is probably a world of difference between the conversational exchanges on social networking sites and true learning on line. Again there is a resonance with the issues raised earlier in the chapter – the idea of matching progression in IT capability with the increasing complexity of history-based activities. If online learning is to be used as an effective tool to support students' understanding in history, it will be necessary to understand not just the history learning that might be taking place but the role of the teacher or e-moderator in the process. Managing the online learning of adults is one thing; managing the online learning of school students raises new questions.

### What the research says

The Office for Standards in Education and BECTa have produced some valuable evidence into the effective, and less effective, uses of ICT in the history classroom. The BECTa key questions used at the start of this chapter provide you with a useful benchmark to assess the effectiveness of ICT in the classroom, a link to which can be found on the companion website.

The focus on VLEs and the way these are used to support the learning of PGCE trainees was deliberate. Developing your own understanding of the pedagogy of e-learning is best done from your perspective as an e-learner. The evaluations by PGCE tutors of their approaches to online learning will provide you with a variety of different perspectives and help you to understand how you learn or work with a VLE. The collection of discussion papers in the Escalate series (see below) is therefore valuable in this respect. They might not provide you with answers for using VLEs in your schools, but they will help you to understand the process of being an e-moderator.

1. 'Using asynchronous discussion to support the reflective thinking of ITE students', Ruth Lee, Leicester University.
2. 'Redefining planning for online interaction with ITT students: what can be learned by separating "discussion" from "board"?' Ruth Lee, Leicester University; Judith Enriquez, Aberdeen University.
3. 'E-learning, history education and the forging of professional identities', Graham Rogers, Edge Hill University.
4. 'Why we value our virtual learning environment', Kerry Jordan-Daus, Canterbury Christ Church University (CCCU).
5. 'VLEs: the new Everest. Do we just use them because they are there?' Ian Phillips, Edge Hill University.
6. 'How do PGCE tutors enable beginning teachers to "connect their learning" through Virtual Learning Environments? Can connections made through the VLE encourage creativity?, Ali Messer: Roehampton University.

All the above can be found at Teacher Education Futures: Developing Learning and Teaching in ITE across the UK: A selection of conference papers presented at St. Martin's College, Lancaster, 19 May 2006. A link to this is available on the companion website.

For a fuller exploration of the project described by Martin et al. (2007) in *Teaching History* see: Coffin (2007). This includes longer extracts from interviews with the students which explore the way they felt they had learnt history and their attitudes to online learning.

## Further reading

Moorhouse, D. (2006) 'When computers don't give you a headache, the most able lead a debate on medicine through time', *Teaching History*, 124: 30–6.

Salmon, G. (2000) E. Moderating: The Key to Teaching and Learning On Line.

## Useful websites

Live links to these websites can be found on the companion website.

Dan Lyndon's use of Web Quests demonstrates how the Internet can be used with students of all ages: www.comptonhistory.com/.

On the Historical Association site the Secondary Resources area explores other useful IT applications: www.history.org.uk/Secondary_Key_Stage_4.asp.

Teachers TV has a good programme which looks at the way a school in Kirby Lonsdale, Cumbria, has developed the use of a VLE in different curriculum areas. The example of an English A level course is particularly encouraging: www.teachers.tv/video/ 21840.

BECTa what the research says: History and ICT www.partners.becta.org.uk/upload-dir/downloads/page_documents/research/wtrs_history.pdf

In final section Web Link to free resources & IWB templates at www.classtools.net/

For using film in History Teaching feature films often have associated websites and resources www.amazinggracethemovie.co.uk/

# 10 A DIVERSE AND CONTROVERSIAL SUBJECT

**This chapter considers the following issues:**

- the ability of history to challenge students to develop different perspectives on the contemporary world
- the relationship between history and citizenship and how history can promote responsible citizenship
- the challenging, controversial and at times emotionally difficult topics, which are nevertheless an important part of history
- teaching approaches to controversial topics, and different standpoints that teachers might take when teaching these topics.

## A DIFFERENT KIND OF CHAPTER?

In some respects previous chapters have had a common theme linked to the pedagogy of history teaching; the 'points for reflection' largely directed your thoughts to 'technical' issues linked to the history classroom and indirectly to the QTT Standards. In this chapter the focus is different; it is very much about the relevance of the history curriculum and the personal nature of history. The larger curriculum aims, 'Civic participation and responsible citizens', featured in the opening chapter. If you approach these 'outcomes' in terms of Michael Riley's depth and overview you will be able to see the real potential for history as a curriculum subject and as an academic discipline to provide exactly the kind of curriculum that the QCA is after. The text in bold is taken directly from Mick Waters's PowerPoint presentation.

History is a subject which can **address difficult issues** which **affect** the individual **person and society** as a whole. History is a subject which should **not shrink from controversy**. Some topics such as the Holocaust or the slave trade **deal with emotions and relationships**. If history is taught well it can **help young people face fears** and develop a more informed and deeper understanding. Significantly history can also help young people to **see things from different view points**. Society today is very different from when Curriculum 2000 was introduced and it is more important than ever before that young people have a real understanding of the **diverse** society we now live in.

In Chapter 2 there was only a brief exploration of the issue of diversity but it is important to understand just how important this idea is. As a key concept diversity is one of the organizing ideas which you will make use of when planning individual lessons and more extensive schemes of work. It will provide a mechanism for exploring the nature of past societies but, with the bigger picture firmly in mind, you might need to ask yourself if diversity could also be one of the overarching curriculum aims or 'outputs'. It is an awful phrase but it is worthwhile considering this in terms of that $64,000 question a head teacher asks you during your interview: 'what should the end product of a historical education be?' The opening line might inevitably be 'real understanding of the very diverse society which young people live in today'. That could certainly meet the ideas of 'civic participation and responsible citizenship'. You might just think that this is another cunning plan which manages to tick the right boxes on a 'QCA new curriculum tick box checklist'. If, however, you begin to take the $64,000 answer apart you can see that, in order to understand modern-day society, students need both a perspective – the past – and the intellectual tools to analyse this past – historical methodology.

There is a pessimistic view which believes that the new curriculum will lead to the demise of history as a subject. Such a view thinks history departments are going to be reduced to delivering citizenship and that, ultimately, we might as well pack up and go home. There are grounds for adopting a more positive approach that simply involves history departments demonstrating how they can be central to delivering the ideas embedded in the new curriculum. The misunderstanding lies in the pessimist's simplistic interpretation of responsible citizenship. They are confusing a big aim with the smaller subject. Responsible citizenship is not the sole responsibility of a citizenship department or citizenship teachers. All traditional subjects have to consider how they can help deliver this larger aim, and history is better placed than most school subjects which might all go under the heading of **Diversity**:

- **difficult issues**
- **affecting the person and society**
- **not shrinking from controversy**
- **dealing with emotions and relationships**

- **helping young people face fears**
- **seeing things from different view points.**

If you consider how these bullet points link to history you may be able to appreciate how you, as history teachers, are in a position to ensure that history's unique contribution to the curriculum is, in fact, stronger than ever. History's hand is also strengthened by its academic maturity. In Chapter 1 a comparison was made between history and citizenship and their respective key concepts and key processes. Hopefully, you have developed an understanding of the nature of the history concepts and processes and the role they play in organizing and structuring students' work. Perhaps you are also in a position to appreciate how relatively insubstantial the equivalent concepts and processes are for citizenship. They are both too broad and too 'fuzzy', a little like Father Dougal's dreamy vision of 'nice things' in *Father Ted*. The slave trade might contribute to the citizenship curriculum but might require the rigour of the history key concepts and key processes to give the study real shape, direction and, more importantly, bite (Figure 10.1). What is equally apparent in the citizenship concepts and processes is the reliance time and again on the importance of the historical perspective and historical method. Rather than packing up and going home, or teaching citizenship, history teachers need to be highlighting the fact that citizenship can only become a rigorous and valid subject if citizenship teachers develop a sound understanding of the key concepts and key processes which underpin the study of history.

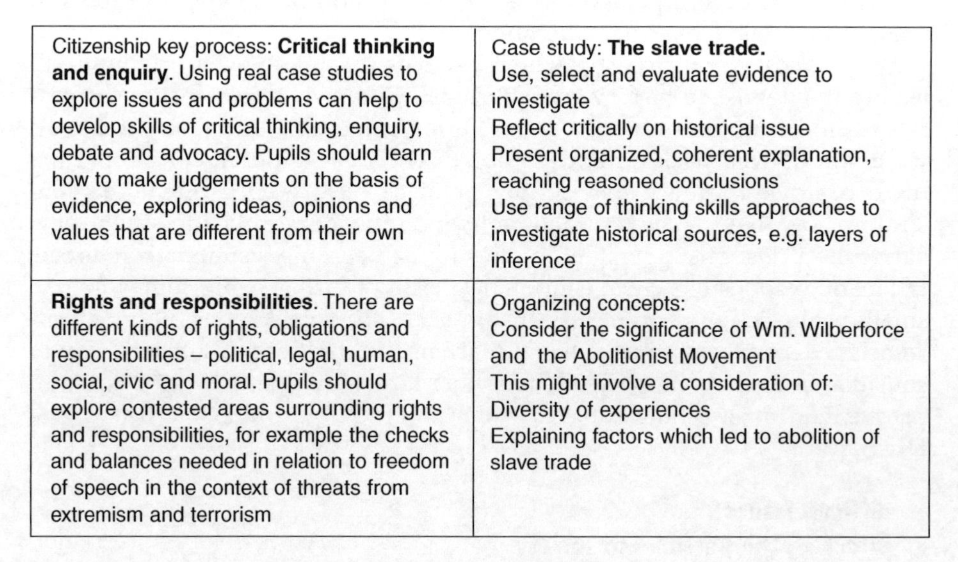

| | |
|---|---|
| Citizenship key process: **Critical thinking and enquiry**. Using real case studies to explore issues and problems can help to develop skills of critical thinking, enquiry, debate and advocacy. Pupils should learn how to make judgements on the basis of evidence, exploring ideas, opinions and values that are different from their own | Case study: **The slave trade.**<br>Use, select and evaluate evidence to investigate<br>Reflect critically on historical issue<br>Present organized, coherent explanation, reaching reasoned conclusions<br>Use range of thinking skills approaches to investigate historical sources, e.g. layers of inference |
| **Rights and responsibilities**. There are different kinds of rights, obligations and responsibilities – political, legal, human, social, civic and moral. Pupils should explore contested areas surrounding rights and responsibilities, for example the checks and balances needed in relation to freedom of speech in the context of threats from extremism and terrorism | Organizing concepts:<br>Consider the significance of Wm. Wilberforce and the Abolitionist Movement<br>This might involve a consideration of:<br>Diversity of experiences<br>Explaining factors which led to abolition of slave trade |

**Figure 10.1** Using historical concepts and processes to structure and shape citizenship study

## THE PERSONAL AND THE CONTROVERSIAL NATURE OF HISTORY

One of the strengths of history as a curriculum subject is the ability of individuals – students and teachers – to relate to, and probably be affected by, the subject matter of history. The issues for reflection in this chapter are certainly different and perhaps more demanding. Their focus is not so much on an analytical response prompted by classroom interaction but might require a more considered, almost philosophical approach. It might be worthwhile considering the proposition that, as a beginning history teacher, you have been developing a reflective approach to history teaching and have developed a more sophisticated understanding of what makes an effective lesson: focused enquiries, good use of source material, activities which both intrigue and challenge. A question raised in this chapter focuses on the different challenges that certain kinds of history present to history teachers. These challenges might therefore be described as 'sensitive', 'emotive', 'emotional' and 'controversial'. The history itself might be controversial: the SHP Modern World study which has as its focus terrorism, has attracted the indignation of the *Daily Mail* but the SHP module on Ireland managed to do the same in the 1980s. Would an examination of the pro-appeasement line of the *Daily Mail* of the 1930s provoke similar outrage? The focus of this next discussion, however, is not to suggest approaches to history teaching which assuage the sensitivities of the *Daily Mail* but to reflect on different approaches to the history that provokes, disturbs or challenges, and to consider how these approaches might be conditioned or influenced by the nature of the history.

## WHY DO WE TEACH SUCH DIFFICULT TOPICS?

This aspect of school history went under a number of guises (and none at all) for many years. It has probably been recognized that there are some issues or topics which are difficult to teach for any number of reasons. The difficult to teach topics demonstrate once again that history is probably a school subject unlike any other. In March 2007 the Historical Association produced a report for the DfES with the appropriately enigmatic acronym *TEACH: A Report from The Historical Association on the Challenges and Opportunities for Teaching Emotive and Controversial History 3–19*. The report is essential reading. It is a dispassionate analysis of the problems associated with teaching 'difficult' history and provides a number of case studies which examine how teachers in a range of schools deal with the issues of emotional or controversial history. Their definition of emotive and controversial history (below) is not necessarily

comprehensive and bears some of the hallmarks of either being written by a committee or of being constrained by a very particular brief.

> The study of history can be emotive and controversial where there is actual or perceived unfairness to people by another individual or group in the past. This may also be the case where there are disparities between what is taught in school history, family/community histories and other histories. Such issues and disparities create a strong resonance with students in particular educational settings. (HA, 2007: 3)

Several things become clear on reading the report. It is eminently sensible; this is not meant in a disparaging way for the report contains good practical advice and highlights why and how some history might be considered difficult to teach. The report's definition, however, is also limiting, and again this can be picked up in terms of the nature of the historical topics which are the focus of discussion. Issues are emotive and controversial when students are forced to confront brutality, inhumanity and injustice: obvious examples are the Holocaust and the transatlantic slave trade. History becomes emotive and controversial when past events have a resonance with current problems faced by society, such as racism, terrorism and Islamophobia. While mathematics teachers might be expected to demonstrate how and where their Programme of Study might coincidentally, accidentally or in a totally contrived manner address all society's problems, you can see where the difficulties lie for you as history teachers.

The TEACH report was accompanied by a short piece in the *Guardian* which best sums up one of the elements identified by the authors of the report as problematic. The article was headlined 'Schools drop Holocaust lessons' and went on to discuss how the sensitivities, or prejudices, of local communities might affect the way that schools dealt with some topics in the history curriculum. A link to this article can be found on the companion website. It would be worth downloading and reading this article as a starting point for your thoughts on this topic

## Points for Reflection

These issues are significant and do represent a real challenge to history teachers but are in some respects limiting. Consider the implications of both the definition of emotive and controversial history and the *Guardian* piece, for your own developing practice.

- Some history is difficult to teach because it requires schools or individual teachers to deal with (or confront) issues such as racism.

- In some instances antipathy to teaching about the Holocaust might come from other minority communities who themselves are, or have been, the victims of racism.
- Some ways of teaching about the transatlantic slave trade or the Holocaust can reinforce a negative view of African-Caribbean people and Jews as victims.
- Teaching Islamic history is difficult: the subject matter might be unfamiliar; teaching about Islam or about terrorism might again harden attitudes rather than develop a sense of understanding.

Thinking about these issues actually demonstrates how relevant history is. The issues themselves and the difficulties they present in developing your philosophy of (or for ) teaching history inextricably link school, community and the wider society.

## Points for Reflection

The next series of prompts considers these issues in terms of aims and purpose: to what extent are the issues raised legitimate.

- Is history being used as a propagandizing tool (however benign)?
- Does the fact that the DfES commissioned the TEACH report imply that there might be a correct way to teach some historical topics?
- Does the report recognize that history teaching has a socially useful role to play both in school and in the wider community?

The points below may appear too trite, too idealistic, too naive or too simplistic; nevertheless they are worth serious consideration:

- History teaches children valuable lessons.
- History can help children to be more understanding, more tolerant.
- If we can learn the lessons of history we might be able to prevent events like the Holocaust happening again.
- Teaching some of these topics encourages respect for all: valuing diversity and challenging racism through the curriculum.

## TEACHING SENSITIVE ISSUES: BARRIERS TO UNDERSTANDING?

The TEACH report has certainly highlighted an aspect of the emotive and the controversial, but it might be useful to consider why history has this ability to engage students with difficult and challenging subject matter. It is largely because history is one 'bloody thing' after another and then a whole subsequent series of other 'bloody things'. History might be about human achievement but it is also, undeniably, about the depths, the outer limits, of inhumanity and barbarity. Why are Hitler and Stalin such fascinating characters? Why might young historians study the Nazis at every stage of their secondary schooling and then some more in university? Why do so few undergraduates decide to follow modules in Renaissance ideas? This is an element of emotive and controversial history which the TEACH report does not necessarily address in any real detail. The shocking, the gruesome, the graphic side of history requires a careful or circumspect consideration for very different reasons: we do need to treat the minds of young people with respect. We might live in a very graphic age, young people might be inured to violent images and there is a school of thought which seeks an immediate engagement with the shocking image or the graphic account. This is not an attempt to develop a particular moral standpoint or an attempt to turn back any particular kind of tide. The issue is about the effective engagement of young minds with subject matter which might be described as challenging. Is shock really the best way to achieve this? Teaching some of these topics, before the days of acronyms, was referred to as teaching sensitive issues: perhaps there is still a place for an appreciation of why some issues can be described as sensitive.

Before examining some of these issues it is worth considering the barriers to understanding: why might some pupils find understanding these topics difficult? This might best be illustrated in the following way. One of the first published survivor accounts of the Holocaust was by Ka-Tzetnik 135633 (Concentration-Camp Inmate 135633). He made an important reference to 'Planet Auschwitz' – a world outside the experience of most people. There was nothing about Auschwitz that connected to the normal world; it was a place where values were turned inside-out, a place that is only possible to comprehend through experience. Understanding Auschwitz, the argument went, was impossible if you had not been not there. Such a view suggests that history teachers might just as well pack up and go home because we cannot really comprehend the past, but Ka-Tzetnik's view does raise an important question: 'Are there areas or aspects of human experience which students could find difficult to understand?' In July 2006, John Browne, Chairman of BP, took part in *Desert Island Discs*. Part of the conversation focused on his mother who was an Auschwitz survivor. Shortly before she died he visited the United States Holocaust Memorial Museum with her; Browne was deeply affected by the experience and wondered if it would be too much for his mother. Much to his surprise she dismissed it as just photographs. There was no smell, no sounds;

from the photographs alone she, at least, felt that you could not really understand what Auschwitz was really like.

It might be that one task, as history teachers, is to try and help pupils understand; but without recognizing that there might barriers to understanding it can be difficult to help students to make sense of aspects of the past. This appears to be an odd stance; it might be that you do not consider this an issue as such topics have an in-built ability to provoke students' interest, resources are accessible and are inherently interesting.

## Points for Reflection

- Using the ideas of Ka-Tzetnik 135633 and Lord Browne's mother do you think it is impossible either to know or understand Auschwitz? If we were not there, is it possible to have the capacity to imagine what Planet Auschwitz was like?
- Are you in a situation to understand what we might mean by 'barriers to understanding'?



One way to think about this issue is to think about the idea of developing an empathetic understanding, but this is a difficult term to pin down and its use in the history classroom is fraught with difficulty: 'Empathy is not a special facility for getting into other people's minds. If understanding people in the past required shared feelings, history would be impossible. We cannot experience the fear felt by people in Britain in 1940 that Hitler might triumph and occupy their country' (Lee, in Donovan and Bransford, 2005).

The aim must always be to develop students' ability to understand aspects of emotive or emotional history. It is important to recognize that learning history in schools involves more than academic exercises and engages students with moral concepts such as humanity and inhumanity, and this inevitably involves the development and exercise of imagination (Husbands, 1996: 65). Empathy or historical imagination both suggest an approach to history which might be less than rigorous, perhaps dangerously subjective and liable to lapse into sloppy value judgements.

This is not the end of the matter. Booth refers to imaginative engagement as probably one of the most 'advanced' skills that a history undergraduate is likely to develop, characterized by: 'the ability to connect with issues and historical agency in ways that seem to bring the past to life and cast new light upon it' (Booth, 2003: 26). Similarly one of the qualities of mind identified in the QAA subject benchmark statements refers to a history graduate's ability to 'read and use text and other source materials, both critically and *empathetically*'.

The implication is that this kind of historical thinking is complex and challenging, something perhaps for undergraduates to aspire to; but where does this leave school history? (Elton, in Ballard, 1978) suggested that working with primary sources was not for school children. Should we add to this list the notion of imaginative engagement with the past? In some respects the difficulties have already been highlighted in earlier discussions about students' understanding of the past – students' ability to 'write off people in the past as not as smart as we are' (Lee, in Donovan and Bransford, 2005: 47). It might be better if we attempt to articulate what we want students to achieve by confronting some of these difficult areas of history; the recognition that in the history classroom we need to engage emotions as well as intellects (Husbands, 1996: 66) and that we want students to care about people in the past. If students treat people in the past as less than fully human and do not respond to those people's hopes and fears, they have hardly begun to understand what history is about. (Lee, in Donovan and Bransford, 2005: 47). It might be for these reasons that it is important to understand the significance of barriers to understanding.

To try to demonstrate what we mean by barriers to learning, it might be useful to focus on an aspect of the First World War. This might not qualify as an emotive or controversial topic but might serve to demonstrate the idea of barriers to learning. Trench warfare is a good subject to teach but students often develop a stereotypical view of the war on the Western Front – mud, blood, mad generals, lice and trench foot, and then over the top. Not only is this 'bad' history in that it reflects both a dated and an oversimplified view of the Western Front; it has a strong focus on the gruesome which is far removed from pupils' experience. They might try to imagine what living in a trench was like, what it was like to go over the top, but they are imagining a world that was 'horrible', 'muddy', 'smelly'. They cannot imagine living in these conditions and therefore it must have been 'awful' with the result that they 'feel sorry' for the soldiers living in these conditions.

The Holocaust is one of the areas of history which is so horrific and possibly beyond rational understanding that it can be difficult to know where to begin. There has to be a purpose to any inquiry as the TEACH report recognizes. There is so much which is horrific that teaching activities might be nothing more than a combination of prurient voyeurism and preaching. The

article by Paul Salmons (2003) 'Teaching or Preaching' is a valuable overview of some of the practical issues involved. There are a number of important considerations. One concerns the images themselves; a common series of photographs frequently found in textbooks uses images of Belsen, taken shortly after its liberation in April 1945: piles of bodies in mass graves, British soldiers bulldozing decomposing corpses into mass graves. Such images, often in grainy black and white undoubtedly have an immediate impact but, from experience, the lasting effect is limited. Often such images are thought of as less real by students. They are old, they are from the past but they lack a certain something. There is a degree of detachment between past, which is black and white, and present, which is in colour. One of the criticisms made by Claude Lanzman in 1994 of *Schindler's List* was that Spielberg's decision to film in black and white made the events less real. The significant issue here, though, is the imagery which is used to support teaching and, in this, Paul Salmons's view is important. Such images reinforce the idea that Jews were simply anonymous victims of the Holocaust – ultimately they represent nothing more than a pile of bodies. Getting young people to engage with a difficult subject like the Holocaust is more effective if a link can be made with real people, in everyday situations, which they can relate to and which therefore have some relevance to their lives.

> The Holocaust can be taught effectively without using any photographs of piles of naked bodies, and the overuse of such imagery can be harmful. Engendering shock and revulsion is unlikely to constitute a worthwhile learning experience. It can, though, have a dehumanising effect and reinforce a view of 'Jews as victims'. Even in mass death, the individual human being needs to be recognised. There is a moral imperative to give victims a face and a name, or – as Shulamit Imber from Yad Vashem has said – 'to rescue the individual from an anonymous pile of bodies'. (Salmons, 2003: 147)

Images can be used in a number of ways. Those which puzzle, which ask intriguing questions, are probably more effective in developing students' awareness of the significance of some of the issues.

## Points for reflection

How can a photograph of a pre-war school trip tell us about the impact of the Holocaust? How do you bring home to students the scale of destruction which the Holocaust had on Jewish communities across Europe? Use the image of the class of Polish schoolgirls on the companion website. This was a photograph which turned up in the 1950s. One of the girls on the photograph is writing to another and the heading is: 'That was a wonderful trip.' Before reading the letter it might be useful to consider what – under more normal circumstances the two girls would write about or remember of a wonderful school trip. This activity begins with something which students, and PGCE trainees, can identify with, and asking them to write their own account of a wonderful trip brings a realization that there might be a link between students now and then.

When students read the real account by Stefa Starszewska, one of the schoolgirls, they are faced with the reality of the Holocaust.

- By using a series of resources like this you might want to consider how the image and the written account made you think about one small episode of the Holocaust.
- It would be useful to consider how you feel these resources provide you with a different perspective about the Holocaust. Might this approach differ from the usual approach you might have followed if you studied this as part of your undergraduate studies?
- If you were to consider this as a teaching approach with a specific aim – that of helping students understand something about the scale of destruction – how might this evidence be useful.

---

If you felt that the previous exercise dealt too much with emotions and consequently the historical element became less significant, you might like to consider the following extract from Alan Booth. It raises very directly this issue of difficult, emotive or controversial content and is something to reflect on, particularly in relation to your own experience of learning history.

> Establishing a personal connection to past events is at the heart of many history undergraduates' rationale for studying the subject. For them linking historical issues to their own concerns and values makes history relevant, inspires interest and generates motivation. It is no coincidence that the topics in the history curriculum most attractive to history undergraduates are those involving issues of civil, political and human rights, for these connect directly to issues of personal identity and provoke emotional as well as intellectual responses. In the history classroom learning is not compartmentalized; rather the emotional and cognitive are interactive. (Booth, 2003: 7)

Booth raises an important issue well worth considering in terms of your own interests in history and your motivation for selecting particular modules or areas of interest. You might also believe that history is the dispassionate examination of historical evidence in the search for one version of the truth but, as Booth suggests, one of the reasons why history has an appeal is the ability of the subject matter to enable the reader or researcher, the undergraduate or the amateur, to engage intellect and emotion: historians have feelings and they can be motivational. The executive summary of the TEACH report recognizes the importance of this element of teaching: 'Emotional engagement is a feature of effective teaching of controversial issues. The students have to want to care enough about the issues to arouse both their curiosity and their willingness to engage fully with the questions that are likely to require hard thinking and problem-solving' (HA, 2007: 4).

The crucial issue here is, how do you trigger that emotional engagement? The text below helps to demonstrate how this emotional engagement might work at different levels. In 1985 the French film-maker Claude Lanzman was making a ground-breaking documentary about the Holocaust, entitled *Shoah.* It was largely an oral history but at a number of key points in the film the historian, Raul Hilberg, provided further explanation about the significance of particular episodes in the Holocaust. Hilberg used a simple railway timetable produced by the German authorities running the railway network in occupied Poland. First, Hilberg points out the banality, the everyday nature, of the documents – *Fahrplananordnung* – the timetables for the 'special trains' were not kept particularly secret, *'nur für Dienstgebrauch'* – for internal use only which Hilberg claimed to be a 'very low classification for secrecy'. He even speculates that by not marking the document *Geheim* (secret) it raised little curiosity. This document went to every station on the route – in this case from Warsaw to Treblinka — a large number of people would therefore be aware of the constant traffic of *PKRs* the special trains. Hilberg talks Lanzman through the German Railway shorthand explaining what was happening at each step of the way:

> We are going from (train number) 9228 to 9229, to 9230, to 9231. Hardly any originality here. It's just very regular traffic. (Lanzman - 'Death traffic') Death traffic. And here we see that starting out in one ghetto which obviously is being emptied, the train leaves for Treblinka. It leaves on the thirtieth of September, 1942, eighteen minutes after four o'clock — by the schedule at least — and arrives there at eleven twenty-four the next morning. This is also a very long train, which may be the reason it is so slow. It's a 50G — *fünfzig Güterwagen* — fifty freight cars filled with people. That's an exceptionally heavy transport. Now once the train has unloaded at Treblinka — and you notice there are two numbers here: 11.24, that's in the morning, and 15.59 ... in that interval of time the train has to be unloaded, cleaned and turned around. And you see the same numbers appear as *Leerzug*: the now empty train goes to another place. (Lanzman, 1985: 138-40)

In terms of thinking about your emotional engagement with this document it would be useful to consider the significance of the language. We are used to the language of the Holocaust, the euphemisms the Nazis employed to disguise murder – from *Endlosung* – the final solution which described Nazi policy, to *Sonderbehandlung* – special treatment – the fate of most Jews who arrived at Auschwitz. What is unremarkable about the terms used in the timetables is that they are probably still in use. The key to this document, and the key to understanding what we mean by emotional engagement is where

Hilberg makes the comment: 'If you count up the number of not empty trains but full ones – *PKRs* – we may be talking about ten thousand dead Jews on this one *Fahrplananordnung* here'.

There are also a number of different layers where your abilities as graduate historians can take you. This is what Booth means by the engagement of the emotional and the cognitive. One informs the other to develop a deeper, more complex understanding of history. Does such a document challenge a particular understanding of the Holocaust? To what extent were the timetablers working for German Railways complicit? Is there something odd or banal about the very precise time that the train was due to leave a particular Polish ghetto? Was Treblinka or Auschwitz simply a destination?

It is not suggested that this is a way to engage students in Year 9 or Year 10 with the Holocaust. The significance of the exercise is to help you model the way your own thinking developed, the way your understanding grew as you read Hilberg's analysis. This practical way of demonstrating how the different elements of your graduate understanding might help you to develop a more nuanced awareness of the issues. Hopefully, you can see how what we might call emotional intelligence can unlock that deeper realization of the historical significance of a relatively simple document. In the film, Hilberg holds up the piece of paper and says emphatically 'we may be talking about ten thousand dead Jews on this one *Fahrplananordnung* here'. As history teachers, claims we might make about helping students to work like historians could be difficult to sustain. It is, however, more credible to believe that our teaching can help students to relate to the past in ways very similar to Hilberg in *Shoah*.

Teaching about the Holocaust presents you with a number of challenges in your teaching career and does need you to be clear about the nature and purpose of your teaching and your students' learning, but as we have tried to demonstrate, this kind of teaching can be transformative, particularly if it is in a whole-school context rather than within the confines of the history classroom. There are more controversial topics that present an entirely different challenge which is recognized by the authors of the TEACH report.

> History helps students to ask and answer questions of the present by engaging with the past. It fires their curiosity and imagination, moving and inspiring them by the dilemmas, choices and beliefs of people in the past. It helps them to develop their own identity through an understanding of history at personal, local and international levels. (QCA Introduction to KS3 history curriculum, quoted in HA, 2007: 11)

> In contemporary Britain, where – (recent) – events have led to heightened racial tensions, learning about (the) relationship between the West and Islam are potentially the most controversial and challenging aspects of the Key Stage 3 history curriculum. (HA, 2007: 11)

## BARRIERS TO TEACHING: SUBJECT KNOWLEDGE AND TEACHER CONFIDENCE

The 'Diversity and divisions' issue of *Teaching History* is a valuable starting point for exploring some of these issues and as a beginning teacher it would be useful to consider the art of the possible. Again the key issue is the nature, the integrity of the historical enquiry or activity which you might be involved in. Teaching Islamic history is clearly complex and Kinloch's article contains a timely health warning: 'The understandable attempts – made by many schools in the days and weeks after 11 September – to give students a crash course in Middle Eastern current affairs risked presenting Islam simply as that which opposes and is opposed by, the West' (Kinloch, 2005: 26).

There are clearly different challenges in different schools. In almost exclusively white areas history teachers could well be faced with challenging stereotypical views which might be Islamaphobic, racist or both. In schools with significant numbers of Muslim students the issues might relate to feelings of isolation or persecution. There might also be an issue which was raised in the *Guardian* article, mentioned at the beginning of this chapter, which referred to one school deciding not to teach the Crusades because it conflicted with the view of events presented by a local mosque. This is a challenge and history teachers might rightly feel apprehensive about tackling such a difficult area, but such issues can be taught in a very direct way. From the same *Teaching History* issue, Alison Stephen (2005), who teaches at Abraham Moss School in Manchester, describes how she teaches the Arab–Israeli conflict in Year 11.

Abraham Moss School is ethnically very diverse and, significantly, 60 per cent of the school population is Muslim. The department's approach to teaching history emphasizes the importance of the students' own roots and traditions, but also aims to develop their students' understanding of the opinions and beliefs of others (Stephen, 2005: 5). Conventional wisdom might suggest that studying the Arab–Israeli dispute in the current climate is decidedly risky, however, a number of comments by students referred to in Stephen's article provide useful anecdotal evidence: for example, 'the crisis is still going on today … you need to know the background before talking about it in the future' and 'I now feel confident to join in a conversation about the conflict'. (Stephen, 2005: 5) The comments are valuable, demonstrating as they do the ability of good history teaching to empower students, who felt that their history GCSE lessons were enabling them to develop their own understanding of issues which had a relevance to them.

The Stephen (2005) article also demonstrates that the perceptions of adults and students can sometimes differ in ways which are completely unexpected. Conventional wisdom would identify the influx of Jewish immigrants to Palestine in the 1930s as a factor in the rise of hostility between the different communities; however, Alison Stephen's observation is valuable: 'I encountered some interesting attitudes. For example, there was shock at the Arab fears about Jewish immigration. Most students saw immigration as a positive thing, and found it hard to understand Arab fears of possible economic or political threats' (Stephen, 2005: 6).

It might be hard to understand what was going on in these lessons about the Arab–Israeli conflict but perhaps another article in the same issue of *Teaching History* has something to offer in the way of explanations. Over a number of years Alan McCully has been researching the differing attitudes of young people in Northern Ireland to the Troubles. Community history is partisan and Catholic and Protestant communities have very different histories, but it is the attitude to school history which might be relevant to what was happening in a multi-ethnic school in Manchester:

> The majority of students also demonstrated an awareness that the history they encountered in popular representations, especially in the community, was often partial and fragmented, and frequently politically motivated. In contrast school history was almost universally recognised as different, more comprehensive, objective and multi-perspective. Students valued school history and consciously and explicitly expected it to provide a more balanced alternative to community influences. Particularly they sought formal study that related directly to an increased understanding of contemporary issues. (Kitson and McCully, 2005: 32)

The significance of some of these issues will be considered later because there is another side to the equation. Kitson and McCully's article goes beyond examining students' opinions and attempts to identifies how students have come to express their views in such a forthright way. It is down to teaching – or to a particular kind of teaching. The article identifies a range of attitudes among history teachers which they characterize as avoiders, containers and risk-takers (Figure 10.2). This

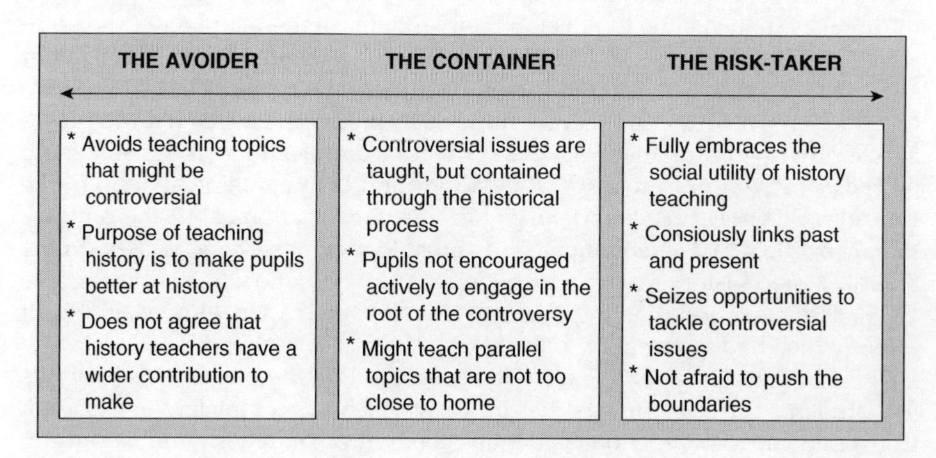


**Figure 10.2** Avoiders and risk-takers (Kitson and McCully 2005)

classification is exceptionally useful if you are considering teaching a controversial topic like Islamic history. You might initially feel that such a topic is difficult to teach or too controversial to tackle but if you read the summary of students' views from Northern Ireland with the ideas in Figure 10.1 you might understand how and why Alison Stephen was able to tackle such a controversial topic in inner-city Manchester.

## Points for reflection

- If you were teaching Islamic history how do you think the evidence from the study of students' attitudes in Northern Ireland and the observations from the students at Abraham Moss could influence the way you decide to approach the topic?
- How do you think the teaching approaches of avoiders and risk-takers might differ in the way they dealt with a topic like Islamic history?
- As a beginning teacher, one of your aspirations should be to develop a teaching style of your own. How has this discussion challenged you?



Teaching Islamic history quite possibly exemplifies the notions of 'difficult' history and 'controversial' history. The following checklist might not be complete but it typifies many of the reservations which teachers might have about teaching aspects of Islamic history:

- unfamiliar or inaccessible subject matter
- Islamic historiography
- teachers not comfortable with subject
- lack of resources and lack of time to create resources
- worthy but dull history
- tokenistic
- reinforces stereotypes
- teaching the Crusades is divisive
- lack of relevance.

These issues, real and perceived, are undoubtedly barriers to effective teaching but they are not necessarily insurmountable and in the following discussion it might be useful to consider how some of the points under consideration link to these barriers to effective teaching. Kinloch's article, referred to earlier, begins by considering the wisdom of using Islamic history as a lens to understand current events in the Middle East. The remainder of the article appears to dwell on obstacles which experienced history teachers are likely to encounter. While Kinloch is ultimately optimistic in his exploration of Islamic historiography there is one huge caveat in the discussion which could cast a degree of uncertainty in the minds of teachers about the 'correct' way to approach Islamic history.

> Western teachers ought to feel confident that they can undertake the teaching of Islamic history; they need only bring to it the same respect that they would bring to any form of historical enquiry, and a willingness to obtain guidance, where necessary, from Muslim authorities as well as Western ones. They need confidence in themselves as teachers; they have the expertise to help their students make sense of this aspect of the past. (Kinloch, 2005: 28)

Equally, history teachers might make too much of the perceived difficulties of understanding Islamic historiography and are perhaps either worrying unduly or being oversensitive. History written from different perspectives is important, but this observation by Carole Hillenbrand is important in restoring a sense of balance:

> It is vital to avoid viewing Islamic history exclusively from the western perspective. Even Orientalists (have) often been rightly criticised in the past for having a colonialist agenda and for being unable to represent the views of the indigenous peoples of the Middle East. Thus it might be argued that the writing of the Islamic view of the Crusades should be left on the whole to Muslim scholars themselves. This is, of course a reasonable point of view but it is a sad fact that the best Muslim historians have, as it happens, specialised in other areas. (Hillenbrand, 2006: 4)

The alternative perspectives are out there and they are accessible. The other significant barrier to the effective teaching of Islamic history is uncertainty or unfamiliarity with the subject matter itself. There are a number of preconceptions or misconceptions which are worth exploring. One of these is the assumption that Islamic history inevitably means a study of the Crusades. In some schools it is the case that the only Islamic history students might undertake is tangential or coincidental to a study of the Crusades. This without doubt reinforces the idea that the history curriculum is Eurocentric and the emphasis is on the impact of the Western crusading armies on the Muslim inhabitants of the Middle East. Another difficulty is the accessibility of suitable resources. Again this is not an insurmountable problem but the QCA Scheme of Work for the topic is decidedly thin. The suggested activities might be placed firmly in the 'worthy but dull' category.

A new text by Byrom, Counsell and Riley in the Longman Pearson series might provide some useful ideas. The example referred to in the Kinloch article is also useful in that it demonstrates the scope and range of Islamic history: the Ottoman Empire played a significant part in European history certainly from the fifteenth through to the twentieth centuries, but again we tend to view it from a series of Western perspectives, from the Bulgarian atrocities to the 'Sick Man of Europe'. It is quite reasonable to argue that one popular view – a Western interpretation of the Crusades – was a product of a growing antipathy to the Ottoman Empire combined with a romantic Gothic view of the Crusaders. The illustrations of Gustave Doré might be said to typify this mid-nineteenth-century attitude, a link is available on the companion website, www.sagepub.co.uk/secondary.

It is not the purpose of this chapter to offer advice on how to teach particular topics but to help you reflect on issues of principle which ought to influence your approach to teaching. Again it might be useful to revisit the Kitson and McCully article (2005). One key to the effective teaching of controversial topics was the sense of relevance to students and their developing sense of identity but the important factor is the willingness of teachers to be risk-takers. In the context of teaching Islamic history, perhaps the risk comes from challenging perceptions.

We also tend to like our history neat and tidy; divided up, compartmentalized. History begins and ends at determined points; 1485 to 1603 for example. Our histories are also histories of regions and areas. But history is not always well behaved and it is the fuzziness, the blurred edges, which offer opportunities to challenge our preconceptions and the way we might package the history we present to students. A typical history of the Crusades might, then, make assumptions about 'the Holy Land' just as we make assumptions about the Middle East today. It was then, and is now Islamic. The truth is clearly different; Damascus was, and still is, home to one of the oldest Christian communities in the world. Society in the Middle East was very diverse. Muslims, Jews and Christians lived together in a state of reasonable toleration. Even more unusual is the fact that the different Christian churches more or less tolerated each other, but then the Roman Catholics were not represented at the end of the eleventh century. This level of complexity still exists as the following press release, concerning the visit of the Archbishop of Canterbury to the Middle East in October 2007 demonstrates:

> In Syria and Lebanon the Archbishop spent time with other Church leaders, including the Patriarchs of Antioch and All the East for the Greek Orthodox, HB Ignatius IV, the Syrian Orthodox, HH Zakka I, the Maronites, HB Cardinal Sfeir, and the Melkite Greek Catholics, HB Gregorios III, as well as the Armenian Catholicos of Cilicia, HH Aram I. These encounters enabled the Archbishop and those accompanying him, to develop a deeper understanding of the

challenges facing these communities. (www.archbishopofcanterbury.org/releases/071005a.htm)

The scope of Islamic history can be challenging simply because it is unfamiliar but it has a great deal to offer in the way that it can challenge preconceptions. It also can serve to illustrate that link, and relevance of the distant past, with recent history and challenge some of our contemporary misconceptions, or preconceptions. This complexity is at the heart of *Ornament of the World* by M.R. Menocal (2002); the sub-title of the text is revealing: 'How Muslims, Jews and Christians created a culture of tolerance in Medieval Spain'. Perhaps Menocal tries too hard to paint a picture of an Andalusian golden age where the three religious communities could and did live together in relative harmony. The text is useful and demonstrates how we have a number of ingrained European, Christian preconceptions – perhaps not 'us' individually but our collective Western views. The events which ended with the fall of Granada in 1492 is known as the *reconquista* – the re-establishment of Christianity in Spain. It suggests a particular view of the history of Iberia: that Spain had been subject to military occupation by Islamic conquerors since the eighth century and that a Spanish, Roman-Catholic society was either driven out or suppressed for almost 800 years. Was it a *reconquista* or just a more straightforward conquest? Does *reconquista* somehow imply that the Islamic civilisation which thrived in al-Andalus for 800 years was not a native European Islamic civilization, merely a temporary foreign import?

What is certain is that by the end of the fifteenth century the new Spanish monarchy had effectively set in motion a process of ethnic cleansing. Jews and Muslims who refused to convert to Christianity were forcibly expelled and even those who had converted were viewed with suspicion. It the case of the Spanish Muslims, the Moriscos, it is inevitable that many of their ancestors were originally Christian converts to Islam.

Our compartmentalized view of history then notes: the Jews were expelled from Spain and they become a footnote in Spanish history because they disappear from one part of the Mediterranean. In time they become an interesting feature of another history. Many of the expelled Sephardic Jews were welcomed in the Ottoman Empire, in Constantinople and in particular in Salonika where, by the middle of the sixteenth century they made up 50 per cent of the population. But this is more than a footnote; the Sephardim were welcome and openly encouraged, because they brought with them their skills, their contacts and their aptitude for trade. They play a significant role in the history of another geographical space. In time Salonika became the most important European city of the Ottoman Empire, and the Jewish community was at the heart of this prosperity. By the early twentieth century Salonika had become Thessalonika, a Greek regional capital, and the Jews had become Greek Jews. The Muslims were less welcome and, in the 'population exchanges' which took place in the Balkans and in Turkey following the First World War, the 'Turks' of old Salonika were resettled in Anatolia.

The point was made earlier that we like our history tidy; we like certainties, and complex and confusing detail is unhelpful. In our teaching we will pass over this Balkan history despite the fact that it came back to haunt Western Europe at the end of the twentieth century. If the Ottoman Empire might be held up as an alternative or different model of diversity, but never an ideal model, it is possible to identify the factors or forces which held the different provinces of that empire together. There are always exceptions in time and place, and generalization is never a precise, or desirable, historical tool but it is possible to ask how the many different groups did manage to live together in varying degrees of harmony for relatively long periods of time. Our Western view of the Ottoman Empire is that is was either an Oriental threat and Eastern Europe was conquered and ruthlessly suppressed, or that it was the 'Sick Man of Europe', in a state of advanced and continuous decay. Louis de Bernieres's (2005) portrait of the closing years of the Ottoman Empire in a small village in Western Anatolia provides one insight. It perhaps presents too idyllic a view of a community of amiable peasants part Turkish, part Greek, their identities shaped by religions that reflected custom rather than zealous belief. They were all Ottoman but Turk Ottoman or Greek Ottoman, and this puzzle of diversity and identity is at the heart of the novel.

The events in the Balkans and the near East are peripheral to our history. We often refer to the complexities of the Balkans at the start of the twentieth century, and the two Balkan Wars in the years immediately preceding the First World War served to increase hostility between Austria–Hungary and Russia. We rarely look at these wars and yet are surprised by the violent nationalism which tore the region apart in the 1990s.

Both Menocal and de Bernieres present an essentially optimistic view of what was possible in the recent or not so recent past. Their respective histories demonstrate the nature of the complex relationships between the three Abrahamic religions. The absolutist certainties which are a feature of Middle Eastern politics today were not typical of the Ottoman Empire or of al-Andalus. It might be possible to argue a convincing case for a culture of tolerance, which is central to Menocal's argument; certainly Moslems and Jews appeared to have a level of mutual understanding which was not always apparent between Christians and Moslems and Christians and Jews. This throws a different light on the idea of diversity. Our Western or British view of diversity tends to focus on the notion of difference rather than the connections and the links which make the diversity less of a problem. Again, the history of al-Andalus or the history of the Ottoman Empire provides a very different model of cultural transmission and of cultural and social relations. A Eurocentric view of diversity tends to emphasize the importance of the dominant culture which imposes its view on a nation or an empire. In the UK the terms English and British are used almost interchangeably by the English, but to the Welsh, the Scots and the Irish the word English often means 'the other'. Such a model of diversity reflects the cultural dominance of one group, and this historical view.

The TEACH report has some useful general guidelines that demonstrate that there is even more need for rigour in the planning stage to make the activities engaging and challenging:

> Activities are more likely to be successful when
>
> - students are given specific investigations, geared around enquiry questions that require engagement with the historical process.
> - students have to work independently; when there is sufficient time for indepth analysis.
> - teaching emotive and controversial issues is unlikely to succeed where little attention is paid to the precise learning objectives that link the key concepts to specific content. (HA, 2007: 7)

## Points for reflection

Points for reflection

You might be tempted to think that some emotive or controversial history lessons simply require students to express views or react to powerful images or texts. The Historical Association on the other hand feels that such approaches might be counter-productive and that the focus for any work which might be termed emotive or controversial needs to be sharply focused and, if anything, more carefully planned than usual.

Can you think of arguments for and against the Historical Association view?

On further reflection, can you understand the perspective of the Historical Association?

## USING THE PAST TO UNDERSTAND THE PRESENT: USING THE PRESENT TO ACCESS THE PAST

This final discussion focuses on the issue of relevance. One of the common questions history teachers are challenged with is 'what's the point of studying the past?' or variations on that theme. The Historical Association uses these lines and these arguments very effectively in their promotional material which goes out to secondary schools each year to help raise the profile of the history department and encourage more students to continue with their history at the end of Year 9. In some ways this goes back to some of the points raised in the first chapter, which asked you to justify the place of history in the curriculum. One of the posters uses the images of 9/11 to make the link. Immediately after these events students wanted answers to questions: why did these shocking events happen? History teachers were able to provide some of the answers. There has always been a realization that this is an important aspect of history teaching and it is perhaps one which you will need to be more aware of. An important element of the SHP GCSE course has been a Modern World study. This part of the course has a very explicit aim – to help students develop a deep and informed understanding of a contemporary issue. Earlier in this chapter you saw how one head of history in Manchester taught the Arab–Israeli conflict in the Middle East as a way of making the subject relevant for her GCSE students.

This aspect of history teaching has always been controversial. In the 1980s one of the Modern World 'options' was Ireland, and history teachers and the examination boards occasionally had to defend themselves against accusations of teaching IRA terrorism. In just a few years this has become legitimate and relatively uncontroversial. Understanding how the peace process was an eventual consequence of the hunger strikes and the Brighton bombing, even in the eyes of the *Daily Mail*, is now a legitimate historical enquiry. Chris Culpin now has to defend teaching about terrorism as students are 'exposed' to al Qaeda propaganda.

It is also possible to use contemporary events as a means to developing a deeper understanding of the past. Each year, at the start of the course, one of the fieldwork activities Edge Hill University trainees take part in is a town trail in Liverpool. The focus is on the home front, and the May blitz of 1941. The trail uses a range of primary sources to develop an understanding not just of the history but the changing townscape. The first source is an extract from *The Cruel Sea* by Nicholas Monsarrat (2002) which we read at the Pier Head. It narrates the arrival of the *Compass Rose* back to its home port, Liverpool, shortly after the blitz. Monsarrat describes the scene, more or less from the same place, as it appeared in 1941. The activity began as an attempt to show how novelists use language not just to describe a scene, but to use sound and smell as well. This makes the history more personal and more real. The first time this trail ran was a week after 9/11. The fictional experience of the crew of *Compass Rose* was seen through the eyes of everyone who had witnessed the events in New York a week earlier. The sights, sounds and smells of the clouds of smoke and dust rising up from the city; the loss of familiar landmarks had an impact on the New Yorkers, just as the destruction of much of the city centre had an impact on the crew of *Compass Rose* in 1941. The eventual loss of life in New York on 9/11 closely matched the civilian casualties in Liverpool in 1940 and 1941. By throwing some more figures into the equation you can develop almost a double perspective. Total US losses on D-Day were 1465 dead, 3184 wounded and 1928 missing.

The ability to make these links is neither fortuitous nor phoney, but demonstrates how history is able to provide a means of using the familiar to link past and present. Having the ability to make links in this way is important. The May blitz is still a significant event in Liverpool's recent past; photographs taken at prominent places in the city enable the students to judge the scale of destruction and personal letters remind them of the human cost. They are able to develop that link between New York and Liverpool and have some understanding of what New Yorkers must have been feeling. The connections between past and present almost become blurred. In 2005, undertaking the same field visit there was a new point of reference, trying to develop an understanding of the problems which Liverpool faced in the immediate aftermath of the May blitz became clearer as the story was unfolding in New Orleans after Hurricane Katrina. In one week in May 1941 40 per cent of the housing stock of Liverpool was destroyed or so badly damaged as to make the houses uninhabitable. Despite this, the local government continued to function, people were rehoused and fed, and the city and its docks continued to operate.

Kitson and McCully make reference to this past–present–past approach but you should be able to see the real power of this way of teaching difficult history. Not only does it make the subject more relevant, but it can actually be empowering. It provides a way into discussions, and it might help students understand and articulate their ideas in situations which might be quite difficult to cope with. This does not meant that it is possible to summon up some historical parallel to put the present into perspective. We should not aim to be time conjurers performing neat tricks for every difficult occasion, but in a careful and sensitive manner it might just be possible to help students develop responses which consider different perspectives and contexts.

### What the research says

Teaching Emotive and Controversial History: How the research is developing

This aspect of history teaching is one that is very much in the hands of the practitioners: the history teachers themselves. Over the years there has been a great deal written from the perspective of using topics such as the Holocaust as a vehicle for delivering citizenship. Ian Davies et al. in *Teaching the Holocaust: Educational Dimensions, Principles and Practice Continuum* (2001) considers a wide range of ethical and pedagogical issues but this text was more a reflection on existing practice. A review article in *Teaching History* by Kinloch (1998) is worth careful re-reading because it raises important issues about the way history teachers might – should or could approach teaching the Holocaust. Clearly the events of 9/11 changed attitudes and perspectives and added another dimension to the idea of emotive and controversial history. As teachers we are told we have a duty to promote community cohesion but there is little out there to guide us. We run the risk of our teaching becoming bland and anodyne for fear of offending cultural and/or political sensitivities. The *Teaching History* article by Kitson and McCully (2005) suggests that effective teaching in this area is down to teachers who are willing to take risks. Alan McCully and Keith Barton (2005), examined pupil attitudes in a divided society and their work provides some valuable insights into the ways that different communities view their histories. Their work might provide you with some ideas about approaching controversial history. For a very different perspective a recent Teachers TV programme 'Teaching History – How Do They Do It In Bosnia provides a valuable perspective. http://www.teachers.tv/video/21611

## *Further reading*

Booth, A. (2003) Teaching History at University: Enhancing Learning and Understanding. Abingdon: Routledge.

Kitson, A. and McCully, A. (2005) '"You hear about it for real inschool." Avoiding, containing and risk-taking in the history classroom', *Teaching History*, 120: 32–7.

McCully, A. and Barton, K. (2005) 'History, identity, and the school curriculum in Northern Ireland: an empirical study of secondary students' ideas and perspectives', *Journal of Curriculum Studies,* 37(1), 85–116.

## *Useful websites*

Live links to these websites can be found on the companion website.

Nicolas Kinloch's (1998) review of Michael Burleigh's Ethics and Extermination, in *Teaching History*, 93.

Kinloch, N. (2001) 'Parallel catastrophes? Uniqueness, redemption and the Shoah', *Teaching History*, 104: 8–14.

The pointers here are very much focused on approaches to teaching. You might want to explore issues relating to teaching black history: the following link will take you to Dan Lyndon's Black History site which explores teaching approaches and develops a strong philosophical approach which might be useful if you are trying to articulate your ideas: www.blackhistory4schools.com/blog/.

If you go to the Teachers TV website you will also be able to watch or download two programmes which focus on approaches to teaching black history.

To develop a more sympathetic perspective on the Crusades you might like to go to the following weblink to the film, *Kingdom of Heaven*: www.apple.com/trailers/ fox/ kingdom_of_heaven/.

This link takes you to a discussion item on the BBC News website about the contemporary significance of the Crusades: http://news.bbc.co.uk/1/hi/world/ 4938202.stm.

This link takes you to a discussion on the BBC history site and places the events of 9/11 in a historical context: www.qca.org.uk/history/innovating/history_matters/ worked_for_ me/ks3/cameo9.htm.

# 11 WHERE DO YOU GO NOW?

**This chapter considers the following issues:**

- your transition from graduate historian to beginning history teacher
- growing your pedagogical craft knowledge and how to think in a more instinctive way about your teaching
- developing a more reflective perspective within your day-to-day practice
- how the aspects of advanced study in your PGCE programme can both inform your practice and make your teaching a more rewarding experience.

One defining feature of your professional development is the move from the possibly less structured world of researching and writing your dissertation to the more structured and methodological world of social sciences. You cease to be a 'footnoter' and reluctantly become a Harvard 'referencer'. As you might expect, making the transition from student to teacher is down to how you feel about your professional development and your capacity to be evaluative and reflective. This is not a Cartesian model, 'I reflect therefore I must be a teacher', but it is recognizing how you feel differently about being in school and teaching history. There will be a number of external references which indicate that you are making progress:

- You feel comfortable in the classroom.
- You relate well to the students you are teaching and the teachers you are working with.
- You are making sense of, and coping with, the course documentation (this last bit might be a lie).
- You can manage most groups with a degree of confidence and competence.
- You are beginning to understand how to put a lesson together.

These factors are all outward signs of your developing confidence but a key marker will be your ability to reflect and evaluate over and beyond the: 'that seemed to go alright, no major riot, I think the kids got what I was saying or most of it'. Evaluating lessons can be a chore, particularly if you view it in a mechanistic way. Developing an appropriately reflective and evaluative approach is akin to talking to yourself – or asking yourself questions. You might like to consider that evaluations take place on two different levels:

- Impressionist. You evaluate the lesson based on how you feel it went, you might take into account a number of reactive features of the lesson: did the students behave, did they complete the work, did you come away with a 'good feeling'?
- Reflector. The impressionist position is your starting point. You instinctively feel that the lesson went well but you want to know why. Were the students better behaved because Fred was absent or was it because the starter activity had captured their imagination?

Making the move from impressionist to reflector is one of the stages you will reach where you begin to think like a history teacher. The idea of professional reflection is at the heart of teaching at every level and it might be valuable for you to refer back to the diagram of Kolb's model of experiential learning (Figure 5.1). Being able to develop a critical and reflective appreciation of your teaching has to serve a purpose: to improve the quality of your teaching and the effectiveness of your students' learning. Again, if you refer back to Chapter 6, the weakest feature of most teachers' 'teaching' was their ability to make a significant connection between assessment and future planning. Assessment does involve measuring students' progress, but at the level of day-to-day teaching much of this 'assessment' is going to be formative. If you are able to develop the skills of critical reflection one of the aspects of the reflective framework is to ask the questions:

- What did the students learn?
- How do I know that they learnt?
- What made the learning less effective?
- How do I make the learning more effective?
- Finally, what do they need to learn next?

If you refer back to Table 1.3 in Chapter 1, you might like to consider how your capacity for critical reflection is linked to your growing professional craft knowledge, in particular your new 'knowledge of teaching history'. The different elements of this can be seen in Table 11.1. For any history lesson you teach you will consciously or unconsciously take these factors into account.

The example used in Table 11.1 focuses on a Year 7 lesson based on the Battle of Hastings. The prompts in Table 11.1 represent some of the questions you might well consider when constructing the lesson. These questions only focus

**Table 11.1** Thinking about new professional craft knowledge

| **Aspect of craft knowledge** | **Developing reflective questions:** |
|---|---|
| 1. Pedagogical content knowledge about HOW to teach history: | |
| 1a. Structuring approaches to topics. | • How am I going to approach teaching the Battle of Hastings: simple narrative or conflicting perspectives?<br>• What should students know/understand/be able to do?<br>• How do I make evidence accessible to students: move from individual account to individual account *or* reflect phases of battle? |
| 1b. Knowledge of underlying· concepts and procedures | • Develop ideas of causation/ideas of complex causes/hierarchy of consequences<br>• Understanding value/importance of evidence<br>• Communicating understanding via extended writing – PEE/hamburger paragraphs *or*<br>• Group presentation<br>• Previous work on causation? Revisiting concepts and processes |
| 1c. Knowledge of teaching strategies – role plays, group work, etc. | • Focus question William lucky? Harold unlucky?<br>• Writing structured paragraphs<br>• Group work – 4/6 groups examine story from Norman/Saxon perspectives |
| 2. Curriculum knowledge | • Do I know how this topic relates to KS3 Programme of Study GCSE/GCE syllabus?<br>• Where does this lesson appear in a school/personal scheme of work?<br>• Can I use this lesson to link to literacy strategies and develop writing skills or presentational skills? |
| 3. Organizational knowledge | • How do I build in appropriate level of challenge with top set/more able?<br>• How might I vary structure/support to make activity accessible for less able?<br>• How am I going to organize groups in each class? |

on one element of your developing professional craft knowledge: 'the knowledge of teaching history'. It is not that you do not use your 'graduate knowledge of history', which might be considered latent, hiding in the background. Your graduate subject knowledge begins to play a different role in your teaching. Without the hidden foundations, even though they are invisible, you know the whole building is going to fall down if they are not there. If you were to think back to the way you planned a topic earlier in your PGCE year you would have felt the need to place 'pure subject knowledge' nearer the top of the pile. As you become a more effective teacher, thinking about lessons calls on the different types of understandings outlined in Table 11.1. You should have realized that yet again you are drawing on your metacognitive abilities, and critical reflection is another element or another characteristic of the effective teacher. If you self-consciously use these tools to plan your lessons, you are equally going to be able to call on them to evaluate your lesson. By this stage in your PGCE year you should be looking at Table 11.1 as a structure for evaluating your lessons. It may appear to be a long-winded mechanism but it may also help you to move from impressionistic to reflective evaluations.

## MAKING EFFECTIVE USE OF OBSERVATION FEEDBACK

The key influences on your development as a reflective teacher are likely to be your mentor and your university tutor. Feedback from lesson observations provide you with an ability to really get inside your lesson and develop a searching professional dialogue. There is a tendency to view these events as hurdles to be crossed or stumbled over and there is a natural sense of relief when an observed lesson is over. To get the most benefit from these exchanges you do need to develop an awareness of what transpires.

Some of the following points may be of value:

- Do you have a focus for your observation? This might be based on a target set from a weekly mentor meeting or a tutorial. For example, you might be worried that you are using questioning to keep the boys focused on their work. Consequently, girls might feel excluded. Can your mentor/tutor focus on this issue for you?
- How history-specific is the focus of the observation? It would be useful to try and break these down into general issues. These often include working with the less able in mixed-ability groups or maintaining the pace of a lesson. The other focus is on history-specific issues. Are you happy with the way you use evidence in your classroom? Why do you think some students find interpretations difficult – do you find interpretations difficult? Can you use some of the headings in Table 11.1 to focus on history-specific issues?
- If you feel that there are aspects of history teaching which are proving to be particularly problematic, you might like to consult the 'Move me on' section in *Teaching History* – don't be too surprised if some imaginary PGCE trainee has had similar problems.
- Could you use your VLE as a sounding board for your thoughts after the lesson observation? In this way one of your colleagues may be able to provide you with a series of different perspectives.
- You may have 'evaluation templates' to use as part of your course paperwork. These often provide a suitable focus for your ideas and subsequent discussion.
- If something happens in the lesson or if you feel that there is a significant moment, make sure that you make a reference to this – perhaps on your lesson plan for discussion later.
- There is a tendency to focus on management, simply because you are at an early stage in your career. Unless the group is especially problematic try not to make management the significant focus of your observation.

Be prepared to consider the dialogue after the feedback. Again your VLE is valuable. One of the difficulties with lesson feedback is that it does not necessarily provide you with the opportunities to really reflect. At the end of the lesson it can sometimes be useful to take a few minutes to collect your thoughts and ideas about the lesson. Your plan should provide you with a useful starting point to begin your reflections. Very often the opening line from mentors and tutors runs along the lines of, 'How did you feel the lesson went?' This is your opportunity to begin the debriefing process. The temptation is to dwell on what you felt went less well than you anticipated. This can prompt the 'it was all crap' response, or what is being described this year as the 'Britney meltdown moment'.

### A trainee's evaluation of her first full lesson

Second lesson was OK. It was on trench warfare. Used a DVD but was kind of forced into it by the head of history and it wasn't that good. Then told them a bit about conditions in the trenches, using sources on the PowerPoint and asking them questions. This bit was bad. I wanted it to be dead interesting but didn't really hit the mark. I know all the theory behind asking good questions but it was dead hard and I was pretty bad at it. Also I don't think I knew enough stories about the trenches – but I did mention a few. After this they had to write a diary extract for one day. I gave them a day each and when we put it together it'll be a whole month. They seemed to keep on track and actually enjoy it but it wasn't very exciting all the same.

What I'm trying to say is I'm a bit deflated. I knew it wouldn't be a dream lesson or anything but the teacher didn't have anything positive to say about it at all. He said my PowerPoint should have been sharper. This was all stuff that I was aware of during the lesson but didn't really know how to address. I had to pat myself on the back at the end about things that went well – such as classroom management (Year 9 just after dinner), and keeping everyone on task. I know that these were good points and think I just needed to hear him say it.

Is this being a critically reflective history teacher? Can I have a master's now?

The evaluation above was posted on the university VLE later in the day following the lesson. The lesson itself was taught early in the initial placement. The edited feedback below was provided via Web Ct the following day.

### Providing tutor feedback via the VLE

The group are good at sharing experiences and are supportive and very positive but at a very early stage in their PGCE year most had not had the opportunity to teach a full lesson so they were, quite rightly, in awe of Clare for having taught two lessons

*(Continued)*

*(Continued)*

back to back. Under these circumstances it is important to get more focused and more positive feedback. At this early stage of the PGCE year relationships with mentors and members of history department are still being developed and it is important to maintain their confidence. The feedback addresses specific issues related to the lesson but hopefully also gives you an insight into the way a tutor might look at what is being taught and how feedback might be organized into coherent sections. In this case the feedback was a response to Clare's evaluation of her lesson.

**1. Handling feedback**

The trainee's reflections were really very perceptive for someone so early in their practice. There was an awareness of the parts of the lesson which worked less well and an understanding of why these were the weakest aspects of the lesson. Equally there was an honest admission that she did not really know how to turn this around in the middle of the lesson. In some ways this is equally perceptive, recognizing as she does that she has not the depth of experience to devise an improvised response.

The evaluation also highlighted a common feature of trainees' early teaching practice – over reliance on PowerPoint or inappropriate use of the technology. In part this stems from that transitional view of history as a body of knowledge and their role – as transmitters of that knowledge.

**2. Responding directly to trainee's perceived problems or issues**

- I think you were aware of problems you had/you faced. Sometimes it is/can be useful to 'get your retaliation in first', let the mentor know you didn't feel lesson went too well – this was one of your 1st after all.
- Ask mentor about DVD – say you were not too sure about how to use it – how would he/she have done this/used this?
- Similarly ask the mentor for ideas about how he would have tackled the topic – the kind of work he would have asked pupils to undertake.
- PowerPoint – there is a danger that new teachers become too reliant on PowerPoint and you present them with information overload – an illustrated lecture.
- Are you/were you aware of how long your PP went on for?

**3. Reference points: learning from others**

It is also important to remind trainees of the wider experiences they might have had. They often tend to see things in isolation and don't make connections across different elements of their course. Later in their practice the ability to see the bigger picture develops. The reference here is to Peter Duffy's Home Guard lesson in the planning session. Rather than just see the film in relation to planning there are other sequences that can be used to highlight very different aspects of history teaching. In this case the link was being made between the problem of 'transferring information' and the PowerPoint and developing alternative strategies.

- You could try looking at the Peter Duffy's Home Guard lesson – how long did he talk to students for?
- How did he get over 'subject knowledge' to whole class? – via the card sort.

- Look at what they were doing sorting ideas into 2 piles – good things about/ bad things about.
- This point/counterpoint idea is a good way to encourage discussion & debate.

**4. Suggesting alternative strategies**

It is always important to relate one teaching experience to another to develop a comparative approach. If this had been a more formal observation/feedback session a mentor might have asked if they had tried this approach with another group or year. The trainee had identified aspects of her teaching which she either found difficult or was less happy with: the PowerPoint as the source of information and her questioning skills. The bullet points try to suggest alternative ways of managing these aspects of her teaching.

- If in doubt get them working/make them work & use opportunity to question/ talk to individuals/groups/pairs.
- The questioning will always be difficult early on but if you get them doing the work they could then be asking *you* questions and you begin to pick up on what they understand or how they are seeing things.
- If they ask questions try not to just give them answers, try to develop a dialogue. Your opening line might be 'why did you say/why do you think ...?'
- What are they likely to write – would they simply take your information and 'put it in their own words'?
- Could you get them to present a report on the trenches?
- Could you give one half of class positive images/accounts of trench life and the other half more stereotypical views and then get them to make presentations and look at their reactions – What might they conclude about Trench Warfare?

**5. Subject knowledge: analogies and relating personal experience**

The Trench Diary or the Letter from the Trenches is a very popular activity, there is a wealth of good source material easily available but the trainee clearly felt less than comfortable with her own grasp of detail 'the stories of the trenches'. Obviously the students' views of the trenches is going to be conditioned by the worksheets or text books or resources which they work with but it is always worth asking: 'How much of trenches is outside their experience'. Do you think you presented a stereotypical view of trench warfare? Trainees naturally focus on the dreadful aspects of the war in the trenches but if you begin with what the students are familiar with, it can be as easy as relating things to their everyday experiences.

- They might know 'cold'. Have they been fishing in winter? Have they been riding their bikes on a paper round in January? Have they got really cold at a football match?
- On the other hand do they know hot – no sun tan lotion in summer – they get 'done' if they take their shirt off and get sun-burnt. They have to wear a woollen vest and thick woollen shirt in summer.

*(Continued)*

*(Continued)*

- What about spring/summer – could it actually be pleasant in French countryside?
- Winters could be cold and wet BUT there tended to be no big battles, the Somme/Ypres/Arras were all spring/summer offensives and the numbers holding trenches tended to be reduced and turn around times more frequent e.g. 3 days in front line, 5–8 days in billets behind front line.

**End on a positive**

It is always important to emphasize the positive, in this case an evaluation of a first lesson taught in the Autumn Term.

- Teaching two lessons back to back – and producing the PP was a significant achievement and you should feel confident in what you are doing – you will get better – significantly better but you will also have times when things conspire against you.

## DEVELOPING A CRITICAL PERSPECTIVE

Another common feature of PGCE courses is that they sometimes require you to maintain a reflective log or learning journal; the status of these is often problematic and there may be no clear or firm expectation of what is required. One purpose of these learning journals is to help you develop a reflective approach to your development as a history teacher. They can also be used as evidence that you are 'meeting the Standards'. This piece of jargon is about as useful as the 1992 Lancashire National Curriculum guidance on assessment where students had an opportunity to 'visit a level'. Learning journals are a good idea if they help you to develop a more critical, reflective or evaluative perspective; if they simply record progression across Standards in the following way their value has to be questioned: 'Monday – worked with an NTA, spoke to him before the lesson about helping Freda with the causes and consequences card sort. I now understand the importance of working with other adults in the classroom to promote effective learning.'

If, on the other hand, you were to evaluate your interaction with the NTA, explaining how the discussion with Freda went might be more important than the 'right answer'. Your reflection might then consider Freda's subsequent contribution to the lesson, or the relative improvement in her work. Under these circumstances you have something concrete to base your reflections upon. The format of a learning journal or a reflective log should be flexible and enable you to develop an approach which supports and aids the reflective process. In a similar vein, you need to decide what you record and when you record. If the journal is too retrospective, that is, completed when a deadline is approaching, it is being filled in for the sake of compliance. You might like to consider some of the following pointers;

- Do you reflect on Standards or on lessons? Either can work. If you reflect on a lesson you need to be clear at the end of the reflection which Standards you think you are considering.
- Do you develop a series of threads? This might involve identifying a specific issue which you follow through from week to week.
- Do you work on targets? These might be identified by mentors or tutors, or you could set you own targets.
- Do you reflect on a target lesson or on a day's or a week's progress? Focusing on a specific lesson might be appropriate if you are target-setting. A weekly retrospective evaluation enables you to take a more holistic approach, but you would still be able to set targets for the coming week.
- Be clear in your own mind how you think you are improving as a history teacher and ask yourself how the process of reflection and evaluation is contributing to your professional development.
- Be aware of the Groundhog Day effect: do the same issues recur regularly?

Reflection and self-evaluation are not things you have to 'do' just because you are on a history PGCE course. Professional development is now an integral part of your developing career. After successfully completing the QTS Standards you will find that you are required to meet the NQT Standards and at each step on the way you will find that there are further professional Standards which impact on pay and promotion. At each stage you will be required to provide evidence of your ability to meet the different Standards, and learning journals can be a very useful way of recording your evidence. They are not going to be so divorced from your history teaching either. The new coursework proposals at A level require students to keep a learning record of their work and developing ideas as they prepare their personal studies. This replicates good practice in a number of universities where third-year students keep learning logs of the work they are completing for their dissertations.

If you look through the earlier chapters you will see that a common feature of history teaching and learning is this emphasis on thinking and reasoning. A thinking skills approach is not just about employing particular tricks and strategies every once in a while to enliven your lessons. It is about encouraging a particular approach to teaching and learning which is conducive to good history. History at any level is about rigorous enquiry and developing particular attitudes of mind; that these attributes are also highly useful for all young learners is a bonus. Critical reflection is a key element of metacognition and is therefore part of the process of developing as an effective history teacher – but then you know that already.

**Level 6 Honours Degrees**

A systematic understanding of key aspects of their field of study, including acquisition of coherent and detailed knowledge, at least some of which is at or informed by, the forefront of defined aspects of a discipline

**Level 7 Master's Degrees**

A systematic understanding of knowledge, and a critical awareness of current problems and/or new insights, much of which is at, or informed by, the forefront of their academic discipline, field of study, or area of professional practice

**Figure 11.1** National Qualifications Framework

## ACADEMIC ENQUIRY

As part of your PGCE it is inevitable that you will have to complete a number of assignments. In most universities some, most or all of these will be required to be written at a higher level. There has been an attempt to clarify the 'level' of the PGCE. To most of you it is a PGCE, a qualification you do after graduating, hence it is a Postgraduate Certificate. The new National Qualifications Framework placed final year degree work at level 6 – in this respect if you have a BA honours in History this is a Level 6 qualification. If you go on to further study and obtain an MA this is a level 7 qualification. The MA criteria demand a higher level of thinking but the distinctions between level 6 and level 7 are not necessarily that clear as Figure 11.1 demonstrates. The significant words or phrase in the level 7 qualification might then be 'critical awareness' but for someone with a 2.1 in history the level 6 description might not appear to be either particularly demanding or to reflect the nature of the work that they did for their degree.

Before attempts were made to bring these qualifications into line, some PGCEs were described as Professional Graduate Certificates in Education or the more familiar Postgraduate Certificates. To be awarded a Postgraduate certificate now you need to be able to demonstrate that you can work at level 7, which again might be misleading because you gain an MA traditionally after a course of study – usually one year full time and two or three years part time. The PGCE is full time but 36 weeks of the course are spent in schools and it is therefore also a professional qualification. Can this get more confusing? As a consequence it is expected that in some universities you will have an opportunity to demonstrate the ability to work at Level 7 in some areas of your course and consequently gain some M level credits. Under these circumstances you will be awarded a PGCE (Postgraduate) rather than a PGCE (Professional Graduate). This reasoning is clearly inspired by the following: 'All right. It says the, uh, "The first part of the party of the first part shall be known in this contract as the first part of the party of the first part shall be known in this contract"'. Otis B. Driftwood, *A Night at the Opera*, 1935

Despite the 'Marxist' interlude, these changes are having an impact on the nature of the assignments PGCE history trainees might be required to undertake. There will be an expectation, or you will have an opportunity of working at a higher level. You might believe that this is simply another demand imposed on you in a particularly busy programme during the middle of a stressful year. On the other hand, it presents you with an opportunity to develop a deeper understanding of an aspect of history teaching. It is more than likely that one of the level 7 assignments you can complete will have a very practical focus on teaching history in the classroom. The work may also be based on small-scale research activity which enables you to focus on your own practice or on the way that your students perceive, understand or learn history.

There have been a number of frequent reference points in previous chapters: the book *How Students Learn: History in the Classroom*, chapters in *Knowing, Teaching and Learning History* and numerous articles in *Teaching History*. The common factor is that the authors, be they experienced researchers, history teacher educators or history teachers, are seeking to develop a more informed understanding of how students learn history and how their learning can be made more effective – and enjoyable. It is possible to follow lines of development in teaching and learning: the hamburger paragraph, first suggested as a way of engaging less-able students, has moved into the mainstream and the idea has been applied across the age and ability range. Engaging A level students with historical reasoning and argument develops the hamburger paragraph in a more complex and challenging environment. Similarly the BECTa word-processing materials were originally designed for use with KS3 students but first Gerry was able to use similar ideas to improve the way he worked with evidence and again similar ideas can be used to help A level students manage and analyse large bodies of text.

What you can see developing in the articles in *Teaching History* is the community of practice in action: taking ideas, developing variations on a theme, applying them in their own teaching and sharing the findings. The work of some of the practitioners might be viewed in some areas as episodic or anecdotal and their conclusions tentative, but what remains impressive is the very active community of history teachers who are thinking deeply about their practice. Their work is well informed and they are thinking critically and reflectively about their practice. More significantly, these articles have had an impact on the teaching and learning of history, certainly since the late 1990s.The opportunity to investigate an element of your practice can help you to understand something about the process of teaching history and it also places you within that important community of practice.

## HOW DO YOU GO ABOUT INVESTIGATING YOUR PRACTICE?

The beginning of this chapter remarked on moving from a being footnoter to a Harvard referencer. As you may have guessed there is more to working in the social sciences than simply different referencing conventions. If you are researching any aspect of your practice you do need to be aware of the new or different academic conventions that will impact on your practice. It is highly probable that your PGCE course will provide you with guidance on the different research methodologies and on research ethics. It is also inevitable that you will have course-specific guidelines about the precise nature and focus of your research. If you have completed a history research project, be it an undergraduate dissertation or work for a higher degree, the contrast between that and educational research could not be more different.

Research in the social sciences is more 'organized' and deciding on an appropriate approach to researching your practice – the methodology – is important. For example, you might decide that you want to investigate how less-able students work with visual sources and you plan a series of lessons where the students work with photographs or cartoons. Evidence for their understanding will come from work they do in their exercise books and an analysis of your teaching over the series of lessons. This could have the makings of a useful enquiry but you would need to sharpen up the focus of your enquiry. When you come to begin thinking about your research activity you might like to consider these issues:

- *Rationale.* What is the focus? Why is it important? Do you have a hypothesis? Can you draft a statement of purpose?
- *Research questions.* Refine your rationale. What critical questions must you answer? Try and list three?
- *Scope and sample.* Who are you researching? When? Where?
- *Research literature.* Which key texts, journals, documents are relevant? How are they important?
- *Intended research methods.* How will you collect data? Interviews, questionnaires, observations, others?
- *Data analysis.* How will the data collected be used and presented? (Graphs, tables, quotes?)
- *Ethical challenges.* Impact on the researched? How will you inform and protect the researched?

## STRUCTURING YOUR WRITING

Much will depend on the precise format of your postgraduate work but it would be worthwhile considering the structure and formal organization of a journal article. This model might provide you with a sense of direction and it might provide you with a useful end product.

## The abstract

This should provide a very brief overview of the purpose behind your work and its place in an overall academic context (approximately 150 words).

## Introduction

You should use this section to place your work in the context of other work that has been carried out and to demonstrate how your work is looking at specific areas/issues that have relevance to the general body of academic theory and practice.

## Areas of discussion

This section should look at your own findings in detail, considering (where appropriate) any methods used in data collection before describing and presenting your data in appropriate forms and analysing and explaining your findings both in terms of your own interpretations and the previous findings of other researchers in related and relevant areas.

## Conclusion

You should draw together the findings discussed in the previous section to produce appropriate conclusions which should reflect the abstract and provide a cohesion to the whole piece.

It might be worthwhile considering some of the 'titles' listed below in terms of 'good enquiry questions'. In Chapter 3 and again in Chapter 4 discussion focused on the importance of good focus questions to drive a student enquiry forward. Do the potential 'research' tasks or questions meet the criteria?

- The role of focus questions in creating a challenging enquiry: do they enhance learning?
- Use word processing to develop students' abilities to develop an understanding of causation.
- Can the use of a range of VAK activities help improve engagement and assessment scores in SEN pupils?
- Do thinking skills improve historical understanding?
- To what extent does variety of learning styles close the achievement gap between boys and girls in history at KS3?

If you look at this work as an opportunity to pursue an aspect of history teaching which you find interesting, you will naturally be more motivated to pursue your line of enquiry. While the end result should be rewarding and give you a sense of professional pride, it should also make you more curious about your teaching as the project is under way. Ethical considerations mean that you will already have discussed your work with your mentor. It would seem sensible to keep your mentor up to date with your work. Even if your mentor is not directly involved in your work they could act as a useful sounding board, helping you to develop further your own ideas. In some partner schools trainees undertaking work like this have actively collaborated on aspects of departmental practice. The end result benefits both trainee and partner school. As with everything, if you view the research task as yet another hurdle to cross you are simply going to regard it as something which is as inescapable as death and taxes.

## YOUR NQT YEAR: AND BEYOND

If you thought your PGCE year was hard …

There is no doubt that the responsibility of being a full-time history teacher is demanding and you will inevitably find the going hard, but what you have developed over your PGCE year is a quality which might be described as academic resilience. You have the ability to meet the expectations placed on you as a teacher in a school and to gain a more developed understanding of history teaching. The physical demands may be considerable, you might even be surprised to discover that you were to some extent 'protected' during your PGCE year, but you will also have learnt a great deal and those difficult aspects of teaching are now less of an obstacle. As one former trainee remarked:

> You're a proper teacher now, you have your own classroom, the kids know you're for real and you belong to the school. You've got so much more respect. I can't believe things are so much different.

You will still have the Standards to meet and records to keep but these will link to your career entry and development profile (CEDP). At first glance it may appear as the final lock on the gate but the role of the CEDP has changed over the years. Yes, you will have to meet agreed targets during your NQT year but the CEDP is also about recognizing your entitlement to continuing support and continued professional development. As you complete your PGCE year you will be expected to decide your 'training needs' for your NQT year. To some extent these will be influenced by your progress and the interests you have developed, largely in your final placement. You might also like to consider what your new school might need from you, or how you feel your school might need to support you in your early career. A common area is to gain a deeper understanding of the demands of public examination courses. You might, for example, not have had an opportunity to teach on the SHP GCSE course. Your new history department might therefore think it appropriate to send you on some syllabus-specific course. On the other hand, you might want to deepen your understanding of thinking skills. It could be that this is an LA priority and you might get to go to Blackpool for the weekend – which is how one LA in the North West sometimes manages staff development.

It is highly likely that much of the support and the staff development opportunities you can take advantage of during your NQT year will be geared to supporting you in a physically demanding year but, like your PGCE year, you could well find yourself in the company of other NQTs in your school and perhaps in the wider LA.

Staff development is now seen as a continuous process. It is seen as beneficial and helping to motivate staff. It is also an entitlement and the opportunities for staff development are more tailored your needs and more readily available. There is also a link to be made with your PGCE qualification. You may have wondered where the M level work was going; what was the point of all that extra work just to get 'post' rather than 'professional' on your PGCE Certificate? Any M level credits which you were awarded as part of your PGCE qualification now count towards any accredited CPD course you might wish to pursue. Some may view the CPD system as a clever trick to tie in teachers to their university education departments, but I could not possibly comment. From a personal perspective I do know that this is a highly-effective way of developing and extending a community of practice. Former history PGCE trainees become motivated MA students. They are frequently the skilled and enthusiastic mentors who work with beginning teachers. They are also the skilled history teachers who ensure that history will always be one of the best taught subjects in our schools.

**What was professional development like?**

In the good old days before the National Curriculum, local authorities employed subject advisers who often organized in-service courses. The quality and range of courses were variable but they often helped to foster local communities of history practice. They encouraged autonomy and reflective practice.

In the bad old days of the early 1990s with the first version of the National Curriculum and the first Ofsted inspections, teacher autonomy and reflective practice was considered a bad thing and history teachers had to be told what to do. Local authority advisers became Ofsted inspectors to make money for their cash-strapped (then) LEAs. In-service courses were reduced to instruction on how to prepare for Ofsted inspections and how to teach and assess Hi1(a) and Hi1(c). This training was only for heads of department who were then expected to pass on the good news to the rest of the department. This system of in-service was known as the cascade model.

*(Continued)*

*(Continued)*

We also had to attend school Inset days which were initially called Baker days after Kenneth Baker the Secretary of State for Education. During these Inset days which were usually the last day of term, or the day before the first day of term, managerial head teachers would often castigate the rest of the staff about the GCSE pass rate, or infect everyone with his or her Eeyore-like sense of pessimism at the prospect of an impending Ofsted inspection. At times Inset days were used to get the school ready for open night. This gave teachers the opportunity to change their wall displays at least once a year.

The only flicker of light was provided by Ted Wragg who allegedly referred to Baker days as B-days and the cascade system as the piston model.

One might be tempted to say that all this changed on the 2 May 1997 but again Ted Wragg brought a sense of perspective to proceedings with leaks about the latest policy initiatives from the Prime Minister's personal office. Who can ever forget the fictional Greek madman who came up with those implausible ideas: Mr Tony Zoffis – I wonder where he is now!

## *Further reading*

Live links to these sites can be found on the companion website.

*Research Methods in Education* by Cohen, L., Manion L., and Morrison K. Chapter 3, Research design issues – planning research.

*A Newly Qualified Teacher's Manual: How to Meet the Induction Standards* by Sara Bubb.

## *Useful websites*

Live links to these websites can be found on the companion website.

www.teachernet.gov.uk/professionaldevelopment/induction/guidance/
www.standards.dfes.gov.uk/research/
www.centres.ex.ac.uk/historyresource/journalstart.htm

# BIBLIOGRAPHY


Aldrich, R. (ed.) (1991) *History in the National Curriculum*. London: Kogan Page. pp. 62–92.

Arthur, J. and Phillips, R. (eds) (2000) *Issues in History Teaching*. London: Routledge.

Arthur, J., Davies, I. and Phillips, R. (eds) (2001) *Citizenship through Secondary History*. London: Routledge.

Ashby, R. and Lee, P. (1987) 'Children's concepts of empathy and understanding in history', in C. Portal (ed.), *The History Curriculum for Teachers*. Falmer Press. pp. 62–88.

Assessment Reform Group (2002) *Assessment for Learning: 10 Principles*. Available online: www.qca.org.uk/qca_4336.aspx and www.qca.org.uk/libraryAssets/media/4031_afl_principles.pdf. The web address for the Assessment Reform Group is http://arg.educ.cam.ac.uk/.

Asthana, A. (2007) 'Q: What links the British empire, witch-hunts and the Wild West?', *Observer*, 21 October: http://observer.guardian.co.uk/uk_news/story/0,,2196001,00.html.

Atkin, D. (2000) 'How can I improve my use of ICT? Put history first', *Teaching History*, 99: 42–9.

Baker, C., Cohn, T. and McLaughlin, M. (2000) 'Current issues in the training of secondary history teachers: an HMI perspective', in J. Arthur and R. Phillips (eds), *Issues in History Teaching*. London: Routledge. pp. 191–201.

Banham, D. (1998) 'Getting ready for the Grand Prix: learning how to build a substantiated argument in Year 7', *Teaching History*, 92: 6–15.

Banham, D. with Culpin, C. (2002) 'Ensuring progression continues into GCSE: let's not do for our pupils with our plan of attack', *Teaching History*, 109: 16–22.

Banham, D. and Hall, R. (2003) 'JFK: the medium, the message and the myth', *Teaching History*, 113: 6–12.

Barnes, S. (2002) 'Revealing the big picture: patterns, shapes and images at Key Stage 3', *Teaching History*, 107: 6–12.

Barton, A. and McCully, A. (2007) 'Teaching controversial issues ... where controversial issues really matter', *Teaching History*, 127: 4–10.

Benaiges, P. (2005) 'The spice of life? Ensuring variety when teaching about the Treaty of Versailles', *Teaching History*, 119: 30–5.

Birmingham Grid for Learning: Multiple Intelligences: www.bgfl.org/bgfl/custom/resources_ftp/client_ftp/ks3/ict/multiple_int/index.htm.

Black, P., Harrison, C., Lee, C., Marshall, B. and Wiliam, D. (2002) *Working Inside the Black Box*. London: King's College.

Black, P., Harrison, C., Lee, C., Marshall, B. and Wiliam, D. (2003) *Assessment for Learning: putting it into practice*. Buckingham: Open University Press.

Booth, A. (2003) *Teaching History at University: Enhancing Learning and Understanding*. London: Routledge.

Bourdillon, H. (ed.) (1994) *Teaching History*. London: Routledge.

Brett, P. (2005) 'Citizenship and the National Curriculum', *International Journal of Historical Learning, Teaching and Research*, 5(2).

British Educational and Communications and Technology Agency (BECTa) (1999) *History Using IT: Defining Effectiveness in History Using IT: Approaches to Successful Practice*. Coventry and London: BECTa and Historical Association.

Brown, G. and Wrenn, A. (2005) '"It's like they've gone up a year!" Gauging the impact of a history transition unit on teachers of primary and secondary history', *Teaching History*, 121: 5–13.

Burnham, S. and Brown, G. (2004) 'Assessment without level descriptions', *Teaching History*, 115: 5–15.

Butler, S. (2004) 'Question: When is a comment not worth the paper it's written on? Answer: When it's accompanied by a level, grade or mark!', *Teaching History*, 115: 37–41.

Byrom, J. (1998) 'Working with sources: scepticism or cynicism? Putting the story back together again', *Teaching History*, 91: 32–5.

Byrom, J. (2000) 'Why go on a pilgrimage? Using a concluding enquiry to reinforce and assess earlier learning', *Teaching History*, 99: 32–5.

Byrom, J. (2003) 'Continuity and progression', in M. Riley and R. Harris (eds), *Past Forward*. London: Historical Association. pp. 12–14.

Byrom, J. and Riley, M. (2003) 'Professional wrestling in the history department: a case study in planning the teaching of the British Empire at Key Stage 3', *Teaching History*, 112: 6–19.

Byrom, J. and Riley, M. (2007) 'Identity-shakers: cultural encounters and the development of pupils' multiple identities', *Teaching History*, 127: 22–9.

Calder, A. (1992) *The People's War*. London: Pimlico.

Calderhead, J. (1984) *Teachers' Classroom Decision Making*. Eastbourne: Holt, Rinehart and Winston.

Card, J. (2004) 'Seeing double: how one period visualises another', *Teaching History*, 117: 6–9.

Cercadillo, L. (2001) 'Significance in history: students' ideas in England and Spain', in A.K. Dickinson, P. Gordon and P.J. Lee (eds), *Raising Standards in History Education: International Review of History Education*, vol. 3. London: Woburn Press.

Chapman, A. (2003a) 'Conceptual awareness through categorising: using ICT to get Year 13 reading', *Teaching History*, 111: 38–43.

Chapman, A. (2003b) 'Camels, diamonds and counterfactuals: a model for teaching causal reasoning', *Teaching History*, 112: 46–53.

Claxton, G. (2003) *Learning to Learn: A Key Goal in a 21st century Curriculum*. London: QCA Futures.

Claxton, G. Building Learning Power: www.buildinglearningpower.co.uk/blp/Home.html.

Coffin, C. (2007) *The Language and Discourse of Argumentation in Computer Conferencing and Essays: Full Research Report*. ESRC End of Award Report, RES-000-22-1453. ESRC.

Coltham, J.B. and Fines, J. (1971) *Educational Objectives for the Study of History*. London: Historical Association.

Conway, R. (2006) 'What they think they know: the impact of pupils' preconceptions on their understanding of historical significance', *Teaching History*, 126: 10–15.

Counsell, C. (1997) *Analytical and Discursive Writing at Key Stage 3*. Shaftesbury: Historical Association

Counsell, C. (2000a) '"Didn't we do that in Year 7?" Planning for progress in evidential understanding', *Teaching History*, 97: 36–41.

Counsell, C. (2000b) 'Historical knowledge and historical skills: a distracting dichotomy', in J. Arthur and R. Phillips (eds), *Issues in History Teaching*. London: Routledge. pp. 54–71.

Counsell, C. (2003) 'History for all', in M. Riley and R. Harris (eds), *Past Forward*. London: Historical Association.

Counsell, C. (2004a) 'Looking through a Josephine-Butler shaped window: focusing pupils' thinking on historical significance', *Teaching History*, 114: 30–6.

Counsell, C. (2004b) Editorial, *Teaching History*, 114.

Croft, M. (2005) 'The Tudor monarchy in crisis: using a historian's account to stretch the most able students in Y8', *Teaching History*, 119: 15–29.

Culpin, C. (1994) 'Making progress in history', in H. Bourdillon (ed.), *Teaching History*, London: Routledge. pp. 126–52.

Culpin, C. (1999) 'No puzzle, no learning: how to make your site visits rigorous, fascinating and indispensable', *Teaching History*, 97: 29–35.

Culpin, C. (2002) 'Why we must change history GCSE', *Teaching History*, 109: 6–9.

Culpin, C. (2005) 'Breaking the 20-year rule: a very modern history at GCSE', *Teaching History*, 120: 11–15.

Cunningham, D. (2004) 'Empathy without illusions', *Teaching History*, 114: 14–29.
Cunningham, R. (2001) 'Teaching pupils how history works', *Teaching History*, 102: 14–19.
David, R. (2000) 'Imagining the past: the use of archive pictures in secondary school history textbooks', *The Curriculum Journal*, 11(2): 225–46.
Davies, I. (2000) 'Citizenship and the teaching and learning of history', in J. Arthur and R. Phillips (eds), *Issues in History Teaching*. London: Routledge. pp. 137–47.
Davies, P., Lynch, D. and Davies, R. (2003) *Enlivening Secondary History,*. London: RoutledgeFalmer.
Dawson, I. (2004) 'Time for chronology? Ideas for developing chronological understanding', *Teaching History*, 117: 14–24.
Dawson, I. (2006) Reflections on active learning: www.thinkinghistory.co.uk/Issues/IssueReflections.html.
de Bernieres, L. (2005) *Birds without Wings*. London: Vintage.
Department for Education (DfE) (1995) *History in the National Curriculum*. London: HMSO.
Department for Education and Employment/Qualifications and Curriculum Authority (DfEE/QCA) (1999) *History: The National Curriculum for England*. London: QCA.
Department for Education and Skills (DfES) (2000) *History: the National Curriculum for England*. London: HMSO.
Department for Education and Skills (DfES) (2002) *Access and Engagement in History: Teaching Pupils for Whom English is an Additional Language*. London: DfES.
Department for Education and Skills (DfES) (2004) *Pedagogy and Practice: Teaching and Learning in Secondary Schools Unit 5: Starters and Plenaries*. National Strategy. London: HMSO. Available online: www.standards.dfes.gov.uk/secondary/keystage3/downloads/sec_ppt l042804u5 startplen_a.pdf.
Department for Education and Skills (DfES) (2005) *Key Stage 3 National Strategy: Leading in Learning: Exemplification in History*. London: HMSO.
Department for Education and Skills (DfES) (2007) *Diversity and Citizenship Curriculum Review* (Ajegbo Report) (DfES-00045-2007). London: Department for Education and Skills. Available online: http://publications.teachernet.gov.uk/default.aspx?PageFunction= product details&PageMode=publications&ProductId=DFES-00045-2007.
Department for Education and Skills (DfES) Guidelines: www.standards.dfes.gov.uk/giftedandtalented/identification/recognising/.
Department for Education and Skills (DfES) *Teaching History to Students with EAL*: www.standards.dfes.gov.uk/secondary/keystage3/all/respub/fs_hi_eal.
Department of Education and Science (DES) (1991) *History in the National Curriculum*. London: HMSO.
Dickinson, A.K. and Lee, P.J. (1984) 'Making sense of history', in A.K. Dickinson, P.J. Lee and P.J. Rogers (eds), *Learning History*. London: Heinemann. pp. 117–53.
Dickinson, A.K., Gard, A. and Lee, P.J. (1978) 'Evidence in history and the classroom', in A.K. Dickinson and P.J. Lee (eds), *History Teaching and Historical Understanding*. London: Heinemann. pp. 1–20.
Dixon, J. (2003) 'The hidden crisis in GCSE history', *Teaching History*, 110: 41–3.
Donovan, M.S. and Bransford, J.D. (eds) (2005) *How Students Learn: History in the Classroom*. Committee on How People Learn: A Targeted Report for Teachers. National Research Council. Washington, DC: National Academies Press.
Edwards, A.D. (1978) 'The "Language of History" and the communication of historical knowledge', in A.K. Dickinson and P.J. Lee (eds), *History Teaching and Historical Understanding*. London: Heinemann. pp. 54–71.
Edwards, C. (2006) 'Putting life into history: how pupils can use oral history to become critical historians', *Teaching History*, 123: 21–5.
Elton, R.G. (1970) 'What sort of history should we teach?', in M. Ballard (ed.), *New Movements in the Study and Teaching of History*. London: Temple Smith.
Farmer, A. and Knight, P. (1995) *Active History in Key Stages 3 and 4*. London: David Fulton.

Fisher, P. (2002) *Thinking Through History*. Cambridge: Chris Kington.

Freeman, J. (2004) *The Current State of the 4–19 History Curriculum in England and Possible Future Developments: a QCA perspective*. Available online: www.centres.ex.ac.uk/historyresource/journal10/papers/freeman.pdf.

Gardner, H. (1993) *Frames of Mind: Theory of Multiple Intelligences*. London: Fontana.

Gardner, H. (2003) *Multiple Intelligences after 20 Years*: www.howardgardner.com/Papers/documents/MI%20After%2020_Feb-03_HG.pdf.

Gorman, M. (1998) 'The structured enquiry is not a contradiction in terms: focused teaching for independent learning', *Teaching History*, 92: 20–5.

Grovesnor, I. (2000) 'History for the nation: multiculturalism and the teaching of history', in J. Arthur and R. Phillips (eds), *Issues in History Teaching*. London: Routledge. pp. 148–58.

Guy, J. (2004) *My Heart Is My Own*. London: HarperCollins.

Guyver, R. (2006) 'More than just the Henries: Britishness and British history at Key Stage 3', *Teaching History*, 122: 15–23.

Hammond, K. (1999) 'And Joe arrives …: stretching the very able pupil in the mixed-ability classroom', *Teaching History*, 94: 23–31.

Hammond, K. (2001) 'From horror to history: teaching pupils to reflect on significance', *Teaching History*, 104: 15–23.

Hammond, K. (2002) 'Getting Year 10 to understand the value of precise factual knowledge', *Teaching History*, 109: 10–15.

Harris, R. (2001) 'Why essay-writing remains central to learning history at AS level', *Teaching History*, 103: 13–16.

Harris, R. (2005) 'Does differentiation have to mean different?', *Teaching History*, 118: 5–12.

Harris, R. and Foreman-Peck, L. (2004) '"Stepping into other peoples' shoes": teaching and assessing empathy in the secondary history curriculum', *International Journal of Historical Learning, Teaching and Research*, 4(2): 1–14.

Harris R. and Luff, I. (2004) *Meeting SEN in the Curriculum: History*. London: David Fulton.

Harris, R. and Rea, A. (2006) 'Making history meaningful: helping pupils see why history matters', *Teaching History*, 125: 28–33.

Haydn, T. (2004) 'History', in J. White (ed.), *Rethinking the School Curriculum*. London: RoutledgeFalmer. pp. 87–103.

Haydn, T. (2005) 'Pupil perceptions of history at Key Stage 3: final report for QCA': www.qca.org.uk/libraryAssets/media/qca-06-2335-pupil-perceptions-history.pdf.

Haydn, T. and Counsell, C. (eds) (2003) *History, ICT and Learning in the Secondary School*. London: RoutledgeFalmer.

Haydn, T., Arthur, J. and Hunt, M., (2001) *Learning to Teach History in the Secondary School*. 2nd edn. London: Routledge.

Hellier, D. and Richards, H. (2005) 'Do we have to read all of this? Encouraging students to read for understanding', *Teaching History*, 118: 44–8.

Her Majesty's Inspectorate (HMI) (1985) *History in the Primary and Secondary Years*. London: HMSO.

Hibbert, B. (2002) '"It's a lot harder than politics" … students' experience of history at Advanced level', *Teaching History*, 109: 39–43.

Hillenbrand, C. (2006) *The Crusades: Islamic Perspectives*. Edinburgh: Edinburgh University Press.

Historical Association (HA) (2005) *Curriculum Development Project: History 14–19*. London: Historical Association.

Historical Association (HA) (2007) *Teaching Emotive and Controversial History 3–19 (TEACH 3–19)*. Report for the Department for Education and Skills. London: Historical Association. Available online: www.haevents.org.uk/PastEvents/Others/ Teach%20report.pdf.

History Practitioners Advisory Team (2007) *A Way Forward for School History: A Report Presented to the Shadow Secretary of State for Education*. May. Available online: www.historypractitioners.org/docs/HPAT%20Final%20Report.pdf.

'History in British Education', proceedings from various conferences on held at the Institute of Historical Research in 2005 and 2006. Available online: www.history.ac.uk/education/index.html.

Howells, G. (1998) 'Being ambitious with the causes of the First World War: interrogating inevitability', *Teaching History*, 92: 16–25.

Howells, G. (2000) 'Gladstone spiritual or Gladstone material? A rationale for using documents at AS and A2', *Teaching History*, 100: 26–31.

Howells, G. (2002) 'Ranking and classifying: teaching political concepts to post 16 students', *Teaching History*, 106: 33–6.

Howson, J. (2006) '"Is it the Tuarts and then the Studors or the other way around?" The importance of developing a usable big picture of the past', *Teaching History*, 127: 40–7.

Hunt, M. (2000) 'Teaching historical significance', in J. Arthur and R. Phillips (eds), *Issues in History Teaching*. London: Routledge. pp. 39–53.

Hunt, T. (2007) 'What links the British empire, witch-hunts and the Wild West? Radical changes to the traditional A-level syllabus will create a new way of teaching history in schools', *Observer*, 21 October: http://observer.guardian.co.uk/uk_news/story/0,,2196001,00.html.

Husbands, C. (1996) *What is History Teaching?* Buckingham: Open University Press.

Husbands, C., Kitson, A. and Pendry, A. (2003) *Understanding History Teaching: Teaching and Learning about the Past in Secondary Schools*. Buckingham: Open University Press.

Illingworth, S. (2004) 'Purposeful plenaries': http://educationforum.ipbhost.com/index.php?showtopic=1356.

Jack, P. and Fearnham, E. (1999) 'Ants and the Tet Offensive: teaching Y11 to tell the difference (or: preparing pupils to write well in exams)', *Teaching History*, 94: 32–7.

John, P. (1991) 'The professional craft knowledge of the history teacher', Teaching History, 64(July): 8–12.

Kelly, A. (2004) 'Diachronic dancing', on Ian Dawson's Thinking History website: www.thinkinghistory.co.uk/Issues/IssueChronologyDiachron.html.

Kinloch, N. (1998) 'Learning about the Holocaust: moral or historical question?', *Teaching History*, 93: 44–6.

Kinloch, N. (2001) 'Parallel catastrophes? Uniqueness, redemption and the *Shoah*', *Teaching* History, 104: 8–14.

Kinloch, N. (2005) 'A need to know: Islamic history and the school curriculum', *Teaching History*, 120: 25–31.

Kirk, G. and Broadhead, P. (2007) *Every Child Matters and Teacher Education: A UCET position paper*. London: Universities Council for the Education of Teachers, pp. 11–15 Available online: www.ttrb.ac.uk/attachments/60ed1258-aa90-4335-9546-75163c88770c.pdf.

Kitson, A. (2001) 'Challenging stereotypes and avoiding the superficial: a suggested approach to teaching the Holocaust', *Teaching History*, 104: 41–8.

Kitson, A. (2003) 'Reading and enquiring in Years 12 and 13: a case study on women in the Third Reich', *Teaching History*, 111: 13–13.

Kitson, A. and McCully, A. (2005) '"You hear about it for real in school." Avoiding, containing and risk-taking in the history classroom', *Teaching History*, 120: 32–7.

Klemperer, V. (1998) *I Shall Bear Witness: Diaries 1933–1941*. London: Wiedenfeld and Nicholson.

Klemperer, V. (1999) *To the Bitter End: Diaries 1942–1945*. London: Wiedenfeld and Nicholson.

Laffin, D. (2000) 'My essays could go on forever: using Key Stage 3 to improve performance at GCSE', *Teaching History*, 98: 14–21.

Lang, S. (2004) Address to Schools History Project Conference, July: http://educationforum.ipbhost.com/index.php?showtopic=1616.

Lanzman, C. (1985) *Shoah: An Oral History of the Holocaust*. New York: Random House.

Le Cocq, H. (1999) 'Note making, knowledge-building and critical thinking are the same thing', *Teaching History*, 95: 14–23.

Le Cocq, H. (2000) 'Beyond bias: making source evaluation meaningful to Y7', *Teaching History*, 99: 50–5.
Lee, P. (2005) 'Putting principles into practice: understanding history', in M.S. Donovan and J.D. Bransford (eds), *How Students Learn: History in the Classroom*. Committee on How People Learn: A Targeted Report for Teachers. National Research Council. Washington, DC: National Academies Press. ch. 2.
Lee, P. and Ashby, R. (2000) 'Progression in historical understanding among students ages 7–14, in P.N. Stearns, P. Seixas and S. Weinburg (eds), *Knowing, Teaching and Learning History*. New York: New York University Press. pp. 199–222.
Lee, P. and Shemilt, D. (2003) 'A scaffold not a cage: progression and progression models in history', *Teaching History*, 113: 13–23.
Lee, P. and Shemilt, D. (2005) '"I just wish we could go back in the past and find out what really happened": progression in understanding about historical accounts', *Teaching History*, 117: 25–31.
Lee, P., Slater, J., Walsh, P. and White, J. (1992) *The Aims of School History: the National Curriculum and Beyond*. London: Tufnell Press.
Lee, P.J. (1984) 'Why learn history?', in A.K. Dickinson, P.J. Lee and P.J. Rogers (eds), *Learning History*. London: Heinemann.
Leonard, A. (1999) 'Exceptional performance at GCSE: what makes a starred A?', *Teaching History*, 95: 20–3.
Leonard, A. (2000) 'Achieving progression from the GCSE to AS', *Teaching History*, 98: 30–5.
Lomas, T. (1993) *Teaching and Assessing Historical Understanding*. Pamphlet. London: Histotical Association.
Luff, I. (2000) '"I've been in the Reichstag": rethinking role-play', *Teaching History*, 100: 8–17.
Luff. I. (2003) 'Stretching the straitjacket of assessment: use of role play and practical demonstration to enrich pupils' experience of History at GCSE and beyond', *Teaching History*, 113: 26–35.
Lydon, D. (2006) 'Integrating Black history into the National Curriculum', *Teaching History*, 122: 37–43.
MacNamara, D. (1991) 'Subject knowledge and its application: problems and possibilities for teacher educators', *Journal of Education for Teaching*, 17(2): 113–28.
Martin, D., Coffin, C. and North, S. (2007) 'What's your claim? Developing pupils' historical argument through asynchronous text based computer conferencing', *Teaching History*, 126: 32–7.
Mastin, S. and Wallace, P. (2006) 'Why don't the Chinese play cricket? Rethinking progression in historical interpretations through the British Empire', *Teaching History*, 122: 6–15.
Mazower, M. (2004) *Salonika: City of Ghosts: Christians, Muslims and Jews 1430–1950*. London: HarperCollins.
McAleavy, T. (1994) 'Meeting pupils' learning needs: differentiation and progression in the teaching of history', in H. Bourdillon (ed.), *Teaching History*. London: Routledge. pp. 153–68.
McAleavy, T. (1998) 'The use of sources in history', *Teaching History*, 91: 10–16.
McAleavy, T. (2000) 'Teaching about interpretations', in J. Arthur and R. Phillips, (eds), *Issues in History Teaching*. London: Falmer. pp. 72–82.
McCully, A. and Barton, K. (2005) 'History, identity, and the school curriculum in Northern Ireland: an empirical study of secondary students' ideas and perspectives', *Journal of Curriculum Studies*, 37, 1: 85–116.
McGuinness, C. (1999) 'From thinking skills to thinking classrooms: a review and evaluation of approaches for developing pupils thinking': www.dfes.gov.uk/research/programmeofresearch/projectinformation.cfm?projectid=12823&resultspage=1.
Menocal, M.R. (2002) *Ornament of the World: How Muslims, Jews and Christians Created a Culture of Tolerance in Medieval Spain*. New York: Little, Brown.
Michaux, M. (1997) *Enseigner L 'Histoire au College*. Paris: Armand Colin.

Monsarrat, N. (2002) *The Cruel Sea*. London: Penguin.
Moon, J. (2006) *We Seek It Here; a New Perspective on the Elusive Activity of Critical Thinking: a Theoretical and Practical Approach*. Bristol: Escalate.
Moon, J. (2006) *Learning Journals: A Handbook for Reflective Practice and Professional Development*. London: Routledge.
Moore, R. (2000) 'Using the Internet to teach about interpretations in years 9 and 12', *Teaching History*, 101: 35–9.
Moorhouse, D. (2006) 'When computers don't give you a headache: the most able lead a debate on medicine through time', *Teaching History*, 124: 30–6.
Mulholland, M. (1998) 'Frameworks for linking pupils' evidential understanding with growing skill in structured written argument: the evidence sandwich', *Teaching History*, 91: 17–19.
Murray, M. (2002) '"Which was more important Sir, ordinary people getting electricity or the rise of Hitler?" Using Ethel and Ernest with Y9', *Teaching History*, 107: 20–5.
National Academy for Gifted and Talented Youth (NAGTY) (2005) *Supporting High Achievement in History: Conclusions of the NAGTY History Think Tank 28 & 29 November 2005*. Warwick: National Academy for Gifted and Talented Youth.
National Council for Educational Technology (BECTa)/Historical Association (NCET/HA) (1998a) *History Using IT. Improving Students' Writing Using Word Processing*. Coventry: NCET.
National Council for Educational Technology (BECTa)/Historical Association (NCET/HA) (1998b) *History Using IT. Searching for Patterns in the Past Using Databases and Spreadsheets*. Coventry: NCET.
Office for Standards in Education (Ofsted) (2000) *Subject Reports Secondary History*. London: HMSO. Available online: http://www.ofsted.gov.uk/assets/2909.pdf.
Office for Standards in Education (Ofsted) (2004) *Subject Conference Report: History: Interpretations of History*. Available online: www.ofsted.gov.uk/assets/3794.pdf.
Office for Standards in Education (Ofsted) (2004a) *2004 Report: ICT in Schools – the Impact of Government Initiatives: Secondary History*. London: HMSO. Available online: www.ofsted.gov.uk/assets/3645.pdf.
Office for Standards in Education (Ofsted) (2005) *The Annual Report of Her Majesty's Chief Inspector of Schools 2004–5*. London: HMSO. Available online: http://live.ofsted.gov.uk/publications/annualreport0405/subject_reports.html.
Office for Standards in Education (Ofsted) (2007) *History in the Balance: History in English Schools 2003–07*. Available online: www.ofsted.gov.uk/publications/070043.
Pankhania, J. (1994) *Liberating the National History Curriculum*. London: Falmer Press.
Phillips, R. (1998) *History Teaching, Nationhood and the State*. London: Cassell.
Phillips, R. (2000) 'Government policies, the state and the teaching of history', in J. Arthur and R. Phillips (eds), *Issues in History Teaching*. London: Routledge. pp. 10–23.
Phillips, R. (2001) 'Making history curious: using Initial Stimulus Material (ISM) to promote enquiry, thinking and literacy', *Teaching History*, 105: 19–25.
Phillips, R. (2002) 'Historical significance: the forgotten "Key Element?"1', *Teaching History*, 106: 14–19.
Prior, J. and John, P.D. (2001) 'From anecdote to argument: using the word processor to connect knowledge and opinion through revelatory writing', *Teaching History*, 101: 31–4.
Quality Assurance Agency (QAA) Subject Benchmark Statements: History: www.qaa.ac.uk/academicinfrastructure/benchmark/honours/history.asp.
Qualifications and Curriculum Authority (QCA) (1998) *Education for Citizenship and the Teaching of Democracy in Schools: Final Report of the Advisory Group on Citizenship* (Crick Report) London: QCA. Available online: www.qca.org.uk/qca_4851.aspx.
Qualifications and Curriculum Authority (QCA) (2005) *The Annual Report on Curriculum and Assessment in History, 2004/05*. Available online: www.qca.org.uk/qca_10241.aspx.
Qualification and Curriculum Authority (QCA) (2007) *History Programme of Study for Key Stage 3 and Attainment Target*. London: HMSO. Available online: http://curriculum.qca.

org.uk/uploads/QCA-07-3335-p_History3_tcm6-189.pdf?return=http%3A//curriculum.qca.org.uk/subjects/history/index.aspx%3Freturn%3Dhttp%253A//curriculum.qca.org.uk/subjects/index.aspx.

Rayner, L. (1999) 'Weighing a century with a web site: teaching Y9 to be critical', *Teaching History*, 96: 19–22.

Richardson, H. (2000) 'The QCA history scheme of work for Key Stage 3', *Teaching History*, 99: 14–19.

Riley, C. (1999) 'Evidential understanding, period knowledge and the development of literacy: a practical approach to "layers of inference" for key stage 3', *Teaching History*, 97: 6–12.

Riley, M. (1997) 'Big stories and big pictures: making outlines and overviews interesting', *Teaching History*, 88: 20–2.

Riley, M. (2000) 'Into the Key Stage 3 history garden: choosing and planting your enquiry questions', *Teaching History*, 99: 8–13.

Riley, M. and Harris, R. (2002) *Past Forward: A Vision of School History 2002*–2012. London: Historical Association.

Rosenzweig, R. (2000) 'How Americans use and think about the past', in P.N. Stearns, P. Seixas and S. Wineburg (eds), *Knowing, Teaching and Learning History*. New York: New York University Press. pp. 262–83.

Rudham, R. (2001a) 'A noisy classroom is a thinking classroom: speaking and listening in Year 7 history', *Teaching History*, 105: 35–41.

Rudham, R. (2001b) 'The new history AS level: principles for planning a scheme of work', *Teaching History*, 103: 18–21.

Salmon, G. (2000) *E Moderating: the Key to Teaching and Learning On Line*. London Routledge.

Salmons, P. (2003) 'Teaching or Preaching? The Holocaust and intercultural education in the UK', *Intercultural Education*, 14(2): 139–49.

School Curriculum and Assessment Authority (SCAA) (1994) *History in the National Curriculum, Draft Proposals*. May. London: HMSO.

'Schools drop Holocaust lessons' (2007) *Guardian*, 2 April: http://education.guardian.co.uk/schools/story/0,,2048161,00.html.

Scott, A. (2006) 'Essay writing for everyone: an investigation into different methods used to teach Year 9 to write an essay', *Teaching History*, 123: 26–33.

Sellar, W. and Yeatman, R. (1998) *1066 and All That: A Memorable History of England*. London: Methuen.

Shemilt, D. (1976) *A New Look at History*. (Schools Council History Project.) Edinburgh: Holmes McDougall.

Shemilt, D. (1980) *History 13-16: Evaluation Study*. Edinburgh: Holmes McDougall.

Shemilt, D. (1984) 'Beauty and the philosopher: empathy in history and classroom', in A.K. Dickinson, P.J. Lee and P.J. Rogers (eds), *Learning History*. London: Heinemann. pp. 39–84.

Shemilt, D. (2000) 'The caliph's coin: the currency of narrative frameworks in history teaching', in P.N. Stearns, P. Seixas and S. Wineburg (eds), *Knowing, Teaching and Learning History*. New York: New York University Press.

Shulman, L. (1986) 'Those who understand: knowledge growth in teaching', *Educational Researcher*, 15: 4–14.

Slater, J. (1988) *The Politics of History Teaching: A Humanity Dehumanised, Special Professorial Lecture*. London: Institute of Education, University of London.

Slater, J. (1989) *The Politics of History Teaching: A Humanity Dehumanised*. London: Institute of Education, University of London.

Slater, J. (1995) *Teaching History in the New Europe*. London: Cassell.

Smith, P. (2001) 'Why Gerry now likes evidential work', *Teaching History*, 102: 8–13.

Smith, P. (2002) 'International relations at GCSE – they just can't get enough of it', *Teaching History*, 108: 19–22.

Stearns, P.N., Seixas, P. and Wineburg, S. (eds) (2000) *Knowing Teaching and Learning History*. New York: New York University Press.

Stephen, A. (2005) 'Why can't they just live together happily Miss? Unravelling the complexities of the Arab-Israeli conflict at GCSE', *Teaching History*, 120: 5–10.

Stouder, P. (1999) *Enseigner L'Histoire au College avec Les Documents Patrimoniaux*. Paris: Armand Colin.

Stow, W. and Haydn, T. (2000) 'Issues in the teaching of chronology', in J. Arthur and R. Phillips (eds), *Issues in History Teaching*. London: Routledge. pp. 83–97.

Styles, S. and Willoughby, S. (1992) 'History in Lancashire: guidelines for the construction of a departmental policy document', Lancashire County Council Advisory Service.

Sylvester, D. (1994) 'Change and continuity in history teaching 1900–93', in H. Bourdillon (ed.), *Teaching History*. London: Routledge. pp. 9–23.

Tillbrook, M. (2002) 'Content restricted and maturation retarded? Problems with the post-16 history curriculum', *Teaching History*, 109: 24–6.

Timmins, G., Vernon, K. and Kinealy, C. (2005) *Teaching and Learning History: Teaching and Learning the Humanities in Higher Education*. London: Sage.

Traille, K. (2006) '"You should be proud about your history. They made me feel ashamed": teaching history hurts', *Teaching History*, 127: 31–7.

Walsh, B. (1998) 'Why Gerry likes history now: the power of the word processor', *Teaching History*, 93: 6–15.

Walsh, B. (1999) 'Practical classroom approaches to the iconography of Irish history in the classroom', *Teaching History*, 97: 16–19.

Ward, R. (2006) 'Duffy's devices: teaching Year 13 to read and write', *Teaching History*, 124: 9–16.

White, J. (2004) 'Howard Gardner: the myth of multiple intelligences', lecture at Institute of Education, University of London, 17 November: www.ioe.ac.uk/schools/mst/LTU/phil/HowardGardner_171104.pdf.

Wineburg, S. (2000) 'Making historical sense', in P.N. Stearns, P. Seixas and S. Wineburg (eds), *Knowing, Teaching and Learning History*. New York: New York University Press. pp. 306–25.

Wineburg, S. (2001) *Historical Thinking and Other Unnatural Acts*. Philadelphia, PA: Temple University Press.

Woodcock, J. (2005) 'Does the linguistic release the conceptual? Helping Year 10 to improve their causal reasoning', *Teaching History*, 119: 5–14.

Wrenn, A (1999a) 'Build it in, don't bolt it on: history's contribution to support critical citizenship', *Teaching History*, 96: 6–12.

Wrenn, A. (1999b) 'Substantial sculptures or sad little plaques? Making interpretations matter to Y9', *Teaching History*, 97: 21–8.

Wrenn, A. (2004) 'Making learning drive assessment: Joan of Arc – saint, witch or warrior?', *Teaching History*, 115: 44–51.

www.bbchistorymagazine.com/education.asp?id=26547

www.blackhistory4schools.com/.

www.heirnet.org/ is the website of the History Educators International Research Network, *International Journal of Historical Learning, Teaching and Research*, with useful articles, particularly on the curriculum.

www.nagty.ac.uk/thinktanks, the NAGTY history think tank.

www.nc.uk.net/gt/history/examples_ks3.htm, for the QCA/National Curriculum.

www.teachers.tv/.

http://ygt.dcsf.gov.uk/HomePage.aspx?stakeholder=3, the new Young Gifted and Talented website.

# INDEX